P9-CDB-746

The Arno Press Cinema Program

THE THEORY AND PRACTICE OF THE *CINÉ-ROMAN*

William F. Van Wert

ARNO PRESS
A New York Times Company
New York • 1978

This volume was selected for the
Dissertations on Film Series
of the ARNO PRESS CINEMA PROGRAM
by Garth S. Jowett, University of Windsor, Canada

Editorial Supervision: Maria Casale

First publication 1978 by Arno Press Inc.

Reproduced from a copy in the Indiana University Library

THE ARNO PRESS CINEMA PROGRAM
For complete listing of cinema titles see last pages

Manufactured in the United States of America

Library of Congress Cataloging in Publication Data

Van Wert, William F
The theory and practice of the ciné-roman.

(Dissertations on film series) (The Arno Press cinema program)
Thesis--Indiana University, 1975.
Includes bibliographies and filmography.
1. Moving-pictures--France. 2. Moving-pictures and literature. I. Title. II. Series. III. Series: The Arno Press cinema program.
PN1993.5.F7V3 1978 791.43'0944 77-22912
ISBN 0-405-10756-0

THE THEORY AND PRACTICE OF THE *CINE-ROMAN*

BY

William F. Van Wert

Submitted to the Faculty of the Graduate School
in partial fulfillment of the requirements
for the degree of Doctor of Philosophy
in the Comparative Literature Program
Indiana University
August 1975

Acknowledgements

I wish to give thanks especially to Professor Harry Geduld who pioneered the development of film courses at Indiana University at a time when such courses were generally not thought to be academically acceptable in university curricula. Without him this dissertation would not have been possible. I wish also to thank Charles Eckert, Breon Mitchell, Emile Snyder and Walter Mignolo for their academic support and Johanna Van Wert for her emotional support. Writing the dissertation was easy. Getting it typed in an acceptable form was more difficult. Accordingly, I wish to thank the many typists who took a crash course in French film to help me complete the present study. Finally, I wish to thank Grove Press and New Yorker films for their cooperation with film-viewing and analyzing film stills.

Contents

Critics of French film generally agree that an aesthetic revolution took place in France in 1959 with the success of several first features at the Cannes film festival. The scope of these films extended far beyond the festival. In terms of output alone, the number of first features was remarkable: Claude Chabrol had made his first feature in 1958 (*Le Beau Serge*), but he personally accounted for three feature films in 1959: *Les Cousins*, *A Double Tour* and *Les Bonnes Femmes*. The other films seen in connection with those of Chabrol in 1959 were François Truffaut's *Les Quatre Cent Coups*, Jean-Luc Godard's *A Bout de Souffle*, Eric Rohmer's *Le Signe du lion* and Alain Resnais's *Hiroshima mon amour*. That all of these films appeared in 1959 and that all of these directors except Resnais were critics for *Cahiers du Cinéma* before making films themselves added to the general feeling of a *nouvelle vague* or New Wave in French film.

Resnais is the exception and the exception is crucial. His name became temporarily associated with Truffaut and Godard because all three had won awards at Cannes. In reality there were two New Waves begun in France in the 1950's. The first and better known of the two is that of the former *Cahiers* critics: Truffaut, Godard, Chabrol and Rohmer.[1] There was another New Wave related both in theory and in practice which included Resnais, Chris Marker, Agnes Varda, Henri Colpi, Armand Gatti, Jean Cayrol and later Alain Robbe-Grillet and Marguerite Duras. If the first group can be designated as the *cinéma des critiques* (cinema of critics or critics' cinema), then the second group can be set apart by contrast. They have alternately been called "les intellectuels" (referring both to the temperament of these directors and to their formal and plastic concerns in film), "Rive Gauche" ("Left Bank," referring both to their residence in Paris and to their politics) and "the literary New Wave" (referring both to a real connection with literature outside of film and to their desire to transpose literary techniques in their films). As an alternative to "the literary New Wave," we might propose the term *cinéma des auteurs*, which has the advantage of setting these directors apart from the *cinéma des critiques* more clearly than does "literary New Wave". The disadvantage to calling them the *cinéma des auteurs* is the possible confusion of that term with *auteur* theory, which was espoused by the *Cahiers* directors but rejected by the literary New Wave directors. Yet, that confusion is essential to our discussion, for the whole question of authorship has preoccupied the French cinema since 1946. When the *Cahiers* directors used the term *auteur*, they intended two things: (1) that *auteur* should mean "author" in the sense that the director of a film distinguishes himself from the rest of the community involved in the making of that film by the degree of aesthetic control he/she exerts; and (2) that *auteur* should mean "artist" in the sense that the director, because of his possibilities for aesthetic control over his film, is as much an artist as the novelist or painter. In the term *cinéma des auteurs*, *auteur* carries the general sense of "author" and "artist"; it also carries the specific meaning of "writer", for Resnais and the other directors of the literary New Wave were interested in finding cinematic equivalents for literary devices and in using those equivalents to "write" directly in film.

Both New Wave groups signify a confrontation between film and literature, and their films can be seen either in reaction to literature or in relation to it. For the younger *Cahiers* directors, whose education had been a film education, the *auteur* theory was a vehicle for viewing film as an art form: that is, in order to make comparisons with other art forms, they first had to make film analogous to the other art forms. By positing that a good director could achieve a world view in his films similar to that of a Balzac in literature, for example, the young critics were in effect denying that film is also an industry, a collective enterprise involving more people than the director. Their emphasis upon the director was an attempt to gain respectability for film as art. In addition, the *auteur* theory was an attack, a reaction against the pre-war tradition of well-made films, dominated by their script-writers as much, if not more than, their directors.[2] They blamed the mediocrity of such films on the script-writers, whose adaptations, they argued, prevented such films from developing their own (filmic) language. They saw the secure positions of such script-writers in French films of the 1930's as being symptomatic of film's inferiority complex toward, and dependency on, literature. Their espousal of the *auteur* theory was an attempt to shift responsibility in the form of praise or blame from the studio and from the script-writer to the director. This shift implied that film should not be seen as an adjunct to literature. Thus, espousing the *auteur* theory also implied a critical aesthetic based on attacking filmed adaptations of literature, especially when those adaptations invited comparisons between the film and the original work. Adaptations of little known novels or best-sellers were acceptable, because they did not burden the director. Truffaut felt no constraint to be faithful to David Goodis' novel *Down There* when he filmed *Tirez sur le pianiste* (1960), just as Godard's *Bande à part* (1964) bears little resemblance to Dolores Hitchens' *Fool's Gold*. Indeed, as critics at *Cahiers du Cinéma* they had tended to admire as *auteurs* directors who were also screenwriters themselves (Renoir, Rossellini, Welles) and directors who adapted little-known works in such a way that their world view within the films was the same, regardless of the original works adapted (von Sternberg, Hitchcock).

On the other hand, Resnais and the other directors of the *cinéma des auteurs* wished to make films which would be equivalent to writing at the level of the director and to reading for the spectators. This desire to advance a literary cinema was fulfilled in three stages: first, the transposition of literary devices into film, which implied adaptations of technique, not content (of methods, not works); second, the recruiting of poets and novelists on the part of Resnais to write directly for film; finally, the passage from screenwriter to director of three of Resnais's collaborators. The first step is especially apparent in the first films of the literary New Wave directors. Resnais, for example, had made a 16 millimeter adaptation of Proust's Les Yeux d'Albertine in 1945. It was his only adaptation. But when he made Muriel (1963), he acknowledged his indebtedness to Proust by subtitling the film "ou le temps d'un retour". That indebtedness was to Proust's method, not to any individual work of Proust nor to the content (story) of any of Proust's works. Specifically, Resnais transposed Proust's method of linking time past with time present through association. Associative editing is Resnais's equivalent for Proust's mémoire involuntaire. When Resnais cuts from a close-up of the hand of the Japanese lover in bed to a close-up of the hand of the dead German lover in the past at Nevers in Hiroshima mon amour (1959), Resnais is transposing Proust's method of using sights, smells and objects (the madeleine, for example) to trigger a complex network of past memories in the mind of the narrating Marcel in A la Recherche du temps perdu (1913-1928). The mind of Riva in Hiroshima and of Marcel in Proust's work objectify memory in the object of association that links past with present, so that the world is the character's idea of the world. Once that trigger has sparked the dormant Memory, the voluntary memory of the protagonist/narrator relives those past experiences, which are often traumatic, through an intellectual effort or an effort of will. Alain Robbe-Grillet's novels (like Dans le labyrinthe - 1959) and films (like L'Immortelle-1962) alter time-space relationships and multiple points of view by this same device of associative editing.

When Agnes Varda made her first feature film, La Pointe courte (1954-1955), it was the device of fusing two otherwise unrelated stories that Faulkner had used in The Wild Palms (1939) that Varda was transposing. Varda admired the structure of the work and adapted that structure, not the work itself. Faulkner's novel is really two novels whose connections are left open by Faulkner for the reader to fill in. Varda's La Pointe courte is correspondingly two films: the "objective" film of candid photographs of poor fishermen in northern France and the "subjective" film of two actors hired from the theater to play the roles of lovers in a theatrical way: exaggerated gestures, literary dialogue delivered in the manner of a recitative. The viewer must make the connections between the two kinds of film here.

The second step toward a literary cinema was initiated by Resnais, who has collaborated with a novelist on each of his feature films: with Marguerite Duras on Hiroshima mon amour, with Alain Robbe-Grillet on L'Année dernière à Marienbad (1961), with Jean Cayrol on Muriel (1963), with Jorge Semprun on La Guerre est finie (1965) and Stavisky (1974) and with Jacques Sternberg on Je t'aime je t'aime (1968). There was a precise method to each collaboration. Once the novelist in question had accepted to write an original scenario for film, Resnais worked closely with the novelist, meticulously planning the inter-relationships between the spoken text, the musical soundtrack, the camera angles and the editing. Thus, Resnais participated in the scenarios while they were being written rather than after the scripts were completed as is more commonly the case in this country. Resnais encouraged his writers to produce the equivalent of a novel, often requiring an elaborate synopsis of characters' personalities, even when such detail would never appear in the film. Further, he encouraged them to give the characters highly literary dialogue without worrying about whether or not such speech would be realistic or even plausible in real life.

If Resnais co-participated in the writing of these scenarios, his collaborators co-participated in the process of filmmaking. They learned to write in terms of film and film in terms of writing through their association with Resnais. The passage from screenwriter to director was for them a relatively easy one, since the two functions had been so inseparable. Thus, Jean Cayrol (Le Coup de Grace - 1965), Alain Robbe-Grillet (L'Immortelle - 1962) and Marguerite Duras (La Musica - 1967) joined the literary New Wave as directors as well as screenwriters in this third step toward a literary cinema.

The roots of this literary cinema envisioned by the cinéma des auteurs were present in the years immediately following World War Two. A side-effect of that war was the crisis it produced among artists and intellectuals in France who reassessed their positions after the war. There was a general feeling that the pre-war existential literature of Sartre, Malraux and Camus had been rendered somehow impotent or less relevant after the war. Artists were looking for new forms as well as new ideas, and they saw in the cinema possibilities for rejuvenating literature. Thus, Sartre wrote in 1948:

> Il faut apprendre à parler en images, à transposer les idées de nos livres dans ces nouveaux langages. Il ne s'agit pas du tout de laisser adapter nos oeuvres à l'écran ou pour les émissions de Radio-France: IL FAUT ECRIRE DIRECTEMENT POUR LE CINEMA, POUR LES ONDES... 3

In the same year, Alexandre Astruc published his prophetic article "Naissance d'une nouvelle avant-garde: la caméra-stylo," in which he affirmed: "Le cinéma n'a d'avenir que si la caméra finit par remplacer le stylo."[4] Astruc was reacting to adaptations in which the dialogue and overall sound track were subservient to the visuals, often offering little more than a duplication of those visuals. Astruc stressed that the "tyranny of the visuals" prevented film from developing its own language, its own way of writing, and the visuals' necessary emphasis on the anecdotal subject kept film tied to literature at the level of the text:

> Le cinéma s'arrachera peu à peu à cette tyrannie du visuel, de l'image pour l'image, de l'anecdote immédiate, du concret, pour devenir un moyen d'écriture aussi souple et subtil que celui du langage écrit. 5

Claire Clouzot notes that pronouncements like that of Astruc eased the way for the <u>cinéma des critiques</u> to confront literature in their films: "Style de cinéma romanesque, avec narration à la première personne en 'off' et caméra fluide restant toujours à l'extérieur des personnages."[6]

If Astruc was an inspiration for the <u>Cahiers</u> directors, Jean Cocteau and the Surrealists who made films (Marcel Duchamp, Man Ray, Bunuel, Jean Vigo) were an inspiration to the <u>cinéma des auteurs</u>.

From his first film (Le Sang d'un poète - 1930) to his last (Le Testament d'Orphée - 1959), Jean Cocteau had always urged a "literary" cinema, a cinema in which word and image would have equal importance.

> Pour que l'art cinématographique devienne digne d'un écrivain, il importe que cet écrivain devienne digne de cet art, je veux dire qu'il ne laisse pas interpréter une oeuvre écrite de la main gauche, mais s'acharne des deux mains sur cette oeuvre et construire un objet dont le style devienne équivalent à son style de plume. 7

By stressing equivalency over adaptation, Cocteau made it more possible for later writers to turn from literature to film.

But it was André Bazin, one of the founders of Cahiers du Cinéma and spiritual father to the New Wave, who most addressed himself to the "tyranny of the image" of which Astruc wrote and to the changing relationships between film and literature. Bazin believed that from film's beginnings until 1950 the history of film had been in large part the history of film's technical achievements and mechanical sophistication.

> Jusque vers 1938 environ, le cinéma (en noir et blanc) a été en constant progrès. Progrès technique d'abord (éclairage artificiel, émulsion panchromatique, travelling, son) et, par voie de conséquence, enrichissement des moyens d'expression (gros plan, montage, montage parallèle, montage rapide, ellipse, recadrage, etc.). 8

With a relative plateau in technological achievement, Bazin argued, film could only progress in terms of human input: specifically, in terms of the scenario:

> Tout se passe donc comme si la thématique du cinéma avait épuisé ce qu'elle pouvait attendre de la technique. Il ne suffit plus d'inventer le montage rapide ou de changer de style photographique

> pour émouvoir. Le cinéma est entré insensiblement dans l'âge du scénario; entendons: d'un renversement du rapport entre le fond et la forme. 9

What Bazin urged, then, was a more concerted use of the technological advances to further new and better scripts whose degree of sophistication would justify the technology.

That language should "live" again in film was also the aim of the cinéma des auteurs in the 1950's. They were concerned with integrating a highly poeticized text with an image track that would alternate between a sometimes vertiginous mobile camera (long traveling shots) and a rigidly fixed camera (freeze frames) and an editing of dialectical montage (montage of attractions) that had not been seen in France since the silent films of Eisenstein.[10] The credo of equivalency for the cinéma des auteurs could be summed up in the following statement of Jean Cayrol:

> Le langage ne cesse pas d'être combattant: du moment que quelqu'un parle, il engage le film. Il n'y a que la parole pour remettre en actualité une situation. Il faut redonner au texte son premier rôle qui n'est pas d'expliquer ou de répéter, mais celui d'une parole libre, libératrice d'images en détention. 11

Seeing in film an alternate way of writing a novel meant liberating the film from the "tyranny of the visuals" by a shift of emphasis from films to be seen to films to be read. As Agnes Varda pointed out: "Je crois vraiment que j'ai entrepris La Pointe courte comme on écrit un premier roman... C'est un film 'à lire.'"[12]

Varda's statement seems in retrospect an almost immediate response to Bazin's prophecy of 1952:

> Le temps viendra peut-être des résurgences, c'est-à-dire d'un cinéma à nouveau indépendant du roman et du théâtre. Mais peut-être parce que les romans seront directement écrits en films. 13

Ironically, it was not Bazin's protegees at *Cahiers* -- Godard, Chabrol, Truffaut and Rohmer -- who would fulfill his prophecy of novels written directly as films, but Resnais, Varda and the rest of the *cinéma des auteurs*. It is to them and their concept of a literary cinema that this present study is devoted.

The term "literary" New Wave refers as much to the past careers of these directors as to their present preoccupation with developing a literary cinema. Thus, literature is the first influence upon the *cinéma des auteurs*. Several worthwhile studies could be done on individual influences and transpositions within the group. We have already noted the influence of Proust on Resnais and Robbe-Grillet and that of Faulkner on Agnes Varda. We might add the influence of Kafka on Robbe-Grillet and Virginia Woolf on Marguerite Duras to the list as well. The two main literary influences, however, are the Surrealist poets, playwrights and novelists (Breton, Cocteau, Desnos, Eluard, Queneau)[14] and the *nouveau roman* or "new novel," of which Robbe-Grillet, Duras and Cayrol were leading proponents.

The theater exerts another influence. Whereas the *Cahiers* directors (with the exception of Jacques Rivette) deliberately set out to dedramatize film narrative and to destroy theatricality in film acting, the *auteurs* group steadfastly maintained its theatrical roots. Resnais's first avocation was that of an actor. He studied with Marcel Marceau and toured with Marceau's mime troupe during the war. Agnes Varda was the official photographer for the TNP (Théâtre National Populaire) of Jean Vilar prior to making La Pointe courte. Armand Gatti, Marguerite Duras and Henri Colpi have written plays which the TNP has produced. Even Robbe-Grillet, who has never written a play, is influenced by the theater in that he writes highly theatrical dialogue and demands theatrical gestures and looks from his actors. Of this influence of the theater upon the literary New Wave, Clouzot notes:

> Le théâtre exerce, avec la littérature, l'influence dominante sur La Pointe courte, Une Aussi Longue Absence, L'Année dernière à Marienbad, L'Enclos, La Musica, L'Homme qui ment et Détruire dit-elle. 15

In addition, the dramatic theories and plays of Bertold Brecht find their echo in the films of the cinéma des auteurs.

A third influence, which falls somewhere between theater and literature, are the comics (bandes dessinées). Resnais is deadly serious about the influence of the comics upon his films:

> Ce que je sais au cinéma, je l'ai autant appris par les "comics" que par le cinéma. Les règles du découpage et du montage sont les mêmes dans les "comics" qu'au cinéma. Bien avant le cinéma, les comics ont utilisé le "scope," et ils ont toujours pu changer le format. De même pour la couleur, ils savent l'utiliser à des fins dramatiques. Bien d'autre procédés devraient être soulignés. Par exemple, cette façon de mettre un personnage en évidence en le détachant sur un fond uni. 16

Resnais admired the comics' freedom to expand or contract image size; their freedom to understate or exaggerate for dramatic impact; their freedom, through montage-boxes, to play with time and space and join together logically unrelated times and spaces; their freedom, through color, to underexpose or overexpose for dramatic effect; finally, their freedom of framing, whereby objects surrounding a comic character (long shot) become symbolic of that character or whereby an object or face may be enlarged to fill up the whole box (extreme close-up) for psychological impact. In connection with Resnais's passion for the comics, one thinks of Fellini's love of _fumetti_ strips and their influence on his early films. Chris Marker was alluding to the comics when he subtitled _La Jetée_ (1963) "un photo-roman". The _photo-roman_ was a form of strip-cartoon very popular in France and Italy at that time, which employed photographs (with the story conveyed in tableaux form by actors) instead of drawings.

Contrary to that on the _Cahiers_ directors, filmic influences on the literary New Wave are relatively few. The most important single influence in this context is that of Eisenstein whose politics, editing style of dialectical montage (in which two images clash to form a third which is not on-screen but in the mind of the viewer, prompted by the clash of the first two) and desire for the cinema to be a total work of art the literary New Wave directors admired. To a lesser degree, they were also influenced by the Surrealist filmmakers of the 1920's: Cocteau, Buñuel, Man Ray, Germaine Dulac.

The fact that the _Cahiers_ directors were critics of the cinema and had seen thousands of films prior to making any of their own is at the heart of the _auteur_ theory and goes far to explain the tendency in their films toward films-within-the-film, allusions to favorite directors, imitations of those directors' styles and autobiographical (or should we say auto-filmographic) allusions. We should perhaps reiterate the differences between the two New Waves on both *auteur* theory and adaptation theory before analyzing in depth the literary cinema of the *cinéma des auteurs*.

Auteur theory (*la politique des auteurs*) is usually accredited in terms of origin to Truffaut and the publication of his "Une certaine tendance du cinéma français" in 1954.[17] Its real roots, however, are in Bazin, particularly in his analyses of Renoir in France, Chaplin in America and the Italian neo-realists. Even though Bazin would reject the *auteur* theory prior to his death in 1958, his writings formed the basis for its application by the *Cahiers* directors. Thus, an *auteur* came to mean a director whose essential personality could be perceived, regardless of the format or genre of the film. The essential Howard Hawks could be deciphered, for example, through all his films without regard to the individual film being a western, a war film, a musical. An *auteur* was a director who could transcend a bad script to infuse that script with his own personality. Thus, Eric Rohmer wrote:

> Louons donc ces cinéastes, qui, méprisant les fausses valeurs du scénario, du bon goût, de l'unité de ton et de la raison, conservent un peu de ce fol génie qui s'autorise une pure plaisanterie de mise en scène sur le papier absolumment gratuite et denuée de sens. Sternberg s'amuse. C'est donc sérieux. 18

Carlton Tanner has further noted that "a good scenario, clearly, is no advantage; but more fundamentally, a bad one is no disadvantage for a good director."[19] As the theory developed, it came to mean that an *auteur* could conceivably make a bad film, but that his bad film would probably be better than a good film by a director who was not an *auteur*. Thus, Jacques Rivette wrote:

> Un cinéaste qui a fait dans le passé de très grands films peut faire des erreurs, mais les erreurs qu'il fera ont toutes chances, à priori, d'être plus passionnantes que les réussites d'un confectionneur. 20

An interesting but perverse kind of narcissism among the *Cahiers* critics also dictated that the master's touch could best be seen in the director's self-revelation: Orson Welles and Jean Renoir acting in their own films; Hitchcock's fleeting appearances in all of his films. Truffaut defined such appearances as those of the master with his puppets, in which the camera lens becomes an inwardly-turned mirror:

> Mais néanmoins nous éprouvons une pointe de plaisir quand Hitchcock apparait assis à côté du héros dans un bus ou dans un train, ou nous sourions au moment voulu quand le visage criblé de taches de rousseur de Chaplin surgit derrière cette porte de cabine. Car, durant ce bref instant, le maître est montré avec ses marionnettes, l'invisible se matérialise, les lentilles de la caméra sont devenus miroir. 21

Bazin had already set the precedent in his "salvation" of Chaplin's *Monsieur Verdoux* (1947) by a similar mirror-image:

> We see Verdoux next being led away across the prison yard in the dawn, between two executioners. A small man in his shirt sleeves, his arms tied behind him, he moves forward toward the scaffold with a kind of a hop, skip, and a jump. Then comes the sublimest gag of all, unspoken but unmistakable, the gag that resolves the whole film: Verdoux was Charlie! THEY'RE GOING TO GUILLOTINE CHARLIE! The fools did not recognize him. In order to force

> society to commit this irreparable blunder, Charlie has decked out the simulacrum of his opposite. In the precise and mythological meaning of the word, Verdoux is just an avatar of Charlie - the chief and we may indeed say the first. As a result, Monsieur Verdoux is undoubtedly the most important of Chaplin's works.[22]

Bazin's way of reading meaning into the later films of a Chaplin or Renoir was taken up by the other critics at Cahiers too.

Auteur criticism, thus, too easily became a game of director-worship, of asides and allusions, of mirror images of the master. A whole study could be done, in fact, of the interviewing style of the Cahiers critics when they dealt with the directors of the literary New Wave. In their round-table discussion of Resnais's Muriel, for example, everything but Muriel was discussed. They focused primarily on the allusion to Hitchcock on the menu in the restaurant scene. A discussion of Hitchcock, Rossellini, Hegel, Kant and others ensued. When Cahiers interviewed Agnes Varda, they digressed from a discussion of La Pointe courte to talk about Rossellini's Voyage en Italie (1953). Their point seems to have been that behind every good film is the influence of a previous good film done by an auteur director.

After they turned filmmakers, the Cahiers critics gradually rejected auteur theory, Truffaut and Chabrol on aesthetic grounds (the theory had become corrupted by those who "invented" auteurs), Godard and Rivette on political grounds (auteur criticism exists in an ideological void and thus furthers bourgeois forms/content in the cinema).

Because of their insistence upon collaboration and the collective nature of the literary cinema envisioned, the literary New Wave directors had rejected it from the outset.

Their differences in terms of the *auteur* theory also accounted for their differences concerning adaptations. It was perhaps due to the age of the *Cahiers* critics and some measure of insecurity that they sought justification of the director's role vis-a-vis the script and the studio. If that is true, then it is also true that the security that the literary New Wave directors had established in the other arts freed them from qualms of ego when it came to collaborating on a film. Whatever the reasons, the latter directors were committed to writing directly for film. That decision had its impact on literature too, for each successive film script was published in the form of a *ciné-roman*, which was the antithesis of the traditional adaptation, in which the literary work precedes the filmed adaptation. With the *ciné-roman* publication coincided with, or followed, the release of the film. These published texts attest to the literary merit of the film texts at the same time that they serve as program notes (like the libretto for an opera) to be used in conjunction with the film. Significantly, these directors realized that "films to be read" must be taken literally. The publication of their films' texts gave readers the chance to supplement their viewing of the films. Such publications were made possible by the close ties which these artists already had with the publishing houses of Les Editions du Seuil (Cayrol, Marker), Les Editions de Minuit (Robbe-Grillet, Duras) and Gallimard

(Duras, Semprun). The phenomenon of the *ciné-roman* was one of literature accomodating itself to film, while providing an alternate distribution outlet for films whose complex narrative structures and literary sophistication often caused them grave problems within the realm of film distribution. Finally, they attest to a desire shared by all of the *cinéma des auteurs* directors that film (possible publication in book form) be a total work of art, just as Eisenstein had envisioned.

Notes

1
Other names could be added to the list of _Cahiers_ directors, that is, critics who later turned director: Jacques Rivette, Pierre Kast, Jacques Doniol-Valcroze. The phenomenon of a critical film journal first creating an atmosphere in which the critics could see themselves as filmmakers and then actually switch from criticism to filming is unparalleled.

2
They were referring to Jean Aurenche, Pierre Bost, Charles Spaak, Jacques Sigurd and the Prévert brothers.

3
Jean-Paul Sartre, "Qu'est-ce que la littérature?" in _Situations II_ (Paris: Gallimard, 1948), p. 292.

4
Alexandre Astruc, "Naissance d'une nouvelle avant-garde," _L'Ecran francais_, 144 (March 30, 1948).

5
ibid.

6
Claire Clouzot, _Le Cinéma français depuis la nouvelle vague_ (Paris: Fernand Nathan, 1972), p. 7.

7
Jean Cocteau, _Entretiens autour du cinématographe_, ed. Andre Fraigneau (Paris: André Bonne, 1951), p. 20.

8
André Bazin, "Pour un cinéma impur: défense de l'adaptation," in _Cinéma: oeil ouvert sur le monde_, ed. Georges-Michel Bovay (Lausanne: Clairefontaine, 1952), p. 30.

9
Bazin, p. 31.

10
For a discussion of the affinities between Eisenstein and the literary New Wave directors, see _Etudes Cinématographiques_, 64-68 (1968).

Notes

11 Jean Cayrol and Claude Durand, Le Droit de regard (Paris: Seuil, 1963), p. 20.

12 Agnes Varda, Cahiers du Cinéma, 165 (April 1965), p. 42.

13 Bazin, p. 32.

14 Resnais made two of his shorts in collaboration with Eluard and Queneau. Eluard wrote the script for Guernica (1950) and Queneau wrote the poem-script for Le Chant du styrène (1958). See the section on "subjective documentary" for more details.

15 Clouzot, p. 53.

16 Alain Resnais, Image et Son, 129 (February 1960).

17 Francois Truffaut, Cahiers du Cinéma, 31 (January 1954)

18 Cahiers du Cinéma, 86 (August 1958), p. 53.

19 Carlton Tanner, "La Politique des Auteurs as a Critical Aesthetic" (Masters Thesis,University of California, 1968).

20 Clouzot, p. 180.

21 For a compilation of the Cahiers interviews of the auteur directors they favored (Renoir, Rossellini, Lang, Hawks, Hitchcock, Bunuel, Welles, Dreyer, Bresson and Antonioni), see La Politique des auteurs (Paris: Champ Libre, 1972).

22 André Bazin, What is Cinema? II, trans. Hugh Gray (Berkeley, Los Angeles and London: University of California Press, 1971), p. 109.

What is a *ciné-roman*? French critics like Marcel L'Herbier and André Malraux generally agree that it was probably Louis Delluc who first used the term around 1920. Delluc apparently did not intend by it a hybrid-form, but rather a justification of the cinema as an art form. Just as Eisenstein often drew parallels between film and the other arts, citing Joyce and Wagner, Baudelaire and the Kabuki theatre, so too Delluc sought to raise the status of film to the level of esteem that poetry, the theatre and the novel commanded. In other words, the search for a film language for these early theoreticians of the cinema did not involve discussions of photography, from which film sprang technically, but rather discussions of the affinities between film and the "other" arts. André Malraux also discussed the concept of a film-novel in his *Esquisse d'une psychologie du cinéma* (1941) without clearly defining the concept. Like Delluc, Malraux's intent seems not to have been that of formulating a definition for a hybrid or even a new genre. While separating literature and film as artistic media, Malraux discussed the influences of one upon the other. Thus, his interests lay in tracing the development of cinematic literature or "literary" films, the latter being more infrequent than the former. While film had frequently adapted literary works, particularly novels with the advent of sound films, it had not concerned itself with adapting literary techniques. Thus, the relationships between literature and film were drawn either by film writers and critics who wished to gain more respectability for the new medium or by literary writers and critics who wished to note what they had gained from film as a source of inspiration for literature or who wished to demonstrate the inferiority of film, often pointing out the ways in which a filmic adaptation deviated from the literary original. In other words, the term *ciné-roman*, when it was used, emphasized the *roman* and not its prefix.

That definition and emphasis changed in the mid-fifties with a group of filmmakers here designated as the *cinéma des auteurs*: Alain Resnais, Chris Marker, Agnes Varda, Jean Cayrol, Armand Gatti, Marguerite Duras and Alain Robbe-Grillet. With *La Pointe courte* (1955), Agnes Varda was the first to draw critical attention in a feature film to a new literature-film relationship. Varda adapted the form of William Faulkner's *The Wild Palms* but not the content. Her intent was a transposition of literary techniques to film, not a simple borrowing of the novel's plot. The spectator will not recognize any trace of Faulkner in the Varda film, except in the form, which involved the dialectical clash of two different milieu, just as Faulkner had interwoven two different plots in his novel. Varda deliberately juxtaposed the candid portraits of village fishermen with the private "story" of two lovers who differ from those fishermen in their theatrical acting (exaggerated gestures) and in their "literary" dialogue, a dialogue which one might find in a poem or novel but which one would never hear in the streets. Succinctly put, Varda's concern was not with popularizing literature but with advancing film art.

Alain Resnais further developed the technique of advancing film through literature. Refusing to adapt literary works, Resnais, nevertheless, sought to fuse literature and film through collaboration. For his short films, he consciously sought out poets who would write original scripts for him, scripts of the same poetic intensity, complexity and originality that Resnais found in their pre-cinematic literature. Thus, Resnais collaborated with Paul Eluard on Guernica (1950), with Chris Marker (a published poet) on Les Statues meurent aussi (1953), with Jean Cayrol on Nuit et brouillard (1955), and with Raymond Queneau on Le Chant du styrène (1958). Marker, Cayrol and Queneau had also written novels, but it was their poetry that Resnais wanted in the shorter films. When he turned to feature films, he also turned to novelists: to Marguerite Duras for Hiroshima mon amour (1959), to Alain Robbe-Grillet for L'Annee dernière à Marienbad (1961), to Jean Cayrol for Muriel (1963), to Jorge Semprun for La Guerre est finie (1966), and to Jacques Sternberg for Je t'aime je t'aime (1968). Again, Resnais wanted poetry, poetry sustained enough to equal the images in importance. With accumulations of details, repetitions of key words or phrases, rhythm and sometimes even rhyme, Resnais wished to fuse the literary tone of voice-over narration and the dialogue of his actors.

The transposition of literary techniques to the cinema is perhaps the first step in defining the ciné-roman, as the term came to be used by the _cinéma des auteurs_. Yet, even among themselves, they disagree slightly on what the term means. For Agnes Varda, a _ciné-roman_ meant the published text of a film, specifically the scenario without camera indications. In other words, it meant a book, a book which would help those who had seen the film remember it better, a book which could stand upon its own merits and be read as a _ciné-roman_ or film-novel by those who had not seen the film.

> Il s'agit de présenter un livre--aide-mémoire pour ceux qui ont vu le film, ciné-roman pour les autres.[1]

Thus, _ciné-roman_ assumes one's not having seen the film. Yet, the emphasis is also upon the film, for it, and its resultant published text, are more important for Varda than the scenario which precedes the film:

> Et pourtant le film n'a pas été écrit comme un scénario, traduit ensuite en cinéma. J'essaie de travailler bien en désordre, car j'aime que la focale d'un objectif précède parfois dans ma pensée une figure. J'aime aller du site à la "situation," du travelling au tourment, du tempo d'un découpage à une pensée.[2]

Varda, thus, begins with technique and moves toward content. Her implication is that film technique ("site," "travelling," "découpage") involves a specific language, a language with which one can "write"; indeed, Varda explains her reasons for making films and her reasons for publishing the texts of those films in terms of writing: "Nous, cinéastes, qui faisons des films pour ne pas écrire des livres, il nous faut quand même écrire quelque chose sur nos films."[3] "We filmmakers who make films in order not to write books" seems especially significant. Her implication is that she and the other directors of the *cinéma des auteurs* are writers who prefer to "write" films rather than books. This preference seems to hold true for Robbe-Grillet, whose novelistic output decreased as his film output increased, and for Marguerite Duras, who turned to film to expand her literature.

Robbe-Grillet, too, considers the *ciné-roman* to be the published text of the film. In his preface to the publication of *L'Immortelle*, he elaborated upon his concept of the *ciné-roman*. Significantly, he likens the published text of a film to a libretto for an opera, both capable of being read as literature but both depending upon a "performance" for their total impact and amplification.

> Le livre que l'on va lire ne prétend pas être une oeuvre par lui-même. L'oeuvre, c'est le film, tel qu'on peut le voir et l'entendre dans un cinéma. On n'en trouvera ici qu'une description: ce que serait, pour un opéra, par exemple, le livret accompagné de la partition musicale et des indications de décor, de jeu, etc.[4]

Robbe-Grillet seems to agree with Agnes Varda, in the sense that he sees the text as fulfilling a double role: that of accompanying the images of the film in an audio-visual construct and that of a piece of literature which can be read independently of the film, without, however, supplanting the film which is the total work ("L'oeuvre, c'est le film"). Robbe-Grillet further specifies that the *ciné-roman* can be read leisurely or studied, whereas a film cannot, and that a *ciné-roman* appeals directly to the critical intelligence of the reader, whereas the film appeals directly to the senses of the viewer.

> Le livre peut ainsi se concevoir, pour le lecteur, comme une précision apportée au spectacle lui-même, une analyse détaillée d'un ensemble audio-visuel trop complexe et trop rapide pour être aisément étudié lors de la projection. Mais, pour celui qui n'a pas assisté au spectacle, le ciné-roman peut aussi se lire comme se lit une partition de musique; la communication doit alors passer par l'intelligence du lecteur, alors que l'oeuvre s'adresse d'abord à sa sensibilité immédiate, que rien ne peut vraiment remplacer.[5]

Like Varda, Robbe-Grillet thinks of the _ciné-roman_ in terms of those who have not seen the film. This concern reminds me somewhat of André Malraux's projects for disseminating the great masterworks of painting: through books--a portable and inexpensive museum. It seems curiously odd that the directors of the _cinéma des auteurs_ should think of disseminating their films through books, since films seem to have a larger and more immediate audience than books. Are they simply reversing the roles of the two media, realizing that films as adaptations of literary works have usually been used as the portable museum and the merciless popularizer? I think the answer lies elsewhere. Imagine for a moment a director like Jean-Luc Godard, who works from a skeletal script or no script at all, encouraging those who have not seen his films to go read the published texts. Those texts depend largely on stills from the films and not upon the literary merit of the language used in narration or dialogue. In other words, the _ciné-roman_ is in a sense a compensation for distribution. Creating a "literary" cinema is not the same as conforming to a commercial cinema. The films of the _cinéma des auteurs_ have often received limited distribution, having been judged too difficult for most audiences by their distributors. Those distributors are partially correct. Grove

Press, which distributes Robbe-Grille's films in this country, informed me that they would not acquire the rights to any more Robbe-Grillet films, because the two they do have (L'Immortelle and L'Homme qui ment) have been financial failures for them. When I asked Henri Colpi what film projects he envisaged in a questionnaire I sent him, he answered:

> Pas de projets de film, même pour l'année à venir. La situation du cinéma français est difficile. Elle est encore plus difficile pour les réalisateurs qui n'ont pas derrière eux un grand succès commercial.

The ciné-roman is, thus, a compensation for the lack of a market for what Robbe-Grillet calls "art et essai" films. The ciné-roman also implies a particular audience. In other words, the commercial failure of many of the films of the cinéma des auteurs was anticipated by their directors. Rather than trying to attract a mass audience, they have actually appealed to an audience which would think of film in terms of art and not in terms of entertainment. Robbe-Grillet's analogy of the libretto for an opera suggests this restricted audience. Indeed, there are probably more people who have read the published texts of films than people who have read the libretto for an opera. The mention of "l'intelligence du lecteur" is a further indication of the sophistication of such directors' scripts.

So, Robbe-Grillet defines the ciné-roman as a book consisting of a film text, a book especially useful for those who have not seen the film. When I asked Robbe-Grillet to define the ciné-roman in a questionnaire, he replied: "Un livre--partition se rapportant à un film. Le film lui-même n'est jamais un ciné-roman." Jean Cayrol and Henri Colpi gave more extensive answers. Cayrol replied:

> Le cinéma est en avance sur la littérature car les mots ne peuvent pas arriver à exprimer l'inaudible de l'actualité, l'instantané de l'évènement. J'ai toujours peur de la réflexion dans les écrits, il faut qu'un art donne l'impression d'une improvisation. (See Appendix)

Cayrol, thus, insists upon the advantages of film over literature, the immediacy of the image and the possibilities of orchestrating that image aurally being the main differences between film and literature. Henri Colpi sees the film-novel relationship in terms of films which are like the <u>nouveau roman</u> or new novel, that is, in terms of the abolition of the anecdotal subject:

> Que peut être le ciné-roman, sinon un cinéma qui s'articule comme un roman? Le tout est de savoir de quel genre de roman il s'agit. Il y a aussi bien Stendhal qu'Alexandre Dumas ou Robbe-Grillet. Je pense, évidemment, que vous vous référez à un cinéma dont le récit n'est plus uniquement une anecdote qui va de A à Z, comme de nombreux romans aujourd'hui s'évadent de la trame pure et simple. En ce sens, oui, il y a un certain cinéma contemporain auquel on pourrait donner un terme générique, quel qui'il soit, ciné-roman, si vous voulez, ou roman-ciné, ou mieux même ciné-poème. (See Appendix)

In contrast with Varda or Robbe-Grillet, Colpi sees the <u>ciné-roman</u>, not just in terms of a published text for a film, but also in terms of the film itself ("un cinéma qui s'articule comme un roman"). In addition, he reverses the role of prefix or qualifier, suggesting that <u>roman-ciné</u> or <u>ciné-poème</u> might be terms as appropriate as <u>ciné-roman</u>.

The disagreements among the various directors of the <u>cinéma des auteurs</u> seem to be ones of emphasis, not of substance. For instance, they agree that the text for a film should be an original one, not an adaptation, and that the text should be the equivalent of literary writing, thus, worthy of being published after the film is completed. The film is what ties the scenario (with camera indications) and the published text (usually without camera indications) together. Those films are not hybrids which try to assimilate two essentially unlike things, so that there is not the critical danger that Jean Ricardou has pointed out:

> L'influence d'un art sur un autre appartient au domaine de l'illusoire. C'est pourquoi d'hybrides concepts comme "films-romans" utilisés souvent par la critique, me paraissent entretenir une dangeureuse équivoque.[6]

Rather, the ciné-roman, involving a scenario which precedes the film, the film itself, and the published text upon completion of the film, points toward a new art work and a new art form. That new work or form would presuppose an abolition of arbitrary distinctions between genres or between media in favor of a more constructive multiplicity of uses for the work or form. In this context, the attitude of Marguerite Duras is significant. She was asked by Jacques Rivette in a published interview why she "adapted" her own novels and plays into films. Her answer reveals the limits which Duras had reached in her fictional writing:

> Rivette: Il semble que, de plus en plus, vous avez envie de donner des formes successives à chacune des - non pas des histoires, que vous écrivez, que ce soit "le Square," qui a eu plusieurs versions, ou "La Musica," qui a eu aussi plusieurs formes, ou encore "L'Amante Anglaise." Cela correspond a . . .

Duras: Au désir que j'ai toujours de casser ce qui a précédé. "Détruire," le livre "Détruire" est un livre cassé au point de vue romanesque. Je crois qu'il n'y a plus de phrases . . . Je ne peux plus du tout lire de romans. A cause des phrases.[7]

Duras had reached a point of multiple revisions, a point at which she could not longer construct complete sentences nor read novels because of the restrictive grammar of the language. The gesam■■tkunstwerk or "total work of art" to which Duras aspires is also the total art form. That statement deserves clarification. Duras views art in terms of its uses. Thus, the total work of art would be that which could be read or played upon the stage or filmed or thrown away. As she has stated:

> Il n'y avait pas d'idée de film, mais il y avait l'idée d'un livre . . . qui pouvait être à la fois soit lu, soit joué, soit filmé, et j'ajoute toujours: soit jeté.[8]

It was quite natural, since Duras, Robbe-Grillet, Cayrol and Marker were all published novelists, that critics should have related the ciné-roman to the nouveau roman, especially since Robbe-Grillet had written the nouveau roman's principal manifesto, Pour un nouveau roman (1963). Thus, Richard Blumenberg noted the collage-fusion of literary and cinematic elements in the ciné-roman:

> A ciné-roman uses certain techniques of the novel and of the cinema. From the novel come: (1) point of view; (2) symbolic imagery; (3) narrative rhythm; and (4) description. From the cinema come: (1) image (shot) juxtaposition (montage); (2) photographic representation; (3) perceptual imagery; (4) visual description through shot composition; and (5) the inescapability of the present tense.[9]

Perhaps it would be useful here to clarify some of Blumenberg's terms and to elaborate upon others. Point of view exists in all novels but is not the private domain of the novel. Point of view occurs in painting through perspective and also in photography. What is important, in terms of point of view in the _cinéma des auteurs_, is the transposition of the novel's capacity for subjective point of view to the cinema, with the added distinction that film need not sacrifice the objective or denotative level of the image to achieve the subjective or connotative quality of the image. In other words, objective reality exists _a priori_ (the Paris of Varda's _Cléo de 5 à 7_ (1962), the Turkey of Robbe-Grillet's _L'Immortelle_ (1962); in addition, that objective reality can be read as the subjective vision of a particular character (Cléo or N). That coexistence of the objective and the subjective is less possible in the novel, in which one is usually stressed to the detriment of the other. Quite simply put, the novel is a conceptual form, while the film is a perceptual form. The _cinéma des auteurs_ attempts to fuse both the conceptual and the perceptual, without sacrificing one to the other. Similarly, "symbolic imagery" is not restricted to the novel. Films used symbolic imagery before they ever borrowed the structure or the plots of novels. Symbolic imagery, thus, depends upon both technique and perception, not upon specified genres or media. An image becomes symbolic in a film through camera emphasis, as in a close-up, through repetition, or through editing. Even when one or all three of these techniques are used, the image may not be symbolic to all viewers. A symbol, thus, is a construct between author and audience, the responsibility for its success or failure weighing equally on both.

One can speak of "narrative rhythm" in terms of the novels of Cayrol, Duras and Robbe-Grillet, but this is precisely because their prose approaches poetry. All three use repetition and rhythm in the way a poet would. And, through image or text repetitions, through camera mobility or exaggerated fixity, through dialectical and contrapuntal image-text relationships, the _cinéma des auteurs does_ escape the present tense and thus distinguishes itself from other films.

The _ciné-roman_, in other words, can be seen as a "total art form" or as a multiple art form. As Duras suggests, its uses are varied. Its meanings are many. That multiplicity of meaning and the poetic qualities of the text would suggest that _ciné-poème_ might be a more appropriate term than _ciné-roman_. As Anais Nin has affirmed: "Prose is literal. Poetry is dimensional."[10] Her elaboration upon that point elucidates the affinities between poetry and film, and especially in terms of the _cinéma des auteurs_:

> Poets are granted the privilege of mystery and are praised for what they do not reveal, because the poet is content with recreating a flow of images without interpretation. I have only discarded the novel's explicit and direct statement in order to match the way we truly see and feel, in images resembling film sequences.[11]

And Marcel Martin has added:

> Enfin, au point de vue esthétique, c'est de la poésie moderne que je rapprocherais le plus volontiers le cinéma: même volonté de faire parler les êtres directement, même foisonnement d'un réel recomposé, densifié, transfiguré, même fusion de l'image et de l'idée.[12]

Anais Nin discards the novel's "explicit and direct statement" (interpretation), while Martin, like Cayrol, suggests that the cinema is more direct than literature (communication). Both Nin and Martin suggest mystery, in the sense that the cinema reconstructs reality. Both deny the possibility of empirical meaning and exalt the pluridimensionality of meaning in poetry and film. It is this pluridimensionality, both in terms of the work's interpretations and in terms of the work's uses (Duras), that distinguishes the *cinéma des auteurs* from other films and suggests the structure of a *ciné-poème*.

The directors of the *cinéma des auteurs* used "poetry" as a synonym for lyricism and as an antonym for naturalism. They did not pretend to reproduce dialogues that could be heard anywhere outside of the cinema (or literature), nor did they infer that people "act" in the same way that Sylvia Montfort acts in *La Pointe courte* (1955), in the same way Emannuelle Riva acts in *Hiroshima mon amour* (1959), in the same way Delphine Seyrig acts in *L'Année dernière à Marienbad* (1961). Theatrical gestures and a poetic text are superimposed upon a realistically plausible situation to create a new reality.

Their concept of poetry goes hand in hand with their use of counterpoint between the image track and the sound track. Indeed, counterpoint is one of the main techniques by which their films become *ciné-poèmes*. In terms of the films, themselves, the directors of the *cinéma des auteurs* placed a great deal of importance on the poetic quality of the text, often suggesting that the images of the film would play against the text, not vice versa. Thus, Resnais avowed:

> I had asked Marguerite Duras for a love story set in Hiroshima which would not seem too ridiculous in the context of the atomic bomb. I have even encouraged her to "write literature," without worrying at all. I was intending to compose a sort of poem where the image would serve only as a counterpoint to the text.[13]

The film's meanings are thus multiplied through the multiplication of simultaneously communicating texts: the language of the images, the language of the spoken text, the language of the musical themes. Counterpoints between image and text abound in Hiroshima mon amour. Riva speaks at one point in the film about the horrors of the bombing of Hiroshima and all that perished under the bombing, including inanimate objects such as rocks, stones, metals. But the ultimate in destruction was the altering of the earth's ecological balance. In the midst of so much death, new forms of flowers sprouted everywhere, the radio-activity of the bombs and the ashes on the earth having fertilized the soil. Like the Phoenix, continually reborn from its own destruction, flowers bloomed in Hiroshima. As André Malraux once put it, "fire is born of what it burns."

> Elle: Hiroshima se recouvrit de fleurs. Ce n'étaient partout que bleuets et glaïeuls, et volubilis, et belles d'un jour qui renaissaient des cendres . . . avec une extraordinaire vigeur inconnue jusque-là chez les fleurs. Je n'ai rien inventé.

While she says this, the image on the screen (and seen from her point of view) is a vast expanse of asphalt pavement upon which nothing grows. At another point in Hiroshima, Riva and Okada are walking down the evening streets of Hiroshima. She walks ahead of him and so cannot see him. But Okada cannot hear Riva speak, for her voix intérieure fills the sound track. Both of them are, thus, deprived of one of their senses. Better put, the spectator is privileged to see what Riva cannot see and to hear what Okada cannot hear. Riva's voice makes it clear that she expects Okada to touch her at any minute and that she would surrender to that touch. The visuals, however, show Okada stopping and actually increasing the distance between them. The monologue with scenario indications is as follows:

> Voix intérieure d'Elle: Il va venir vers moi, . . . il va me prendre par les épaules . . . il m'em-bras-se-ra. Il m'embrassera . . . et je serai perdue.
>
> "Perdu" est dit dans le ravissement. On revient à lui. Et on s'aperçoit qu'il marche plus lentement pour lui laisser du champ. Qu'au contraire de revenir vers elle, il s'en éloigne. Elle ne se retourne pas.

The development of a "literary" cinema through counterpoint is thus an integration through opposition. As Marie-Claire Ropars-Willeumier has pointed out:

> C'est que la véritable intégration de la littérature au cinéma s'opère au niveau de l'écriture, non de la parole; et c'est en orchestrant au maximum les possibilités contrapuntiques de l'expression cinématographique que Resnais parvient, en un exemple unique, à combiner tous les pouvoirs de la littérature at tous ceux du cinéma, qui s'unissent dans le mesure où ils restent opposés.[14]

In L'Année dernière à Marienbad, the interior monologue passes directly to the image track. Resnais has stated: "There are moments when the reality is completely invented or interior, as when the image corresponds to the conversation. The interior monologue is never on the sound-track, it is almost always in the image. . . ."[15] The voice-over narration still refers to a subjective point of view (usually X's), but it is used to describe events or people visually, that is, spatially from multiple perspectives. It is the images which give subjective "life" to the monotone of the narrator. His narration of "It was not by force" is orchestrated by the invented or interiorized simulation of a rape in the images: A raises herself up on the bed six times in succession, while X is not physically present in the image. He "rapes" her through the camera which assumes his angle of vision, just as Diego makes love to Nadine in La Guerre est finie (1966) via the camera, which moves between her legs without Diego ever being visually present in the scene. The "absence" of X in the "rape" scene, the abrupt repetition of A's arms being raised and the insistent narration on the sound track--all indicate the subjectivity of the scene and the obsession (either repetition or image immobility in a Resnais or Robbe-Grillet film usually denote the obsessive nature of the narrator's or protagonist's mind) with which X "persuades" through monotony and persistent repetition.

Since the images in Marienbad come in clusters, accumulating perspectives in a spiralling movement, description cannot be said to be communicative in the film; rather, it is expressive. Like a cubist painting by Picasso ("Les Demoiselles d'Avignon," for example) description in Marienbad gives the viewer a sense of vertigo, for he is allowed to perceive events from all possible visual angles. Selectivity gives way to succession. Indirect and expansive expression rather than direct communication is the forte of the cinema, according to Metz: "C'est en fait un moyen d'EXPRESSION beaucoup plus que de communication."[16] Judith Gollub cites Gerard Genette as noting that this technique in Robbe-Grillet's fiction and films owes more to metonymy than to metaphor:

> S'inspirant des distinctions de Roman Jacobsen entre l'aspect sélectif du langage, la métaphore, qui est substitution d'un signifiant à un autre, et l'aspect combinatoire, la métonymie, qui est glissement à partir d'un sens, d'un signe à un autre, Genette conclue que toute l'oeuvre de Robbe-Grillet est une métonymie. Il cite comme l'exemple le plus fragrant de cette technique le début du Labyrinthe où à la situation décrite dans la première ligne: "Je suis seul ici, maintenant bien à l'abri" s'oppose la situation inverse en quatre versions différentes suivant les quatres saisons: "Dehors il pleut . . . Dehors il fait froid . . . Dehors il y a du soleil . . . Dehors il neige . . . Le sélectif est devenu successif.[17]

Multiple point of view, through succession rather than selectivity, and multiple spatial perspectives encourage a multiplicity of readings, since they do not allow the spectator to orient himself from one specific vantage point. The effect of so much spatial description is that of confusing the viewer by putting him in all angles of vision at once and the result is poetry, not truth (expression rather than communication). How does one view the Picasso painting of "Les Demoiselles d'Avignon?" Does one "read" it linearly from left to right? Does one read it chronologically from left to right? Or can one momentarily forget one's normal selectivity of vision and submit to the possibility of seeing the progression from all angles at once? The same questions apply to Marienbad. As Judith Gollub has stated: "En partant de la distance scientifique dans la description des objets, il aboutit à un langage tout entier métaphorique et à la poésie."[18] And André Téchiné adds: "L'accumulation des détails, des objets fonctionnels ou décoratifs, précise moins les pistes qu'elle ne les brouille."[19]

As with Hiroshima, Resnais saw in Marienbad the possibility of composing a poem, in which the images would serve in a dialectical or contrapuntal relationship to the text: "Je tenais à composer une espèce de poème où les images ne serviraient que de contrepoint au texte."[20] His intention, Resnais added, was to destroy the feeling of naturalism in the cinema by juxtaposing realism with poetry through counterpoint:

> Le présent film ne prétend pas supprimer radicalement toute INTRIGUE, mais plutôt s'en servir, avec désinvolture aussi bien, pour édifier autre chose: un récit cinématographique . . . les images et les sons et leurs enchainements espèrent s'imposer avec une force assez grande, une nécessité assez évidente, pour définir un REALISME CONTEMPORAIN, surmontant la vielle opposition entre le cinéma réaliste et le cinéma poétique, et remplaçant pour de bon le vieux naturalisme.[21]

Counterpoint is not a device in Marienbad within a larger structure of narration. Counterpoint is the narration and the structure of the film. When the image and the text do correspond, revealing an invented or interiorized scene, either the image or the text quickly changes to re-establish the counterpoint. That counterpoint is at three levels: between the image and the text/music, between the text and the image/music, and between the music and the image/text. As Ropars-Willeumier has pointed out:

> Si une séquence se passe pendant un concert de violons, c'est l'orgue qui continue toutefois à se faire entendre; lorsque le narrateur évoque devant la jeune femme une de leurs rencontres en public, c'est une autre image qui apparait sur l'écran, celle, toute onirique, de cette femme errant dans un parc, sa chaussure à la main. . . . Et si par hasard une image correspond un moment à la description ou à la voix qui l'accompagne, très vite un décalage apparait entre ce qui est dit et ce qui est vu, soit que, au début du film, le récit précède, suscite et rectifie l'image, soit qu'au contraire, à la fin, l'image emporte soudain sur le récit, le contredise et finalement le réduise au silence.[22]

In Hiroshima, there are two different movements or films, the first involving rapid editing and dialogue between Riva and Okada in which the images are in the past while the dialogue is in the present, the second involving longer takes and less editing with more interior monologue and less dialogue in which the images are more and more in the present while the monologue is more and more in the past at Nevers. A similar two-part movement is at work in Marienbad. Voice-over narration predominates in the first half of the film, giving us two voices for X, that of the unseen narrator and that of the participating actor, nad the images are edited rhythmically in terms of that voice-over narration. In the second half of the film, X ceases to be a voice-over narrator and speaks through dialogue. The images "take over" and they reinforce the contradictions and lies in the early voice-over narration. They also project other points of view, in particular that of A, whose subjective vision (the multiplied photographs in the drawer, for example, when X is not present) carries the images until the very end of the film, when the voice-over narrator returns.

Multiple point of view (involving counterpoint between the image and the text) is expressed primarily in visual terms in Marienbad. The camera closes in on a fixed X, staring off into the distance. The camera rotates on its axis and pans 180 degrees or 360 degrees, supposedly simulating the field of vision of X. In reality, it is the field of vision of the unseen narrator, for, within those pans, we often see A twice, dressed in different costumes each time, or we end up seeing X again, as if he were staring at himself. Similarly, in L'Immortelle (1962), the mobile camera pans across a bridge laterally, revealing N and L three different times, in different degrees of close-up or long shot and in different degrees of facing the camera or facing away from the camera. At another point in L'Immortelle, the camera pulls back to reveal N and L, their backs to the camera, looking at N and L, facing the camera. The only resolutions to such apparent contradictions are the following: (1) multiple point of view; (2) a switch in time; or (3) the subjective vision of an unseen narrator.

By contrast, multiple point of view in Hiroshima and La Guerre est finie is achieved primarily through the spoken text, often involving a fusion between interior monologue and dialogue. In Hiroshima, Okada assumes the role of the dead German soldier, while Riva switches back and forth between a subjective "je" and a more objective "elle":

Lui: Quand tu es dans la cave, je suis mort?

Elle: Tu es mort . . . et . . . comment supporter une telle douleur? On croit savoir. Et puis, non. Jamais . . . Elle a eu à Nevers un amour de jeunesse allemand . . . Nous irons en Bavière . . . et nous nous marierons. Elle n'est jamais allée en Bavière.

(emphasis mine)

The play of personal pronouns corresponds to a similar tempering with verb tenses. Okada asks if "he" is dead in the present tense, that tense provoking the memory of the past more effectively than the past tense could. For Riva, the present tense becomes a timeless infinitive ("comment supporter") and the present and future tenses ("Nous irons," "Nous nous marierons"), which present the hypothesis of memory, are undercut contrapuntally by the past tense, which presents cold statements of fact and thus calls for Riva referring to herself as "Elle" in the third person ("Elle a eu," "Elle n'est jamais allée").

Similarly, Diego in La Guerre est finie projects his visions into the future (everything is hypothesized in Diego's mind before it is actualized) while using those future projections to comment on his past. The play of pronouns here is with the second-person singular. Where Riva fluctuates between the "je" and the "elle," Diego addresses himself as "tu," as if he were speaking to another person. His verb tenses fluctuate between the future and the simple past, the present tense being surrounded and psychologically squashed by these two tenses. In the scene of the meeting of the underground members, Diego's mind and interior monologue function as a filter between the meeting and the spectator. With the Diego that speaks to the others, the Diego that both sees the others and sees beyond them to a past or future vision, the Diego that speaks to himself in the second-person singular, and the Diego that only half-hears and, thus, fragments the dialogue of the others, Resnais replaces the selective with the successive, just as Robbe-Grillet had in the opening passage of _Dans le labyrinthe_. Marie-Claire Ropars-Willeumier has commented on the multiplicity of languages in this particular scene of _La Guerre est finie_:

> La parole, au contraire, dans cette séquence de _La Guerre est finie_, n'est jamais donnée directement comme un discours; toutes les opinions soutenues dans la discussion ne viennent au jour que fragmentées, filtrées ou reflétées par la conscience de Diego; dialogue en espagnol, traduction OFF par Diego de ce dialogue, interpretation en monologue intérieur à la deuxième personne, de ce qui est en train de se passer pour monologue intérieur pur, mais toujours à la deuxième personne, la parole traverse ainsi tous les degrès de la réflexion critique.[23]

This use of voice-over narration to make audible the interior voice of a character in _La Guerre est finie_, as in most of the films of the _cinéma des auteurs_, allows the authors to incorporate a literary text which does not weigh down the images, and which, through counterpoint, are never superfluous duplications of the images. The transposition of the literary text to the voice-over narration of the film involves an added advantage: that of playing upon the spectator's eyes and ears simultaneously. As Ropars-Willeumier suggests, the biggest difference between the reading of that text and the hearing of the text in the film is the amplified emphasis upon silences in the text and upon the musical quality of the voices, such silences and music remaining approximate or unvoiced in literature.

> La parole en particulier, à partir du moment où elle s'est intériorisée en voix OFF, a permis de multiplier le récit, en suggérant la présence d'un regard; par cette voix OFF, à valeur narrative, des matériaux littéraires ont pu passer dans le cinéma, mais en subissant toujours certaines métamorphoses, qui les toupent de silences, ou les rapprochent du chant.[24]

Perhaps the most noteworthy and most extended use of counterpoint between the image track and the sound track occurs in Robbe-Grillet's L'Immortelle in the sequence which begins with L and N in a cemetary. N begins an extended monologue on false appearances, almost as if N were not there, or as if L's voice were a projection of N's thoughts. She tells him: "Ce ne sont pas de vraies tombes . . . On n'enterre jamais personne." ("These are not real graves/ . . . No one is buried here.") As she says this, we see N, no longer in the cemetary but rather in his room, lying on his couch with his hands folded over his stomach--in the posture of burial! L's voice continues on the sound track: "Quand elles s'écroulent tout à fait, on s'en sert pour paver les rues, ou comme bordures de trottoir." ("When the stones crumble away, they are used to pave the streets or as curbs for the sidewalks.") As she says this, we see N at his window, looking down on the streets and those just-mentioned sidewalks. L's voice continues: ". . . et vous marchez dessus, tranquillement, sans y penser" (". . . and you walk over them, nonchalantly, without thinking about them"). As she says this, we see N. walk across the room, from the window to the table on which are two letters (perhaps signifying two visions of the same scene). In terms of a semiological analysis of this sequence, we have in one succinct example of counterpoint between the image track and the sound track two signifiers and as many, if not more, signifieds. In other words, we have a clear example of the syntagm (the denotative level of the images) being amplified or replaced by anaphoric relations, one of the mechanisms of cross-reference, which will be discussed in a minute.

Before discussing cross-reference, which I will posit as a possible reading methodology for the films of the cinéma des auteurs, I think it important to specify what constitutes the poetry of the spoken text. There are approximately three elements which characterize these texts: (1) repetition, (2) accumulations of details in a set rhythm pattern, and (3) negation. All three derive in French from the Symbolist poets (Baudelaire, Rimbaud, Mallarmé). As Julia Kristeva has pointed out in her study of these poets,[25] their use of repetition, rhythm and negation totally transformed the language of poetry, creating new syntactical relationships and a new concept of the linguistic sign. I have randomly selected several examples of the three techniques in the cinéma des auteurs:

(1) Repetition: Elle: Quatre fois au musée à Hiroshima . . . J'ai vu les gens se promener. Les gens se promènent pensifs, à travers les photographies, les reconstitutions. . . , faute d'autre chose . . . les explications, faute d'autre chose. Quatre fois au musée à Hiroshima. J'ai regardé les gens. J'ai regardé moi-même . . . , pensivement, le fer . . . le fer brûlé, le fer brisé, le fer devenu vulnérable comme la chair . . . J'ai vu des capsules en bouquets. Qui y aurait pensé? Des peaux humaines, flottantes, survivantes encore dans la fraicheur de leurs souffrances. Des pierres. Des pierres brûlées. Des pierres éclatées.

Des chevelures anonymes que les femmes de
Hiroshima retrouvaient tout entières
tombées le matin, au réveil.

(Resnais's _Hiroshima mon amour_, text by Duras)

Au dixième jour d'expérience, des images commencent à sourdre, comme des aveux. Un matin du temps de paix. Une chambre du temps de paix, une vraie chambre. De vrais enfants. De vrais oiseaux. De vrais chats. De vraies tombes. Le seizième jour, il est sur la jetée. Vide. Quelquefois, il retrouve un jour de bonheur, mais différent, un visage de bonheur, mais différent. Des ruines.

(Chris Marker's _La Jetée_--1963)

Même un paysage tranquille.
Même une prairie avec des vols de corbeaux,
des moissons et des feux d'herbe.
Même une route où passent des voitures, des
paysans, des couples.
Même un village pour vacances avec une foire
et un clocher peuvent conduire tout
simplement à un camp de concentration.

(Resnais's and Cayrol's _Nuit et brouillard_-1955)

Et une fois de plus je m'avançais, seul, le long de ces mêmes couloirs, à travers ces mêmes salles désertes, je longeais ces mêmes colonnades, ces mêmes galeries sans fenêtres, je franchissais ces mêmes portails, choisissant mon chemin comme au hasard parmi le dédale des itinéraires semblables.

(Resnais's and Robbe-Grillet's _L'Année dernière à Marienbad_)

(2) Accumulation of details in a set rhythm

Une fois de plus--je m'avance, une fois de plus, le long de ces couloirs, à travers ces salons, ces galeries, dans cette construction-d' un autre siècle, cet hôtel immense, luxueux, baroque,--lugubre, où des couloirs interminables succèdent aux couloirs,--silencieux, déserts, surchargés d'un décor sombre et froid de boiseries, de stuc, de panneaux moulurés, marbres, glaces noires, tableaux aux teintes noires, colonnes, lourdes tentures,--encadrements sculptés des portes, enfilades de portes, de galeries,--de couloirs transversaux, qui débouchent à leur tour sur des salons déserts, des salons surchargés d'une ornamentation d'un autre siècle, des salles silencieuses . . .

(Resnais's and Robbe-Grillet's _L'Année dernière à Marienbad_)

Deux cent mille morts. Quatre-vingt mille blessés. En neuf secondes. Ces chiffres sont officiels. Ça recommencera. Il y aura dix mille degrès sur la terre. Dix mille soleils, dira-t-on. L'asphalte brûlera. Un désordre profond règnera. Une ville entière sera soulevée de terre et retombera en cendres . . . Des végétations nouvelles surgissent des sables. Quatre étudiants attendent ensemble une mort fraternelle et légendaire.

(_Hiroshima mon amour_)

Cette réalité des camps, méprisée par ceux qui la fabriquent, insaisissable pour ceux qui la subissent, c'est bien en vain qu'à notre tour nous essayons d'en découvrir les restes. Ces blocks en bois, ces chalits où l'on dormait à trois, ces terriers où l'on se cachait, où l'on mangeait à la sauvette, où le sommeil même était une ménace, aucune description, aucune image ne peuvent leur rendre leur vraie dimension, celle d'une peur ininterrompue.

(_Nuit et brouillard_)

(3) Negation

Et ce sont de fausses Eves, de faux Adams, de faux amours, de trompeuses Vénus, de fausses grottes et de fausses nymphes.

(Agnes Varda's Du Côté de la Côte--1958)

. . . ces doigts faits pour serrer, ces yeux faits pour vous voir, qui doivent se détourner de vous--vers ces murs chargés d'ornements d'un autre siècle, boiseries noires, dorures, miroirs taillés, portraits anciens,--guirlandes de stuc aux enlacements baroques,--chapiteaux en trompe-l'oeil, fausses portes, fausses colonnes, perspectives truquées, fausses issues.

(L'Année dernière à Marienbad)

Vous arrivez dans une Turkie de rêve . . . Fausses prisons, faux remparts, fausses histoires . . . Vous ne pouvez plus revenir en arrière . . . Et pour vous échapper . . . Ce sont de faux bateaux, aussi, vous voyez bien.

(Robbe-Grillet's L'Immortelle--1962)

. . . se croisent vrais et faux Américains, vrais et faux Méxicains, mais même les vrais sont faux, faux les visages, fausses les couleurs, faux les vêtements, faux les seins, fausses les reconstitutions archéologiques . . .

(Chris Marker's Yo Soy Mexico--1965)

It should be apparent from these examples that all three techniques often appear in the same passage. Thus, the repetitions and accumulations of details by Riva in Hiroshima are instantly and abruptly negated by Okada at every turn: "Tu n'as rien vu à Hiroshima," "Tu n'as pas vu d'hôpital à Hiroshima," "Tu ne sais rien," "Tu ne connais pas l'oubli," "Tu n'es pas douée de mémoire." The dialectical or contrapuntal relationship between the text and ie images is often achieved through this interplay of repetitions, ccumulations and negations. Thus, the text creates its own ssociations, its own caesurae, its own *enjambements*, its own ontage.

Counterpoint or association does not always occur simultaneously etween the text and the image track, however. And, if the films of ie *cinéma des auteurs* cannot be "read" in terms of empirical eanings, they can be read in terms of structure. One reading ethodology that I would propose is that of cross-reference or ross-indexing in the films. In *Hiroshima*, for example, Riva entions to Okada that a man passes by her window every day at four nd coughs. This would seem to be a curious but insignificant etail. Yet, no details are superfluous in this text. That detail an be understood cross-referentially, when we learn that Riva spent so much time in the cellar at Nevers, time when she was leprived of seeing things, time when she learned to listen more acutely and to pick up such seemingly insignificant details.

There is another example of cross-reference in *Hiroshima* that exists solely in the spoken text. To the spectator, Riva seems to enunciate her words perhaps too much at two different points. It is no coincidence that those two points join the themes of love and war, of love and time. In the first, Riva says in her *voix intérieure*: "Il va venir vers moi, . . . il va me prendre par les épaules . . . il m'embras-se-ra. Il m'embrassera . . . et je serai perdue." In the second example, Riva says: "Hi-ro-shi-ma . . .

Hi-ro-shi-ma . . . c'est ton nom." The meticulous enunciation and the breaking up of words into syllables links these two otherwise disparate places in the text.

A third example of cross-reference has to do with love again. In the film, ugliness becomes beauty in a strange kind of reverse masochism. Again, two different places in the text are cross-indexed through this theme of ugliness-love. The first exchange goes as follows:

> Lui: Tu es une belle femme, tu sais?
> Elle: Tu trouves?
> Lui: Je trouve.
> Elle: Un peu fatiguée, non?
> Lui: Un peu laide.
> Elle: Ça ne fait rien?
> Lui: C'est ce que j'ai remarqué, hier soir, à ce café. La façon dont tu es laide.

This exchange becomes cross-indexed with an interior monologue of Riva's:

> Tu me tues. . . , Tu me fais du bien . . . J'ai le temps. Je t'en prie. Dévore-moi. Déforme-moi jusqu'à la laideur.

Such examples are not essential for the understanding of the film. Reading the film cross-referentially, as one must read a poem, merely adds to one's understanding of the film. Perhaps several examples from a more difficult film to "read" would better serve my argument.

Everything is cross-indexed in Resnais's and Jacques Sternberg's _Je t'aime je t'aime_ (1968). Thus, everything has its echo and its resonance for the spectator who actively participates in the film, who "recreates" the film's reality with the filmmakers. At one point in Dr. Haesert's examination of Claude Ridder at Crespel prior to his time travel, the doctor says: "Je ne vous vois pas avec un revolver." He says this in response to the fact that Ridder attempted suicide with a revolver. Later (in terms of the film's running) but earlier (in terms of Ridder's past) Catrine says to Ridder on a train: "Je ne te vois pas avec un revolver." She says this in response to their passing a village he helped liberate during the war. The two scenes, thus, become cross-indexed. The problem for the spectator is to discern whether the dialogue between Catrine and Ridder ever occurred, or whether Ridder imagined the dialogue and gives Catrine Dr. Haesert's line.

At another point, Ridder and Catrine are in bed together. The following dialogue ensues:

> Catrine: Tu as vraiment de beaux yeux . . . on te l'a déjà dit?
> Ridder: Oui. Et j'ai envie de toi. On te l'a déjà dit?
> Catrine: Oui.
> Ridder: Tu vois, nous ne sommes pas des pionniers.

Ridder's use of the word "pionniers" is suspicious, for it reverts back to another scene between Ridder and the doctors at Crespel. The doctors ask if Ridder can tell the difference between two mice seen under a glass bubble. Ridder's response is typical of him. He asks if one is male and the other female. The correct response, as the doctor informs him, is that "la souris B est un pionnier." The key to understanding the love affair between Ridder and Catrine has nothing to do with being male or female, but rather with being a pioneer or not: Claude Ridder is a time-traveler, Catrine is not. Also, Ridder's present (Crespel) transforms the dialogues of his past (Catrine).

The cross-reference with the mouse recalls other cross-indexes: for example, the mouse of the time machine travels in Ridder's past and physically runs across his path at the beach. When Ridder asks Catrine if she has ever seen a mouse run across the beach before, she responds: "Elle est peut-être en vacances." Her answer refers to Ridder's earlier exchange with the doctors at Crespel, in which he tells them that one year ago at the appointed hour he was on vacation and that being on vacation is one of the few things he is positive of remembering, one of his few _points de repère_. The cross-reference with the mouse has yet another extension when Wiana, the confidante of Ridder, says to him in a pontifical way: "Claude Ridder, vous êtes fait comme un rat." The colloquial expression, which has a specific connotative meaning that has nothing to do with a mouse or rat, takes on grotesque overtones, because its denotative or literal meaning is equally valid.

Through cross-referencing, a scene involving two secretaries in the hall of a publicity bureau in 1962 becomes related to a scene involving Ridder and Catrine in the Gorges de Provence in 1966. In the earlier scene, the dialogue is as follows:

> Secretaire A: La couleur de la psychose, c'est bien le rouge?
> Secretaire B: Non, le rouge, c'est le futur.
> Secretaire A: Et la psychose, alors?
> Secretaire B: C'est le vert.
> Secretaire A: Ah! . . . Je les confonds toujours!

Compare this exchange with the following exchange in the second scene in question:

> Ridder: Et puis, ici la nature n'a pas ce vert écoeurant de la campagne.
>
> Catrine: Tu as raison . . . C'est un vert moins écoeurant que celui de la campagne. Et si l'homme était allergique à la couleur verte. . . ? C'est peut-être le vert qui provoque l'usure des cellules, entrainant la vieillesse et la mort. Ce serait drôle, non? . . . Des millions de savants qui s'acharnent à inventer des ouvre-boites, des bouchons . . . j'sais pas moi . . . et qui passeraient complètement à côté de cette idée qui changerait tout. Moi, je crois que le secret est là: tellement simple que personne ne l'a effleuré . . . On va rester un mois sans manger de la salade . . . pour voir.

This exchange, related thus to both psychosis and the future, is further cross-indexed with two other scenes involving food and two other scenes involving the characters' comments on nature and the countryside.

But perhaps the most complex (and most rewarding) example of cross-reference involves the often-repeated scene of Ridder emerging from the water. First of all, the scene recalls the doctor's explanation that the time machine is like a decompression chamber for divers: the decompression chamber is a perfect analogy, since both Resnais and Sternberg have insisted on the sense of falling in their concept of time-travel in the film. We can argue that there is mere repetition in these scenes, yet there are slight variations within the repetitions. Sometimes, Ridder pauses to wash his mask before walking backwards out of the water. At other times, he does not pause to wash his mask. There is at least one other time where he has no mask at all. Ridder keeps returning to this scene, and the reasons are many and complex. For one thing, there is a poetic construct set up between Catrine and the water, which makes it important for Ridder to return: to understand this moment is to understand all of the moments with Catrine. The following dialogue, from a scene which takes place away from the beach, bears this out:

> Ridder: Non, j'aime le trouble, la confusion, ce qui bascule . . .
> Catrine: Je bascule, moi?
> Ridder: Pas tellement! . . . Même pas du tout . . . Au contraire, toi, tu es étale. Tu es un marécage. De la nuit, de la boue, des . . . Toi . . . tu . . . sens la marée basse, la noyade, la pieuvre. D'ailleurs cette plage . . .
> Catrine: Oui, cette plage, c'est moi . . .

Drowning (falling in time, losing oneself in time) actually occurs at another point in the film. And the water's reference to death is also made explicit in the final scenes, in which Ridder re-commits suicide, while sounds of breathing underwater fill the sound track. Where all of these cross-references coalesce is in the time machine itself, the only time that Ridder repeats the lines of the title, insisting to himself that he must concentrate, that he must return to that moment emerging from the water: (1) to comprehend the meaning of Catrine and her death, and (2) to escape from the time machine, by staying in that moment long enough for the scientists to be able to pull him out.

It is curious that critics who are accustomed to cross-references in the poetry of Baudelaire, Rimbaud and Mallarmé should balk at reading the cinematic text of Resnais in the same way. Conditioned to linear narrative in films, to film's legacy from photography of reproducing reality, they tire of the fragmented editing in _Je t'aime je' t'aime_; they are confused by repeated scenes, scenes with apparently no connotative meaning, scenes which follow other scenes without transitions which are immediately logical or palpable. It is important to note that even Metz, while praising the ambiguity in such films (the influence, I would contend, of Bazin on him), offers no constructive reading methodology for such cinematic texts. Cross-reference may involve reading the _ciné-roman_ very closely or it may involve seeing the film in question several times. But this again brings film closer to poetry and the novel. A film which offers new reading possibilities each time it is seen is a film which deserves the same esteem as a novel or poem which must be read several times for any deep understanding.

That multiplicity of readings is suggested even in the titles of the films of the _cinéma des auteurs_. Just as Sartre's Florence was at one and the same time a city, a flower and a woman, so too Resnais's _Hiroshima_ is a city, a time and a man; Marker's _La Jetée_, an airstrip a woman, a ballet term referring to a time jump; Robbe-Grillet's _L'Immortelle_, a woman and two cities; Varda's _Les Creatures_ (1966), the characters of the film, the figures of a chess game, and the characters of the husband's novel. This multiplicity at the level of the art work parallels Marguerite Duras's desired multiplicity at the level of the art form for _Détruire dit-elle_ (1969) to be simultaneously a play, a poem, a novel, a musical fugue, a film, and an opera. In this context, the directors of the _cinéma des auteurs_ have radically redefined the meaning of "adaptation."

It seems a paradox that poetry, which usually addresses itself more directly but to a more restricted audience than the novel, should depend so heavily upon that audience for the "completion" of meaning. Likewise, the _cinéma des auteurs_, while addressing itself to a limited audience (and perhaps because of that), demands an enormous amount of participation on the part of the reader/viewer. They have tried to duplicate the conditions of reading literature. Resnais's pronouncements on _L'Année dernière à Marienbad_ are quite significant in this regard:

> With this film I should like, without theory or manifesto, to recover the conditions of reading, that is to say, the spectator should feel himself alone, like the reader. To interest himself in the story, he should not need the well-known elements of dramatic progression, not need to rely upon the anecdote, witty dialogue, explanation or chronology. I should like the real tension to derive not so much from the script as from the image and sound and to impose itself on the eye and ear.[26]

> (I want) to leave the spectator as much freedom of imagination as the reader of a novel has.[27]

> Nous aimerions que le spectateur se laisse aller et participe en créant son interprétation perpétuellement. Le film est fait pour 50% de ce que l'on montre sur l'écran et pour le reste des réactions et de la participation du spectateur . . . _Marienbad_ est un film "ouvert" qui propose à chacun un engagement, un choix.[28]

The invitation to the spectator is not a frivolous or easy invitation. Rather, it is more of a challenge, since the spectator must often content himself with the perception of precise forms rather than precise meanings, because of "la multiplicité des lectures possibles et l'impossibilité de se limiter à une seule interprétation."[29] As René Prédal has pointed out, watching a film of the _cinéma des auteurs_ involves a restructuring of one's logic (as in reading poetry), whereby the spectator accepts the fact that interior visions and mental time perceptions are just as important as objective reality.

> Brouillant les cartes, Resnais filme en effet de la même manière les images mentales et les représentations de la réalité. Or, il s'agit là d'un A PRIORI totalement faux: sauf cas pathologique, l'homme sait différencier une sensation qui lui vient du cerveau d'une autre provoquée par la vue; il fait la différence entre ce qu'il voit et ce qu'il pense alors que le film ne fait pas ce tri: c'est le spectateur... qui doit s'en charger. Au contraire, un autre spectateur, face à ce même puzzle préférera peut-être se mettre "en état de rêve," c'est-à-dire accepter de ressentir comme tout naturel... l'illogique ou l'absurde! Dans ces deux cas, les deux spectateurs n'auront finalement pas l'impression d'avoir vu le même film car, à partir des matériaux communs, ils auront reconstruit une oeuvre totalement originale: Voici donc ouverte l'ère du film personnalisé où chacun compose le spectacle de son choix. 30

The intent, then, of the _cinéma des auteurs_, whether one calls their work _ciné-romans_ (emphasis on the published text) or _ciné-poèmes_ (emphasis on the film), is double-edged: to create "mille oeuvres en une, toutes les oeuvres possibles en une seule oeuvre mouvante,"[31] and to invite the reader/viewer to participate at the level of creation. As Claire Clouzot has asserted: "Un film de Resnais ou de Robbe-Grillet est UN OBJET existant indépendamment de son auteur et dont le spectateur, an s'en emparant, devient l'un des créateurs."[32] The creation of the _Gesamtkunstwerk_, thus, depends as much upon the audience being co-creators as upon the authors. To that end, this audience must be able to incorporate literature and the other arts in their film viewing/reading, just as these directors have incorporated them.

Notes

[1] Agnes Varda, Cléo de 5 à 7 (Paris: Gallimard, 1962), p. 7.

[2] Ibid.

[3] Varda, p. 8.

[4] Alain Robbe-Grillet, L'Immortelle (Paris: Editions de Minuit, 1963), p. 7.

[5] Robbe-Grillet, p. 8.

[6] Jean Ricardou, Cahiers du Cinéma, 1961.

[7] Jean Narboni and Jacques Rivette, "Entretien avec Marguerite Duras," Cahiers du Cinéma, 217 (November 1969), p. 45.

[8] Ibid.

[9] Richard Mitchell Blumenberg, The Manipulation of Time and Space in the Novels of Alain Robbe-Grillet and in the Narrative Films of Alain Resnais, With Particular Reference to Last Year at Marienbad (Ph.D., Ohio University, 1969), p. 74.

[10] Anais Nin, The Novel of the Future (New York: Macmillan, 1968), p. 12.

[11] Nin, p. 27.

[12] Marcel Martin, Le Langage cinématographique (Paris: Editions du Cerf, 1955) p. 238.

[13] Roy Armes, French Cinema Since 1946. Vol. II (London and New York: A. S. Barnes and Co., 1966), p. 89.

[14] Marie-Claire Ropars-Willeumier, L'Ecran de la mémoire (Paris: Editions du Seuil, 1970), p. 234.

[15] Armes, p. 97.

[16] Christian Metz, Essais sur la signification au cinéma (Paris: Editions Klincksieck, 1971), p. 79.

[17] Judith Gollub, Nouveau Roman et Nouveau Cinéma (Ph.D. UCLA, 1966), p. 84.

[18] Gollub, p. 86.

[19] André Téchiné, "La Fin du voyage," Cahiers du Cinéma, 181 (August 1966), p. 24.

[20] René Prédal, Etudes Cinématographiques, 64-68 (1968), p. 29.

[21] Alain Resnais, Cinéma 61, 53 (February 1961), reprinted in Prédal, p. 169.

[22] Ropars-Willeumier, p. 117.

[23] Ropars-Willeumier, p. 208.

[24] Ropars-Willeumier, p. 234.

[25] Julia Kristeva, Sēmeiōtikē: Recherches pour une sémanalyse (Paris: Editions du Seuil, 1969).

[26] Armes, p. 100.

[27] Armes, p. 99.

[28] Alain Resnais, Le Monde, (August 1961), reprinted in Prédal, p. 167.

[29] Ropars-Willeumier, p. 114.

[30] Prédal, pp. 166-167.

[31] Ropars-Willeumier, p. 114.

[32] Claire Clouzot, Le Cinéma français depuis la nouvelle vague (Paris: Editions Fernand Nathan, 1972), p. 69.

The influence of the _nouveau roman_ on the _cinéma des auteurs_ would perhaps be the easiest of influences to document, were it not for the necessity to redefine both the _nouveau roman_ and the _cinéma des auteurs_ in terms of that influence. Were they thorough, such definitions would take up volumes. The intent of this discussion, therefore, is not to present an exhaustive documentation of either the _nouveau roman_ or the _cinéma des auteurs_, nor to suggest the differences between the two, but rather, as if we were dealing with an analogy, to compare the two skeletally, capitalizing on the fact that three of the most prominent new novelists - Alain Robbe-Grillet, Marguerite Duras and Jean Cayrol - have also made _ciné-romans_ or film-novels.

It should be noted from the outset that neither the _nouveau roman_ nor the _cinéma des auteurs_ reflect strict "schools" of thought or rigid classified movements; rather, they reflect intentions, tendencies, "spirits" of thought. In other words, the reader should recognize that Marguerite Duras's _Moderato Cantabile_ (1958) differs from Alain Robbe-Grillet's _Dans le labyrinthe_ (1959) in the same proportion that _Détruire dit-elle_ (1969) differs from _L'Année dernière à Marienbad_ (1961) or _L'Immortelle_ (1962). Yet, as novelists Duras and Robbe-Grillet reacted against similar things, just as they turned to film for similar reasons. I have felt it necessary to make such a qualifying statement, since there are enough misunderstandings about the relationship between literature and film. I do not want to compound the difficulties already inherent in a discussion such as this one.

André Malraux once asserted that "modernism" depended upon the artist's relationship with his subject.[1] What was truly modern in the arts, he argued, was the appearance of the artist upon his own canvas; the necessary prerequisite for such an appearance was the dissolution of traditional narrative or story-telling. In other words, the appearance of the artist marked the disappearance of the anecdotal subject. The traditional distinctions between fiction and diary in literature would have to be rethought. Antonioni pointed to the emphasis on new narratives when he said: "Plutôt que d'une influence documentaire dans mes films, il me semble plus exact de parler de la tendance narrative de mes documentaires."[2] And Anais Nin suggests in her _The Novel of the Future_ that "D. H. Lawrence's accurate statement that our biggest problem in fiction was how to transport the living essence of a character into the novel without its dying in the process was solved by the diary."[3]

But the diary form per se does not completely explain the reasons behind Robbe-Grillet's _je-néant_ (I-void) narrators, Cayrol's _héros lazaréens_ (Lazarus-like protagonists) or Marguerite Duras's emphasis on _sous-conversations_ (sub-dialogue or inter-dialogue). In other words, their affinities with the diary form are not due to a concern for the preservation of the "living essence" of a character, nor are their manifestations of the artist upon the canvas uniquely due to a desire to break down the traditional boundaries between fiction and documentary. As Robbe-Grillet would have it, the problem is much more labyrinthine than that. According to Robbe-Grillet, the sign that the modern narrator wears upon his chest is that of _larvatus prodeo_ or "I advance masked but revealing my mask." The revolution in fiction accomplished by the new novel, then, seems to be the difference between definition and process analysis: not what the narrator relates but how he relates it.

In this respect, it would be noted that both the _nouveau roman_ and the _cinéma des auteurs_ represent lags in time in the sense that both continue experiments that were begun in the 1920's in fiction and film. Thus, the gradual disappearance of characters' family names towards an anonymity of character and the appearance of the _mise-en-abime_ (literally "placed in the abyss," here meaning "the work mirrored within the work") novel within the novel in Gide's _Les Faux-Monnayeurs_ (1925) is the basis for Butor's novel-within-the-novel in _L'Emploi du temps_ (1966) or the books and film within the film of Robbe-Grillet's _Trans-Europ Express_ (1966). It is Kafka's creation of a parallel universe in _The Castle_ (1926) or _The Trial_ (1925), in which the minute description of objects creates a solid objective reality at the same time that it points to the subjective obsessions of the narrator (Robbe-Grillet calls it the sense of _being there_ before _being anything_ and adds that the culmination of objectivity is subjectivity), is behind the parallel universes of _L'Année dernière à Marienbad_ and _L'Homme qui_ *ment* (1968) as films and *Dans le labyrinthe* and *Le Voyeur* (1955) as novels. Virginia Woolf's and Apollinaire's experiments in dialogue without delineated speakers or in language that captures the rhythms of speech as well as its fragments are the precursors of Nathalie Sarraute's fiction and Marguerite Duras's fiction and films. Proust's experiments in expanding language through associative metaphors and his concept of time as a flow interrupted by moments of *déjà vu* and *moments privilégiés* is the source of Resnais's concept of time and his dialectic between past and present. Faulkner's *The Wild Palms* (1939) was the inspiration for Agnes Varda's *La Pointe courte* (1955). Such documentation could go on indefinitely. Suffice it to say that, without the fiction of Joyce, Proust, Kafka, Gide, Faulkner and Virginia Woolf, there would be no *nouveau roman* and no *cinéma des auteurs*. This statement at least needs no documentation.

To appreciate what is "new" about the new novel (and about the *cinéma des auteurs*), one would have to begin with the author's change of distance, both in terms of the artistic work and in terms of the reader or viewer of that work.

On the one hand, the author has entered his work more directly. Where a Balzac would often interject authorial statements into his fiction, all the while retaining his identity as author or as mover of marionettes, the new novelist, as Malraux predicted, enters his own canvas. The subterfuge of such an entry is that the first-person narrator is not omniscient, not omnipotent, not infallible. He is often "in the dark," as many of Robbe-Grillet's narrators seem to be. He often distorts what he sees or deliberately falsifies his visions, as both the husband in La Jalousie (1957) and Boris Varissa in L'Homme qui ment confess to doing. Yet, he is upon the canvas. As Nathalie Sarraute has pointed out:

> Aujourd'hui chacun se doute bien, sans qu'on ait besoin de le lui dire, que "la Bovary - c'est moi." Et puisque ce qui maintenant importe c'est, bien plutôt que d'allonger indéfiniment la liste des types littéraires, de montrer la coexistence de sentiments contradictoires et de rendre, dans la mesure du possible, la richesse et la complexité de la vie psychologique, l'écrivain, en toute honnêteté, parle de soi.[4]

This entrance of the artist upon his canvas creates a disruption of the well-ordered universe in the traditional novel. Being anonymous, the author as main character pervades the work; being human, often obsessively so, as opposed to god-like (Butor characterized Balzac as a deus ex maquina author) his usurpation of the role of main character often means that all other characters are in some way reflections of him. As Sarraute again points out:

> Aujourd'hui, un flot toujours grossissant nous inonde, d'oeuvres littéraires qui prétendent encore être des romans et où un être sans contours, indéfinissable, insaisissable et invisible, un "je" anonyme qui est tout et qui n'est rien et qui n'est le plus souvent qu'un reflet de l'auteur lui-même, a usurpé le rôle du héros principal et occupe la place d'honneur. Les personnages qui l'entourent, privés d'existence propre, ne sont plus que des visions, rêves, cauchemars, illusions, reflets, modalités ou dépendances de ce "je" tout-puissant.[5]

Thus, the narrator of Robbe-Grillet's Dans le labyrinthe begins with "je" on the first page and ends with "moi" on the last page. In between, he seems to enter the body (without entering the mind, as a

Balzac would have done) of the character designated as "le soldat"; in addition, he appears as a doctor near the end of the novel without any signal that the doctor and the narrator are one and the same. Robbe-Grillet uses the same *je-néant* device in his films. A narrator (with X's voice) begins the film, merges with the voices of the play going on in the chateau and then seems to approximate the character of X, although the voice could not logically refer at all times to X and, thus, refers equally to A and M. In *L'Immortelle* the narrator's voice seems to merge with that of N, the professor. But the spectator must ultimately conclude that there are two N's in *L'Immortelle*, one who narrates the beginning and the end of the film and is invisible to the spectator, the other visualized as an awkward, expressionistic N to signify that he, as well as L and all other characters in the film, is a figment of the invisible narrator's imagination and that he is the sensory filter through which all characters in the film must be seen and interpreted.

At the same time that the author thus enters more closely into the "fiction" of his work, he also distances himself from it, moving closer to the reader or viewer than a Balzac or a Flaubert did, becoming in a sense a fellow-reader or fellow-viewer, a spectator of his own creation. In other words, he stops pulling strings.

> Ou le personnage, tant la croyance en lui de son auteur et l'intérêt qu'il lui porte sont intenses, se met soudain, telles les tables tournantes, animé par un fluide mysterieux, à se mouvoir de son propre mouvement et à entrainer à sa suite son créateur ravi qui n'a plus qu'à se laisser à son tour guider par sa créature.[6]

He begins to believe in his creations as real people, with all the contradictions and ambiguities that real people have. He stops fabricating plots that he knows the reader will find too incredulous or too neatly packaged, plots which, by their very neatness, both falsify and rigidify character:

> Et il (the reader) se méfie des actions brutales et spectaculaires qui façonnent à grandes claques sonores les caractères; et aussi de l'intrigue qui, s'enroulant autour du personnage comme une bandelette, lui donne, en même temps qu'une apparence de cohésion et de vie, la rigidité des momies.[7]

Contrasted with this rigidity of a mummy that might characterize a Eugénie Grandet or a Frederic Moreau is the fluidity of new characters, characters whose make-up is more flux than substance, characters whose very identity is placed in question (the characters in Sarraute's *Portrait d'un inconnu* (1956), the Oedipal detective in Robbe-Grillet's *Les Gommes* (1953), Thérèse and the amnesiac vagabond in Henri Colpi's *Une Aussi Longue Absence* (1961)) or whose identity becomes the subject of inquiry for the whole work (*Dans le labyrinthe*); more often than not, the identity problem is never resolved or is resolved in the kind of ambiguity that a film like *Citizen Kane* (1941) or *Rashomon* (1949) presents. Consequently, new tension is created in these novels and films by the very fact that empirical identity is impossible and, in addition, by the fact that characters admit to flux rather than trying to tell other characters who or what they are, as in the following example from Resnais's and Jacques Sternberg's *Je t'aime je t'aime* (1968):

Wiana: J'en arrive à me demander qui tu es exactement.

Ridder: Quelque chose d'assez flou. De plus en plus flou. Je rétrécis et je déteins au lavage.

For his part, the author places himself at the elbow of the reader or viewer and questions characters along with the reader or viewer. Dorrit Cohn has referred to this phenomenon as the quantum or relativity theory of fiction, which has extended to film.[8] Nathalie Sarraute, herself, uses the analogy of physics to state the changeability of the modern fictional character which produces a new questioning on the part of the reader or viewer:

> Ces états, en effet, sont comme ces phénomènes de la physique moderne, si délicates et infimes qu'un rayon de lumière ne peut les éclairer sans qu'il les trouble et les déforme. Aussi, dès que le romancier essaie de les décrire sans révéler sa présence, il lui semble entendre le lecteur, pareil à cet enfant à qui sa mère lisait pour la première fois une histoire, l'arrêter en demandant: "Qui dit ça?"[9]

This refusal to "know all" about the work of art gives it more a sense of a work-in-progress, as opposed to the fatalistic or deterministic sense that one has reading a novel of the nineteenth century, in which the reader knows that all will be explained to him in due time and that the author does "hold the key" to everything. The new novelists and filmmakers under discussion here respect their characters' new-found depth of personality; they can no more predict the outcome of the work-in-progress or explain characters' behavior than they could foresee the future in real life or explain the behavior of real people. Thus, there is no "outcome" or <u>dénouement</u> to Beckett's <u>Molloy</u> (1949), to Robbe-Grillet's *La Jalousie* (1953), to Sarraute's *Tropismes* (1957), or to Claude Simon's *La Route des Flandres* (1960). In fact, rather than a clarification of what goes on, there is instead a further clouding of the problems raised by the work of art. We don't know if Riva leaves Hiroshima or if she consents to stay in *Hiroshima mon amour* (1959). Contrary to popular opinion, Resnais thinks that she stays, but he admits that he doesn't really know. We don't know whether the vagabond in *Une Aussi Longue Absence* was the missing husband or, as he claims, a stranger suffering from amnesia. We don't know whether *Marienbad* spans two years' time or one year. We don't know whether the husband was writing or dreaming or living out the "novel" of Agnes Varda's *Les Créatures* (1966). We don't know whether Boris Varissa and Jean Robin were one and the same person or not in Robbe-Grillet's *L'Homme qui ment*. Finally, we don't know what the forest represents in Duras's *Détruire dit-elle* or what the exact relationships between Alissa, Max Thor and Stein were. It's not that their creators are refusing to tell us; it's rather that they, themselves, do not know. Implicit in their not knowing all the answers is of course the assumption that the work of art cannot be paraphrased or reduced to any empirical meaning or interpretation. What such authors have sacrificed in omniscience, they have regained in the multiplicity of meanings that their novels and films contain.

Their fictional and filmic universes are opened up by the presentation of hypotheses rather than the ultimate resolution of a single truth which would "close" the work. Indeed, Robbe-Grillet cites the investigation of true and false as one of the major characteristics of modern fiction:

> Le faux -- c'est-à-dire à la fois le possible, l'impossible, l'hypothèse, le mensonge, ... (est) devenu l'un des thèmes privilégiés de la fiction moderne.[10]

Thus, the investigation of truth and lie, of dream and remembrance, and of the real and the imaginary takes the place of the traditional plot or story. For the artist to appear on the canvas, it was necessary that the anecdotal subject disappear. One cannot paraphrase the "plots" of the new novels, just as one cannot accurately paraphrase the "plots" of the *cinéma des auteurs*. With the disappearance of plot, the traditional linear time of cause-and-effect slows down, becomes a more fluid or static time: in either case, a more indeterminant time. Actions give way to feelings or sensory impressions, which are portrayed through description or through dialogue, but which are given as if unexpurgated, that is, without authorial interpretation for the reader. As Sarraute has pointed out:

> Il (the reader) a vu le temps cesser d'être ce courant rapide qui poussait en avant l'intrigue pour devenir une eau dormante au fond de laquelle s'élaborent de lentes et subtiles décompositions; il a vu nos actes perdre leurs mobiles courants et leurs significations admises, des sentiments inconnus apparaitre et les mieux connus changer d'aspect et de nom.[11]

If the narrator has changed places with the reader in a sense, and if actions have given way to feelings, then the style of the writer takes on a much more important significance, since ultimate or empirical meanings have been stripped away. As Robbe-Grillet has stated: "L'écrivain n'a rien à dire, seulement une manière de dire."[12] Indeed, it could even be argued that language has become the main character in the new novel and in the *cinéma des auteurs*. Thus, Judith Gollub has characterized the new novel as "une littérature qui n'est que du langage, dont l'objet est presque uniquement le langage, qui tend donc à la poésie."[13] Marie-Claire Ropars-Willeumier also likens the language of the *nouveau roman* to poetry, insisting that the new novel has almost obliterated the usual distinctions between prose and poetry:

> Il n'est rien de plus statique, en apparence, que *La Jalousie* ou *La Route des Flandres*, et l'envoutement que suscite peu à peu dans l'esprit du lecteur la répétition d'images s'enroulant autour d'un regard absent ou d'une conscience vide ressortit plus à l'incantation poétique qu'au déroulement temporel d'une aventure humaine. Que la poésie soit l'aboutissement suprême de la littérature contemporaine, qu'à la limite toute distinction doive nécessairement s'abolir entre des genres autrefois si séparés, c'est là une question qu'il est possible de poser, non de résoudre.[14]

Thus, Robbe-Grillet, Butor and Cayrol construct circular poems, accumulating details that revolve upon themselves, somewhat as Proust had done before them. Language predominates in a film like *L'Année dernière à Marienbad*, the invisible narrator becoming an integral actor in the film and breaking up the triangle of X, A and M. Thus, *L'Immortelle* and *Trans-Europ Express* begin where they started, just as *La Jalousie* and *Dans le labyrinthe* return to their respective places of departure. Indeed, there is no subject to Robbe-Grillet's _L'Eden et après_ (1970): there are only twelve variations upon the same theme, with the suggestion that there could be an infinite number of variations given, if the filmmaker chose to do so. And his film _N. a pris les Dés_ (1970) is the same film as _L'Eden et après_ with one exception: the characters' names have been changed one more time.

Description for Robbe-Grillet is often a means of tracing the absence between one point and another. His narrator provides us with his eyes, but those eyes are capricious, prone to seeing double, to seeing voids, to seeing visions or hallucination. Marie-Claire Ropars-Willeumier has noted a similar tendency in the camera of Alain Resnais, which, contrary to the traditional mobile camera, shows voids rather than filling them in:

> La description des objets et du décor n'est visiblement pour Resnais qu'un moyen supplémentaire de les rendre absents.[15]

What is absent in this form of fiction or cinema is not the vision of a narrator (that, in fact, is in abundance), but the interpretation of that vision. The narrators in these novels and films refuse to arrange objects neatly into a system of metaphors or symbols with referents. They suppress meaning so that the spectator is forced to provide it himself.

This emphasis on language takes on another form, that is, other than the endlessly circular descriptions of a Robbe-Grillet and Cayrol or the circular tracking camera of Resnais. It also takes the form of a renewed emphasis on dialogue. As Sarraute has stated:

> Mais, à défaut d'actes, nous avons à notre disposition les paroles. Les paroles possèdent les qualités nécessaires pour capter, protéger et porter au dehors ces mouvements souterrains à la fois impatients et craintifs... les personnages de roman deviennent... bavards.[16]

Sarraute goes on to speak of the falseness inherent in the traditional novel's rendering of dialogue: the necessity of denoting the speaker, the necessity of cumbersome punctuation, both of which break up the free-flow of the dialogue and signal to the reader that this dialogue is an artifice. As Sarraute has pointed out:

> Mais plus gênants encore et plus difficilement défendables que les alinéas, les tirets, les deux points et les guillemets sont les monotones et gauches: dit Jeanne, répondit Paul, qui parsèment habituellement le dialogue; ils deviennent de plus en plus pour les romanciers actuels ce qu'étaient pour les peintres, juste avant le cubisme, les règles de la perspective: non plus une nécessité, mais une encombrante convention.[17]

Sarraute cites Ivy Compton-Burnett has having found a way out of the predicament: one need only write a novel in which description gives way to dialogue. In other words, the whole novel is a continuous series of dialogues. Sarraute, herself, with novels like _Tropismes_ (1957) and _Les Fruits d'or_ (1963) has done just that. And Marguerite Duras, in novels like _Moderato Cantabile_, _Le Square_ (1955) and _Le Ravissement de Lol V. Stein_ (1964) as well as in films like _La Musica_ (1967), _Detruire dit-elle_, _Nathalie Granger_ (1972) and _La Femme du Gange_ (1973), has totally restructured the work of fiction or the film in terms of language. Even Robbe-Grillet seems to have forsaken the narrator who describes in _Marienbad_ for the _bavard_-inventor of half-truths and half-lies in _L'Homme qui ment_. Yet, it could be said that all dialogue in the _cinéma des auteurs_ stems from the new novel and from this predominance of language over action. The lovers in Varda'a _La Pointe courte_ or in Resnais's _Hiroshima mon amour_ do not act: they discuss, they chant, they recite. Sarraute could very well be talking about the Varda or Resnais films when she says of Ivy Compton-Burnett's literary conversations:

> Ces longues phrases guindées, à la fois rigides et sinueuses, ne rappellent aucune conversation entendue. Et pourtant, si elles paraissent étranges, elles ne donnent jamais une impression de fausseté ou de _gratuité_.[18]

Sarraute's statement seems to apply even more directly to the fiction and films of Marguerite Duras. It could even be said that language is all that is left in Duras's work. Her characters are not usually described by the author; they describe themselves through speech. Such characters do not act; rather, they react. And their reactions are given in language. One of the most striking features of a Duras character is the _ennui_, the physical and spiritual boredom or lassitude that he or she feels. Action has already occurred somewhere in a past which precedes the reader's or viewer's entry into the work.

There is no plot, properly speaking, in a Duras novel or film. There is only the language of characters who are struggling to find meaning in the present. Indeed, the possibilities of language as communication become whatever plot there is. The essential question in a novel like _Moderato Cantabile_ is whether or not Anne Désbaresdes and Chauvin can communicate. It should be noted that communication between characters in a novel has usually been taken for granted before Marguerite Duras and Nathalie Sarraute. Assuming that language communicates, artists have been more interested in language as expression. Sarraute and Duras have placed the very premise of language in question: does language function adequately as communication? That question is raised to the level of an _ars poetica_ in Resnais's and Duras's _Hiroshima mon amour_, in which Riva and Okada do not act except to react, their repetitions on the past in Nevers and Hiroshima belonging more to poetry or music than to ordinary speech. Duras's next film followed the same pattern. André Téchiné has commented on Duras's and Paul Seban's _La Musica_:

> Dans ce film tout arrive par la parole... Les personnages sont voués à la pratiquer et à ne pratiquer rien d'autre. Etrange fonction du verbe qui donne aux grands films d'aujourd'hui la seule dimension possible, chaque être n'ayant d'autre épaisseur que celle de sa propre langue.[19]

With language as a main character and language as plot, the novels or films of Duras function on repetitions, on one character's language negating or serving as counterpoint to another's, as if they were separate "voices" in a piece of music ("modéré et chantant" is both the translation and the style of _Moderato Cantabile_). Characters use language to rebuild a world around them, and they often betray themselves or others in the process.

> Le dialogue - plutôt les monologues - obéissent à l'unique intention de faire naître un monde, de faire survivre quelque chose... Cette parole créatrice comporte sa propre négation.

> Elle témoigne d'une irrémédiable impuissance, et il lui arrive de dévorer les personnages qui s'imaginent éclaircir les choses. On ne se trouve pas par la parole, elle n'est d'aucun secours.[20]

Thus, Riva in Hiroshima feels she has betrayed her dead German lover, not because she slept with the Japanese, but because she told the Japanese about Nevers. Alissa in Détruire dit-elle accuses Elizabeth Alione of having betrayed both herself and the others (Alissa, Max Thor and Stein) by telling her husband about them.

What becomes stressed in such films and novels is the aural insistence upon point of view. There are no scenes per se; there are, rather, suites of dialogue: variations upon a musical theme. The reader or viewer becomes preoccupied with the question of where the dialogue or monologue is coming from, who the speaker is, and who the intended audience is. Indeed, in Sarraute's Les Fruits d'or, the reader has the impression that he is overhearing a conversation that takes place in another room and perhaps in another time. The voices have no bodies: they float freely in the novel, and the reader's ears must be as tuned as his eyes to appreciate them.

In terms of film, this insistence upon language weighs upon the image. Because the image is no longer the mover of an anecdotal subject, it acquires a quality of stasis or immobility. As Judith Gollub has stated: "Dans un film sans récit, le dialogue a comme fonction de voiler et de déguiser le sens de l'image. L'impossibilité de s'exprimer par les mots est proclamé."[21] With a director like Resnais, the text of Duras found its perfect counterpart, for, even though the images seem static at times, they are never immobilized. There is an alternating play of stop-and-go between Duras's text and Resnais's camera. The latter never duplicates the text, so that when the sound track is filled with the *voix intérieure* (inner voice or monologue) of Riva, the camera is moving back and forth between Hiroshima and Nevers, or else it is moving forward in the streets of Hiroshima, revealing images which have little to do with Nevers. Resnais's camera admits the importance of the aural in the text of Duras. At the same time, it insists upon the visual participation of the spectator as well. This is not the case with *Détruire dit-elle*, in which Duras deliberately decreases the number of shots (less than 150 in the whole film), deliberately expands the duration of the camera takes, and deliberately strips the images of any interest for the spectator. Those images are calculated to convey the *ennui* of the characters and the strangeness of the words those characters speak. The spectator in *Détruire dit-elle* is forced to pay sole attention to the interplay of language, since there is very little movement within the image and very little movement between images. As Téchiné has pointed out, time ceases to play its traditional role in such a film: "Si bien qu'il semblerait que tout flashback, toute image au sens traditionnel du terme n'ait plus sa raison d'être."[22] It is perhaps worthwhile to cite Nathalie Sarraute again here: "Il a vu le temps cesser d'être ce courant rapide qui poussait en avant l'intrigue pour devenir une eau dormante au fond de laquelle s'élaborent de lentes et subtiles décompositions."[23]

Contrasted with this emphasis on dialogue in the *nouveau roman* is another current which emphasizes description. Dialogue is not so different from description, it should be noted, when both end up as monologues. Thus, novels like Robbe-Grillet's *Dans le labyrinthe*, Claude Simon's *La Route des Flandres* and Samuel Beckett's *Molloy* have very little dialogue in them; yet, they are full of *bavardage* carried out by narrators who meander as if by compulsion from one topic to another and from one vision to another. Often, what dialogue there is is repetitive, monotonous, deceptively laconic or cliché-ridden. Such dialogue may by its very simplicity trigger a series of very complex associations or visions, just as the simple mention of a golfer calling his caddie triggers a complex network of sensations and feelings in the mind of Benjy in Faulkner's *The Sound and the Fury* (1929).

What becomes stressed in such novels is the visual insistence upon point of view. Since the new novelists refuse to enter into the bodies of their characters to tell us what such characters are feeling or into their minds to tell us what such characters are thinking, there is a predominant emphasis upon what the narrator or character sees. Claude Simon relates this emphasis upon vision in the new novel with that in film:

> Je ne peux écrire mes romans qu'en précisant constamment les diverses positions qu'occupent dans l'espace le ou les narrateurs (champ de la vision, distance, mobilité par rapport à la scène décrite - ou, si l'on préfère, dans un autre langage: angle de prises de vue, gros plan, plan moyen, panoramique, plan fixe, travelling, etc.). Même lorsque mon ou mes narrateurs rapportent autre chose que des scènes immédiatement vécues (par exemple des

> situations, des épisodes remémorés ou imaginés). Ils se trouvent toujours dans une position d'observateur aux connaissances et aux vues bornées, voyant les faits, les gestes, sous un éclairage particulier et limitatif.[24]

The insistence upon the visual is an insistence upon point of view. In turn, the new novelists and directors of the _cinéma des auteurs_ after them have insisted upon multiple or shifting points of view, in the same way that point of view is fluid and shifting, through dialogue, in the fiction of Nathalie Sarraute, Boris Vian and Marguerite Duras. Thus, the point of Molloy gives way to that of Moran in _Molloy_; point of view (and point in time with it) shifts in _La Route des Flandres_ each time the obsessive image of the horse recurs; point of view and points in time and space shift in _Dans le labyrinthe_ between narrator and soldier, between painting and photograph, between the characters, themselves, since they all bear generic or functional names: "le soldat," "le gamin," "la femme." Marie-Claire Ropars-Willeumier has noted the multiple or shifting point of view in Resnais, relating _La Guerre est finie_ (1966) with novels like André Malraux's _La Condition Humaine_ (1933) and Michel Butor's _La Modification_ (1957):

> En menant une histoire à son terme, mais en refusant de limiter chaque moment de cette histoire à un seul point de vue, Resnais accomplit à la fois la vocation du romanesque et les exigences du nouveau roman. L'exemple le meilleur en est sans doute _La Guerre est finie_, qui réussit à confronter à chaque instant du récit l'esthétique de _La Condition Humaine_ et celle de _La Modification_: pendant la réunion de comité des parti, le discours politique, transmis directement en espagnol, est en même temps saisi à travers la conscience critique de Diego, qui soit en résume la substance en voix OFF, tout en cédant à de brèves vues subjectives de sa vie privée, soit au contraire en refuse la portée en s'évadant dans un monologue intérieur, qui cependant, parce qu'il est à la seconde

> personne, ne s'immobilise jamais en une meditation close et s'allie le plus souvent à des vues objectives de la discussion.[25]

Robbe-Grillet has explored this multiple or shifting point of view in film perhaps even more than Resnais. It is interesting to note, in this respect, that a published scenario of Robbe-Grillet is much more explanatory than one of his novels, for, in the scenario, Robbe-Grillet exposes his technique. Thus, in L'Immortelle, Robbe-Grillet explains the use of the mobile camera to indicate the shift in point of view from that of L (or the narrator-camera watching L) to that of every other person in the room, ending up with L again:

> Et elle se retourne, sitôt sa phrase prononcée, vers le bord droit de l'écran, d'une brusque volte-face. La caméra, qui a cessé de reculer, commence une lente rotation, régulière, vers la droite, comme pour montrer ce qui a attiré de ce côté l'attention de la jeune femme; celle-ci se trouve ainsi rapidement éliminée, sur la gauche, tandis que l'on découvre, après un couple lointain qui converse sur le palier, un homme beaucoup plus proche dont la direction de regard semble indiquer qu'il regardait L. Mais, à peine atteint par l'objectif, il tourne la tête avec lenteur vers la droite de l'écran, accompagné donc par le mouvement de caméra qui se poursuit, l'élimine à son tour, passe sans plus s'attarder sur d'autres invités plus ou moins figés, retrouve Catherine debout près du chambranle de la seconde porte, et regardant vers la caméra. Dès qu'elle est dans le champ, Catherine, de même, détourne la tête vers la droite de l'écran, tandis que le mouvement d'appareil se poursuit, sans modification, dans la direction de son regard. Plus au fond, dans la pièce voisine, qui est assez nue, on aperçoit encore un homme debout, immobile, qui regarde aussi vers la droite.
>
> Tous ces personnages ayant été éliminés l'un après l'autre, on retrouve enfin L, et la caméra s'arrête, pour rester fixé ensuite jusqu'à la fin du plan.[26]

If Marguerite Duras's insistence upon dialogue changes the whole concept of time and the traditional use of flashbacks in film, then so also does

Robbe-Grillet's insistence upon the camera as a narrator and upon subjective visions produced within the scene. Where Resnais uses editing to juxtapose Hiroshima and Nevers temporally and spatially, Robbe-Grillet achieves the same juxtaposition within the scene. Thus, a guest who blocks the narrator's vision in L'Immortelle is employed as a cutting device:

> La caméra commence à s'avancer vers elles, mais elle s'arrête presque aussitôt, deux personnes s'étant interposées en gros premier plan: un homme et une femme allant à la rencontre l'un de l'autre et s'immobilisant pour échanger quelques mots juste dans l'axe de la prise de vue... Ils masquent entièrement Catherine et L qui se trouvent dans la pièce voisine; et, lorsqu'ils poursuivent leur chemin, libérant de nouveau la vue, les deux jeunes femmes ont disparu: il n'y a plus que le fauteuil vide, toujours à la même place, dans la pièce vide vers laquelle on s'avance en vain.
>
> La caméra renonce donc à poursuivre dans cette direction... Un buste d'homme passe de nouveau devant l'objectif, obstruant tout le champ... Et cette fois, lorsque ce buste, continuant son mouvement, a disparu sur la gauche, on s'aperçoit que le décor a complètement changé.[27]

This use of the subjective camera for shifting time-space frames and shifting point of view is not restricted to Resnais and Robbe-Grillet. It is a characteristic trait of the entire cinéma des auteurs. Jacques Rivette has commented on this same manipulation of the camera in Duras's Détruire dit-elle:

> Cela frappe dès les premiers plans: des plans que j'ai vus comme commençant comme le regard, justement, d'un personnage, et qui, finalement, dans le mouvement même du plan, deviennent regard sur ce personnage même que l'on croyait, au début du plan, lui-même en train de regarder.[28]

In both the novels which emphasize description and those which emphasize dialogue, the _nouveau roman_ has completely transformed the usual idea of what a character should be and how the novelist should paint that character. The character of a new novel or a film of the _cinéma des auteurs_ often comes without a well-defined job, without a family tree, without a name. Such characters are dressed in their tics and their thoughts: dialogue-thoughts for Sarraute, description-thoughts for Robbe-Grillet. Since these novelists and filmmakers have stripped their works of the anecdotal subject and, with it, of action, their characters often seem to be cold or hollow or abnormally passive. Yet, while passive, these characters are also more open "to the inside," that is, more open for the purpose of translating subjective states of being, because they are more open to change and to the contradictions involved in change. Robbe-Grillet ridicules the well-made characters of the traditional novel, showing how they have been distorted, how they become predictable and mummified:

> Un personnage, tout le monde sait ce que le mot signifie. Ce n'est pas un IL quelconque, anonyme et translucide, simple sujet de l'action exprimée par le verbe. Un personnage doit avoir un nom propre, double si possible: nom de famille et prénom. Il doit avoir des parents, une hérédité. Il doit avoir une profession. S'il a des biens, cela n'en vaudra que mieux. Enfin il doit posséder un "caractère," un visage qui le reflète, un passé qui a modelé celui-ci et celui-là. Son caractère dicte ses actions, le fait réagir de façon déterminée à chaque événement. 29

For Jean Cayrol, the anonymous and passive characters of the _nouveau roman_ are prisoners in a world that resembles the concentration camps.

He calls his anonymous and solitary wanderer _le héros lazaréen_. Claire Clouzot has commented on Cayrol's use of characters and how that use affects his novel's or film's themes:

> A partir de la "déshumanisation" qu'il a subie lui-même dans les camps, Cayrol dévéloppe ce qu'il nomme le "romanesque lazaréen," c'est-à-dire un art de ressuscité, "sans histoire, sans ressort, sans intrigue." Les thèmes de la mémoire, de l'oubli, du temps revécu, du refus du passé hantent ses livres, comme ils hanteront le cinéma de la Rive Gauche dans son entier.[30]

Cayrol, himself, explains that this character "est si vulnerable qu'il prendra l'habitude de la solitude comme un seul moyen de protection, de la seule arme."[31] This explanation, which would characterize the anonymous characters in Kafka's novels, would seem to apply equally to the _unijambiste_ (one-legged) Molloy in Beckett's novel and to the soldier in robbe-Grillet's _Dans le labyrinthe_. Robbe-Grillet, however, explains the new character in less social terms. For him, the real world and the world of fiction are already too anthropomorphic. Robbe-Grillet attacks those metaphors which have no basis in reality and which bend or twist that reality to the image of man. Critics of the _nouveau roman_ and the _cinéma des auteurs_ have stated that these artists have totally depersonalized man, that they have stripped him of everything but his vision or his words, and that they have proportionately placed more and more importance on the role of objects: thus, the early critics of Robbe-Grillet called him a _chosiste_. Robbe-Grillet has responded that he has only returned the balance between man and the objects which surround him to a state of more authentic equilibrium.

In other words, he has restored to objects their autonomy and independence from man: what Maya Deren once called "the malevolent vitality of inanimate objects." Jean Cayrol would respond in a similar way, saying that the cinéma des auteurs restored "le sens initial des choses." And both have argued that the most authentic representation of objects is also the most subjective, thus reacting against the attack of depersonalism in their works. Nathalie Sarraute, in the same vein, has stated that, if the novelist has moved closer to the side of the reader, that novelist also insists that the reader move closer to the artist, thus making the novel a work of interior exploration for both:

> Alors le lecteur est d'un coup à l'intérieur, à la place même où l'auteur se trouve, à une profondeur où rien ne subsiste de ces points de repère commodes à l'aide desquels il construit les personnages. Il est plongé et maintenu jusqu'au bout dans une matière anonyme comme le sang, dans un magma sans nom, sans contours. S'il parvient à se diriger, c'est grace aux jalons que l'auteur a posés pour s'y reconnaitre.[32]

In effect, characters in the nouveau roman and the cinéma des auteurs are drawn in such a way that the reader or spectator must become a co-creator of the work. In other words, there is identification with the author but not with the characters. And the distance created by these authors between their characters and their audience forces that audience to react to the characters critically, that is, intellectually as well as emotionally. If there is an affinity between Brecht and the nouveau roman, it is certainly intentional on the part of the directors of the cinéma des auteurs. Claire Clouzot has noted this affinity:

> L'ombre de Brecht et du Nouveau Roman plane sur leurs thèmes. L'anonymat de certains personnages, le "flou" des situations, le refus du metteur en scène de tirer les ficelles, la distanciation des spectateurs par rapport aux êtres dépeints sur l'écran, la description simultanée du temps de l'action et du temps de la pensées, tout cela en est issu. Le "courant Rive Gauche" s'affirme comme un cinéma de la non-identification, un cinéma de la non-intervention de l'auteur.[33]

There remains the question of why writers like Jean Cayrol, Marguerite Duras and Alain Robbe-Grillet have turned to film. That Resnais brought all three to film is too simplistic an answer, for it does not explain why all three went on to write and make films of their own.[34] What did film offer them that the nouveau roman did not?

Jean-Louis Bory cites four traits in the new cinema that he sees as indications of the camera wanting to emulate the pen ("la caméra se veut stylo"):

> (1) le recours systématique au présent de l'indicatif contre l'imparfait et le passé simple "spécifique" du récit
> (2) le montage par séquences avec ou sans flashback
> (3) la volonté de s'en tenir au visuel
> (4) l'emploi de fondus enchainés[35]

Perhaps in expanding upon Bory' list, we can ascertain the degree to which the cinema offered writers like Cayrol, Robbe-Grillet and Duras more than their fiction.

Both the first and second traits listed by Bory refer to time. In their fiction, both writers who emphasized sous-conversations like Sarraute and Duras and writers who emphasized description like Robbe-Grillet, reverted to a simpler syntax than that which they found in novels written prior to theirs. The accent on the present tense and indicative mood in their work is unmistakable. It is not possible to do a study of the difference between the use of the *passé simple* and the use of the *imparfait* in Robbe-Grillet in the way such studies have been done on Flaubert. One will not find the pluperfect subjunctives of Gide in the fiction of Marguerite Duras. Casting verbs in the present tense for such writers is an attempt to break down the stranglehold that the past tense has held on fiction: the feeling on the part of both creator and reader that the author already possesses the whole story and, thus, that the act of story-telling is simply one of sharing just enough to keep the reader going while withholding just enough to keep the ending more meaningful than the rest of the work. Further, it is an attempt to actualize the dialogues or descriptions, so that they appear to be taking place at the time of reading, not sometime prior to the reader's opening the book. It is also an attempt to spatialize time. The novel has always been referred to as a temporal art, in which moving from space to space is "approximated" by moving from one point in time to another. In the same way, film has been said to create the illusion of temporal fluidity by moving from one point in space to another. Roland Barthes has emphasized in the fiction of Robbe-Grillet in particular, and in that of the entire *nouveau roman* in general, the "regard d'homme qui marche dans la ville."[36] That "regard" has as one of its functions the rendering of time spatially. But these writers did not turn to film simply because it offered more concrete possibilities for rendering time spatially.

The answer lies rather in the possibilities that film offered for achieving a higher degree of objectivity (real voices on the sound track being more authentic than the transcription of those voices in fiction, and real objects captured in the images being both more authentic and more economical than descriptions in fiction) without sacrificing the possibilities for a heightened subjectivity as well (those dialogues and images existing apart from any character at the same time that they may convey a particular character's vision or point of view.).

With their fiction, the problem was either one of the reader or one of the creator. In terms of the reader, the problem lay in the somewhat naive belief by some critics and readers alike that the degree of authenticity was not worth the price. In the same way that critics have reacted against structuralism and semiology, saying that too much effort is expended in order to arrive at the same conclusions that a lay person might arrive at in half the time, they have also questioned the experiments of a Sarraute or a Robbe-Grillet. The argument seems to be as follows: Sarraute shows us that she can capture the minute nuances that exist between speech and thought in _Tropismes_; why does she go to all the bother and why does she persist in that vein in the novels which follow? Robbe-Grillet shows us that he can admirably observe things and people; why does he persist in doing so and what ultimately is the point of so much observation?

In terms of the authors, themselves, the problem is more complex. It involves the dilemma that Robbe-Grillet found himself in with those early critics like Barthes who found him to be completely objective and those later critics like Bruce Morrissette and Ben Stoltzfus who found him to be extremely subjective. How could one portray the objects and people surrounding a character objectively without sacrificing the possibilities for subjectivity in that character? Conversely, how could one effectively explore the subjective states of a character without distorting, in the process, the world of objects and people surrounding him? For Robbe-Grillet, film offered a resolution to those seemingly unanswerable questions. As Marie-Claire Ropars-Willeumier has pointed out:

> S'il est un point commun aux nouveaux romanciers, c'est bien la volonté de détruire la continuité temporelle pour engendrer une composition spatiale qui rende chaque vision à sa présence immédiate et à son insignificance. Mais ce qui mène le roman à s'achever en poésie - telles ces variations de Robbe-Grillet autour de quelques images obsédantes - peut coexister au cinéma avec le maintien d'un récit. Ainsi se développe une polysémie dans laquelle le temps de l'homme peut s'exprimer au même titre que l'espace objectif, et qui permet au cinéma d'accomplir les ambitions contradictoires que le nouveau roman ne pouvait aborder sans perdre sa nature romanesque.[37]

This spatialization of time also explains Bory's indication of the desire to limit oneself to the visual on the part of the <u>nouveau roman</u>. As Michel Butor has stated: "Nous sommes plus visuels qu'aux dix-neuvième siècle - et cela se retrouve dans nos efforts pour saisir les scènes de la vie dans leur totalité, dans leur intégrité, comme le fait l'oeil de la caméra."[38] Jean Cayrol has written that film has made it possible to give time back its fullness, its "actualité." And Jean Ricardou has further noted that the writer of fiction, by the mere mention of an object in a room, places an inordinate amount of emphasis upon that object, since it is clear that he has chosen that object over others for mentioning. Thus, novelistic description is as much what it does not describe as what it describes. Ricardou adds that film simultaneously describes what fiction must render in degrees or succession; at the same time, film divorces the object described from the author describing much more effectively than is possible in fiction. And, whereas the novel usually must admit to some artifice or invasion of privacy in order to depict the subjective states of a character, the camera in film can achieve the same subjectivity by mere displacement. As Ropars-Willeumier suggests, the movement of the camera seems to say: "Suivre les personnages pour dévoiler leurs pensées les plus cachées."[39] The use of fondus enchainés achieves the same results, as Bory seems to suggest.

We might add to Bory's list the use of the freeze frame in the films of the new novelists. In a novel of Marguerite Duras where conversation preoccupies the reader, the physical placement of characters becomes static, because characters' words are their main vehicles of transport. In a novel of Robbe-Grillet in which description takes the place of dialogue, the stasis is the same. Narrators/characters do not describe from movement; they describe from a temporarily fixed vantage point. The very length and minute precision of those descriptions reinforces the fixed state of the narrators/characters. Consequently, in their films Robbe-Grillet and Duras both emphasize the freeze frame or fixed pose: Robbe-Grillet fixes characters within the frame, allowing the editing to be fast and discontinuous (disrupting smooth transitions); Duras fixes the camera itself, allowing for very little movement toward or away from characters. Robbe-Grillet relates this fixing of frames to the subjective vision of characters:

> Lui il est là, il regarde ça, et j'ai l'impression qu'on sent naître chez lui le désir d'arrêter ça... Cet homme qu'on voit dans mes romans et dans mes films, c'est quelqu'un qui effectivement a besoin de voir et d'immobiliser, les deux choses étant constamment liées.[40]

Marguerite Duras's camera indications for La Femme du Gange (1973) attest to the same relationship of fixing the frame in order to force the spectator to see what the narrator or characters see: "Il n'y a rigoureusement aucun movement de caméra. Tous les plans sont fixes (152 plans)."[41]

Finally, film also offers the possibility of counterpoint, a counterpoint that is simultaneous, whereas it must be successive in the novel. This counterpoint, so characteristic of the cinéma des auteurs, expands the possibilities for simultaneously playing the text of a film against the images of a film, and the results are more immediate and more accessible to the reader/viewer than in the novel. Thus, Jean Cayrol explained his intentions in making Le Coup de grace (1965) before he made it:

> On choisira les mots les plus succulents, les images précieuses et faciles. Le tout, ce n'est pas d'exprimer la vérité d'une action ou d'un sentiment, c'est plutôt de dessiner autour de telle action ou de tel sentiment une aura, de leur donner un lustre inimaginable, une résonnance comme un cristal dont on prolongerait le tintement pour le plaisir. Le personnage ainsi décrit apparaitra comme un affreux dilettante, un amateur ennuyé, un esthète qui, dans une situation donnée, détournera la tête pour écouter brusquement le chant d'un oiseau ou le vent dans un arbre. Il croit pouvoir reculer ainsi le moment de choisir, de s'engager. Il musarde en attendant alors que le danger peut être imminent. Il prend la position d'un esclave aux pieds de son maître et qui chanterait d'une voix faible ses airs favoris pour l'apaiser, le rassérener. Il deviendra une victime de charme, si j'ose m'exprimer ainsi.[42]

Alain Robbe-Grillet has perhaps expressed the polyphonic possibilities of film better than anyone else. His explanation for the exodus from the novel to the cinema seems significant enough to conclude this discussion:

> L'attrait certain que la création cinématographique exerce sur beaucoup de nouveaux romanciers doit, lui, être cherché ailleurs. Ce n'est pas l'objectivité de la caméra qui les passionne, mais ses possibilités dans le domaine du subjectif, de l'imaginaire. Ils ne conçoivent pas le cinéma comme un moyen d'expression, mais de recherche, et ce qui retient le plus leur attention c'est, tout naturellement, ce qui échappait le plus aux pouvoirs de la littérature: c'est-à-dire non pas tant l'image que la bande sonore - le son des voix, les bruits, les ambiances, les musiques - et surtout la possibilité d'agir sur deux sens à la fois, l'oeil et l'oreille; enfin, dans l'image comme dans le son, la possibilité de présenter avec toute l'apparence de l'objectivité la moins contestable ce qui n'est, aussi bien, que rêve ou souvenir, en un mot ce qui n'est qu'imagination.[43]

That emphasis on imagination explains the new novelists' fascination with film; it also explains the thematic and technical difficulties (in terms of audience response) of their films. Unfortunately, the production costs and distribution risks for their films are much greater than those for their novels. Man Ray once said that the artist needed only one other person who understood his work for the work to be successful and justified, for the artist to know he is "right" in what he is doing. Unfortunately, more than a one-person audience is needed for a film to be successful.

Notes

1 For a thorough discussion of Malraux's critical definition of modernism, see Joseph Frank, *The Widening Gyre: Crisis and Mastery in Modern Literature* (New Brunswick, New Jersey: Rutgers University Press, 1963) and Lucien Goldmann, *Pour une sociologie du roman* (Paris: Gallimard, 1964).

2 Marie-Claire Ropars-Willeumier, *L'Ecran de la mémoire* (Paris: Seuil, 1970), p. 74.

3 Anais Nin, *The Novel of the Future* (New York: Macmillan, 1968).

4 Nathalie Sarraute, *L'Ere du soupçon* (Paris: Gallimard, 1966), p. 69.

5 Sarraute, p. 57.

6 Sarraute, p. 56.

7 Sarraute, p. 63.

8 Sarraute, Robbe-Grillet and Butor have all related changes in modern fiction with changes in modern physics.

9 Sarraute, p. 69.

10 Alain Robbe-Grillet, *Pour un nouveau roman* (Paris: Gallimard, 1963), p. 177.

11 Sarraute, p. 65.

12 Ropars-Willeumier, p. 119.

13 Judith Podselver Gollub, "Nouveau Roman et Nouveau Cinéma" (Diss. UCLA, 1966), p. 89.

14 Ropars-Willeumier, pp. 119-120.

15 Ropars-Willeumier, p. 120.

16 Sarraute, p. 102.

17 Sarraute, p. 105.

18 Sarraute, p. 108.

19 André Téchiné, "De trois films et d'une certaine parole," Cahiers du Cinéma, 189 (April 1967), p. 49.

20 Téchiné, p. 48.

21 Gollub, p. 136.

22 Téchiné, p. 49.

23 Sarraute, p. 65.

24 Claude Simon, "Enquête Alain Resnais," Premier Plan, 18 (October 1961), p. 32.

25 Ropars-Willeumier, p. 235.

26 Alain Robbe-Grillet, L'Immortelle (Paris: Minuit, 1963), p. 43.

27 Robbe-Grillet, L'Immortelle, pp. 44-45.

28 Jean Narboni and Jacques Rivette, "Entretien avec Marguerite Duras," *Cahiers du Cinéma*, 217 (November 1969), p. 46.

29 Robbe-Grillet, *Pour un nouveau roman*, p. 31.

30 Claire Clouzot, *Le Cinéma français depuis la nouvelle vague* (Paris: Fernand Nathan, 1972), p. 50.

31 René Prédal, *Etudes Cinématographiques*, 64-68 (1968), p. 106.

32 Sarraute, p. 74.

33 Clouzot, p. 56.

34 Jorge Semprun has joined the list of Resnais's screenwriters who have also made films. In 1973 he completed two films: *L'Attentat* and *Les Deux Mémoires*.

35 Jean-Louis Bory, *Des Yeux pour voir* (Paris: 10/18, 1971).

36 Ropars-Willeumier, p. 86.

37 Ropars-Willeumier, p. 233.

38 Michel Butor, *La Nuit* (Paris: Buchet-Chastel, 1961), p. 16.

39 Ropars-Willeumier, p. 76.

40 Alain Gardies, *Alain Robbe-Grillet* (Paris: Seghers, 1972), p. 74. See also William Van Wert, "Structures of Mobility and Immobility in the Cinema of Alain Robbe-Grillet," *SubStance*, 9 (1974), pp. 79-95.

41 Marguerite Duras, *Nathalie Granger/ La Femme du Gange* (Paris: Gallimard, 1973), p. 102.

42 Jean Cayrol and Claude Durand, *Cahiers du Cinéma*, 179 (June 1966), p. 79.

43 Robbe-Grillet, *Pour un nouveau roman*, p. 161.

IV

The Structural Limits of the Cinematographic Novel: Alain Robbe-Grillet's *Dans le Labyrinthe*

1959 was a banner year for French film. It was also an important year for Alain Robbe-Grillet. While Truffaut, Rohmer, Godard, Chabrol and Resnais were making their presence felt at the Cannes film festival, Robbe-Grillet was publishing _Dans le labyrinthe_. The link between these two events is more than chronology or coincidence, for, if _Dans le labyrinthe_ represents the culmination of a radically innovative novelistic technique which Robbe-Grillet had begun in _Les Gommes_, then it must also be seen as the one novel of Robbe-Grillet which most closely foreshadows his films: _L'Immortelle_ (1962), _Trans-Europ Express_ (1966), _L'Homme qui ment_ (1968), _L'Eden et après_ (1970), _N. a pris les Dés_ (1970) and _Glissements progressifs du plaisir_ (1974). The crisis in the form-content relationship in _Dans le labyrinthe_ can only be resolved by switching media. With the novel Robbe-Grillet realized that he had reached an impasse in his literary career, a labyrinth that could only be traversed by pushing his research even more -- but in the film medium. _Dans le labyrinthe_ represents the limits of the cinematographic novel. Whereas other novelists like Steinbeck, Dos Passos, Isherwood and Malraux had previously used cinematographic techniques in their novels to clarify or heighten meaning, Robbe-Grillet uses them to emphasize form and often to obscure empirical meaning. Therein lies the difficulty of "un roman qui est en même temps sa propre théorie" when carried to an extreme.

Semiologists like Julia Kristeva, Christian Metz, Roland Barthes and Umberto Eco have demonstrated that we can speak of a cinematographic language which is distinct from all other languages: for example, the language of poetry or painting or still photography. They assert that film's language is a translinguistic language. Metz proposes a _grande syntagmatique_, an organizational schema of syntagms which roughly corresponds to all of the possible sequences in films. His diagram deals with film narration on the level of denotation. Eco proposes cultural codes which place denotation in a specific context, thus treating film narration on the level of connotation. The _grande syntagmatique_ of Metz has already been used very fruitfully to analyze cinematographic techniques in Robbe-Grillet's _La Jalousie_.[1] But the problem at hand is not one of finding analogies between the media (examples of embracing sequences, parallel sequences, episodic sequences and the like in Robbe-Grillet's novels), but more precisely one of determining critical and theoretical differences in the way narration operates in the two media.

Proceeding from this distinction in methodology, we could assert that visual expression tends to dominate or preclude verbal expression. "The word was made flesh" when it was made visible. From this stems the need for repetition and analogy in spoken language, the need for the speaker to ask the listener: "Do you _see_ what I mean?" From this also stems the use of language books through pictures: French through pictures, Spanish through pictures, etc. The advantage in such books lies in the pictures themselves, based somewhat on the mistaken premise that both Pound and Eisenstein had of the Chinese ideogram: that word (its hieroglyphic) and image could be equated. The disadvantage lies in the fact that a large portion of any language is made up of conceptual, not perceptual words for which there is no visual equivalent. Figurative language (metaphor, personification, metonymy, symbol, allegory, paradox, overstatement, understatement, irony), is, in this context, compensation for defects in the dictionary, for language that can be used (communication) but which paradoxically cannot express itself (visualization) in any other way, without recourse to this figurative language. Thus, one can see the problems facing the filmmaker who "adapts" into film a novel which exploits these properties of language to the extreme. How to adapt, for example, the following "descriptive" passage from Joyce's Ulysses?

> Mr. Leopold Bloom ate with relish the inner organs of beasts and fowls. He liked thick giblet soup, nutty gizzards, a stuffed roast heart, liver slices fried with crustcrumbs, fried hencod's roes. Most of all he liked grilled mutton kidneys which gave to his palate a fine tang of scented urine.[2]

The objective "description" is not really a description at all, but rather a subjective narration in disguise. The novelist here exploits the fact that we "envision" in literature (that is, we conceive and do not perceive; we do not demand a literal "picture" of the passage), whereas we "see" in film. The first and last sentences in the passage are capital for the understanding of the rampant eroticism and the tendency toward sado-masochism in Joyce's Bloom. Culinary tastes are here obviously symbolic of sexual tastes. Neither of these sentences has a visual equivalent in the filmed version of the novel. The second sentence, a catalogue of denotative objects that are related more by their visceral sounds than by their visualization, is equally impossible to adapt. Denotation and connotation, and thus signifier and signified, are radically different in the two media.

We may assert here that language is denotatively poor (that is, non-specific) and connotatively rich (varied and specific with each variation), while cinematographic language is denotatively rich (specific, immediate, actualized) and, by comparison, connotatively poor (non-specific, dependent on added meaning, meaning that goes beyond expressive denotation from knowledge gained extra-cinematically, knowledge that is both cultural and ideological).

> The words CHILDLIKE and CHILDISH both mean "characteristic of a child," but CHILDLIKE suggests meekness, innocence, and wide-eyed wonder, while CHILDISH suggests pettiness, willfulness, and temper tantrums. If we name over a series of coins: NICKEL, PESO, LIRA, SHILLING, SEN, DOUBLOON, the word DOUBLOON, to four out of five readers, will immediately suggest pirates, though one will find nothing about pirates in looking up its meaning in the dictionary.[3]

That the denotative level of the word is weak is evidenced by the fact that its lexical or dictionary meaning is often based on a repetition of the root of the word to be defined ("characteristic of a child") or defined by way of analogies, similes and metaphors, that is, by way of figurative language which is not denotative but connotative. Thus, the denotation of a word like _petit_ in French is "little" or "small." But in the following examples

> Elle a son _petit_ caractère.
> Il prend son _petit_ café dans son _petit_ coin.
> C'est un _petit_ bourgeois.
> Je suis aux _petits_ soins pour mon argent.
> C'est un homme bien _petit_.
> Voilà le _petit_ peuple.

Petit, used figuratively and connotatively, means neither "little" nor "small." Thus also the dictionary definition of "red" ("any of a group of colors whose hue resembles that of blood") or "blue" ("any of a group of colors whose hue is that of a clear sky") differs drastically from the visual representation (definition on the denotative level) in the cinema of "red" or "blue": in the cinema they are immediately actualized, and they may or may not have anything to do with blood or a clear sky. In spoken language, these words, whose denotations are weak and imprecise, have rich and varied connotations (thus, red = revolutionary; communist; Indian; a kind of plague--"The Masque of the Red Death"; an amphetamine, etc.). These connotations are specific, not because they have anything to do with the color red, but because they stem from cultural and ideological usage.

If we look closely at various passages of "camera-eye" literature (before Robbe-Grillet), we notice immediately several things: when there are complete sentences (often there are instead a string of associative phrases or sentence fragments), they contain verbs which are in the present tense, active voice, indicative mood; the subject is often suppressed or implied. The emphasis here is on what the camera could easily capture: specific visual nouns (buildings, trees, armchairs, etc.); descriptive, perceptual adjectives (adjectives that denote size, shape, color and texture): active verbs or verbs of motion (run, hit, throw, catch, etc.). Such passages are expressed sequentially, whereas in the cinema, they may be expressed all within a single shot or within a single sequence. As Metz has pointed out, the cinematic shot does not equal the word; at the very least, it equals the phrase, the self-contained *énoncé*. For instance, a shot, whether in long shot, medium shot or close-up of a house does not correspond to the word "house"; at the very least, it corresponds rather to a complete statement: "Here is a house."

Given these preliminary distinctions between envisioning and seeing and between denotation and connotation in the two media, we can now proceed to show how Robbe-Grillet differs from the previous examples of camera-eye literature: how he employs cinematographic devices in _Dans le labyrinthe_ (close-ups, fades, dissolves, jump-cutting, associative editing, etc.): and how he transcends them, reversing the distinctions mentioned earlier between seeing and envisioning, between connotation and denotation. In order to prove this point, we will analyze the following: (1) structures of repetition (that is, making denotation poetic and thus connotative: _hallucination vraie_); (2) structures of geometric configurations (meta-denotation); (3) structures of depersonalization (false perspectives, hallucinations, the use of the definite article in the place of the possessive adjective, that is, making the individual generic); (4) structures of negation and immobility ("_vertige fixé_"); (5) structures of negation, immobility and indecision in the dialogue; (6) echo structures and metaphor; (7) associative editing and the creation of _mise-en-abime_; (8) triadic structures in description (exterior, denotative) and hypothesis (interior, connotative) and their relation to the labyrinth; and (9) point of view and temporality.

(1) Structures of Repetition

With Robbe-Grillet narration (communicative, temporal, sequential) becomes description (expressive, spatial, asynchronous and asequential). And description in his novels fulfills the same function that the mobile camera (tracking shots, pans, reverse pans) fulfills in his films: a pluridimensionality of meaning. In other words, there is no empirical reading of a Robbe-Grillet text. Where many critics have pejoratively used the term "ambiguity" (lack of meaning), we would prefer to use the term "multiplicity" (many meanings: that is, no ultimate truth, only hypotheses, all contradictory and all probable). Thus, traditional narrative, based on figurative language (metaphor, analogy, what Robbe-Grillet calls "anthropomorphic" adjectives which destroy denotation by persuading the reader to "envision" that which cannot physically and objectively be present), becomes description, based on observation. Our interest passes, then, from that which is described to the process of description and the perspective or angle of vision from which the description takes place. Our reading passes from the omniscient, ubiquitous and past-tense narrator to the partially obscured (but always visible), restricted and fallible (often unreliable) observer: from the absent story-teller who appeals to our minds to the participatory and often voyeuristic observer (because in Robbe-Grillet we are always simultaneously conscious of both the observed and the eye that observes); from a passive reading of a closed text to an active participation (we are forced to affirm <u>signification</u> since Robbe-Grillet's narrator-eye consistently denies any) in an open-ended text.

Because Robbe-Grillet's descriptions are so copious and so meticulously precise, they immediately establish a denotative level in the text that, although it is questioned, contradicted, denied or erased, is nevertheless never broken. It needs no figurative language, since it is its own metaphor, its own analogy. What distinguishes these descriptions from those found in books of mathematics or in operational catalogues (how-to catalogues) which also employ description as narration is the tenor of the voice describing (its rhythm, the poetic accumulation of associative phrases and clauses) and the repetition involved (the thin line between vision and hallucination). We are invited to read such descriptions in the same way that we would read a poem of Baudelaire, Rimbaud or Mallarme: that is, cross-referentially. For the purposes of this study, I have underlined all of the repetitions in the opening passage of *Dans le labyrinthe*:

> Je suis seul ici, maintenant, bien à l'abri. *Dehors* il pleut, *dehors* on marche sous la pluie en courbant la tête, *s'abritant les yeux d'une main tout en regardant quand même devant soi, à quelque mètres devant soi, quelque mètres d'asphalte*, mouillé; *dehors* il fait froid, *le vent souffle* entre les branches noires dénudées; *le vent souffle* dans les feuilles, entrainant les rameux entiers *dans un balancement, dans un balancement, balancement*, qui projette son ombre sur le crépi blanc des murs. *Dehors* il y a du soleil, il n'y a pas un arbre, ni un arbuste, pour donner de l'ombre, et l'on marche en plein soleil, *s'abritant les yeux d'une main tout en regardant devant soi, à quelques mètres* seulement *devant soi, quelques mètres de'asphalte* poussiéreux où le vent dessine des parallèles, des fourches, des spirales.[4]

The repetitions create an incantatory aura, a ritualistic trance or hallucination in which the denotative level, although intact (expressive), becomes suspect (becomes connotative). Julia Kristeva affirms this relationship between repetition and connotation when she states:

> Si dans la langue courante la répétition d'une unité sémantique ne change pas la signification du message et contient plutôt un effet fâcheux de tautologie ou d'agrammaticalité (mais en tout cas l'unité répétée n'ajoute pas un sens supplémentaire à l'énoncé), il n'en est pas de même dans le langage poétique. Ici les unités sont non-répétables ou, autrement dit, l'unité répétée n'est plus la même, de sorte qu'on peut soutenir qu'une fois reprise elle est déjà une autre. La répétition apparente XX n'équivaut pas à X. Il se produit un phénomène inobservable au niveau phonétique (manifeste) du texte poétique, mais qui est un effet de sens proprement poétique et consiste à lire dans la séquence (répétée) elle-même _et_ autre chose. Disons que ces phénomènes _inobservables_ du langage poétique . . . sont les effets de connotation dont parle Hjelmslev.[5]

Thus, in the passage under discussion, an example of repetition like "dans un balancement, dans un balancement, balancement" is to be read in the same way that Kristeva reads repetition in the poetry of Baudelaire (in "Le Balcon" the repetition of the first line of the stanza in the last line: "Mère des souvenirs, maitresse des maitresses"), in the poetry of Mallarmé (in "L'Azur": "Je suis hanté. L'Azur! L'Azur! L'Azur! L'Azur!"), and in the poetry of Poe (in "The Raven": the repetition of "never more"): _la répétition apparente XX n'équivaut pas à X_. Kristeva concludes: "Baudelaire "répète" souvent des phrases, des vers et des mots, mais jamais la séquence "répétée" n'apparait avec le même sens."[6] As with Baudelaire, so too with Robbe-Grillet: the repetitions throughout the novel of single words, phrases and whole sentences is never purely repetitious, never redundant (it could only be so if read uniquely at the level of denotation). Each repetition must be read cross-referentially, as must all echo structures, and in a multiplicity of contexts. Thus, "s'abritant les yeux d'une main tout en regardant quand même devant soi" does not equal "s'abritant les yeux d'une main tout en regardant devant soi": the first must be understood in the context of rain, while the second refers to sunlight. This opening passage merits such detailed analysis, for as Richard Blumenberg has pointed out:

> Specifically, the opening shots can serve two traditional narrative purposes: (1) they can act as exposition, showing what is happening; (2) they can prefigure subsequent action descriptively and by association with object referents, and they can hence establish contact.[7]

The second (2) is, of course, the purpose that all opening passages or shots fulfill in any Robbe-Grillet text. Thus, the opening of Dans le labyrinthe can and should be read in the same way that the narration (with repetition) that begins L'Année dernière à Marienbad (1961) or the visuals (with repetition) that begin L'Immortelle (1962) should be read: that is, cross-referentially, as one would read a poetic text, and vertically, not horizontally, the distinction between the two terms being that employed by Maya Deren:

> Whereas, in what is called a "horizontal" development, the logic is a logic of actions, in a "vertical" development, it is a logic of a central emotion or idea that attracts to itself even disparate images which contain that central core, which they have in common.[8]

In this way, incongruities within these structures of repetition can be reconciled. For example: "Dehors il pleut" versus "Dehors il y a du soleil"; "le vent souffle entre les branches noires dénudées" versus "il n'y a pas un arbre, ni un arbuste, pour donner de l'ombre." Just as the narration which begins L'Année dernière à Marienbad vaporizes and summarizes the whole film into a mise-en-abime (this is reinforced by the fact that the narration actually ends in a visual *mise-en-abime*, the words of the narrator being repeated by, that is, assimilated by the actor in the play), so too the opening passage in *Dans le labyrinthe*, which comprises and summarizes the whole novel into a *mise-en-abime* (reinforced by the fact that the transition from outdoors to indoors is provided by elements common to both: "poussiéreux," "parallèles," "fourches," "spirales"). This is one way to read the text: that is, as a prefiguration of the whole work, as a series of "even disparate images which contain that central core, which they have in common." But they can also be read in another way, as suggested by Blumenberg:

> The repeated shot is another way to use, and has a similar extra-chronological effect as, slow motion. It is not so much that "thought" is externalized" as that the external (spatial) is internalized *and* temporalized.[9]

Thus, the temporal incongruities can be explained, not in terms of description alone, but rather in terms of point-of-view; the narrator-observer's "thought" is his angle of vision (spatial), which is internalized and temporalized. We shall return to this point in our discussion of temporality and point-of-view.

(2) *Structures of Geometric Configurations*

The novel abounds with examples of geometric forms observed and described, as in the following passage: (I have added emphasis for clarification)

> Au-delà se dresse la lampe, dans *l'angle* *droit* de la table: un socle *carré* de quinze centimètres de côté, un *disque* de même *diamètre*, une *colonne* *cannelée* portant un abat-jour

> sombre de conicité très faible. Sur le cercle supérieur de l'abat-jour, une mouche se déplace avec lenteur, d'un mouvement continu. Elle projette au plafond une ombre déformée, où ne se reconnait plus aucun élément de l'insecte initial: ni ailes, ni corps, ni pattes; l'ensemble s'est changé en un simple trait filiforme, une ligne brisée régulière, non fermée, comme un hexagone auquel manquerait un de ses côtés: l'image du filament incandescent de l'ampoule électrique. Ce petit polygone ouvert touche, par un de ses angles, le bord intérieur du vaste rond de lumière produit par la lampe. Il s'y déplace avec lenteur,mais d'un mouvement continu, tout au long de la circonférence. Lorsqu'il arrive à'la paroi verticale il disparait dans les plis du lourd rideau rouge. (pp. 14-15)

The use here (and throughout the novel) of geometric terminology constitutes an attempt at meta-denotation (pure denotation, denotation of denotation, denotation which cannot be altered by connotation, which can only reverse itself by (1) an internal change or metamorphosis, since Robbe-Grillet's geometry is never completely solid and, thus, his labyrinth is mobile; by (2) a change in the amount of light or darkness, which either deforms the object perceived or the perceiving eye, or both; and by (3) a physical change in the angle of vision of the observer: one geometric form seen from a prone position on the bed gives way to another when seen from a seated position at the table.)

Geometric forms and descriptions are especially dear to Robbe-Grillet, since they alone remain uncorrupted by the language that represents and expresses them; in other words, they are in direct opposition to the anthropomorphic language that Robbe-Grillet attacks so vehemently in *Pour un nouveau roman*. Thus, they force seeing, an effort of actualized visualization, where anthropomorphic language forces envisioning (comprehension without literal vision, conception without perception). They create a physically spatialized and geographically determinate labyrinth, in which cohabitation with a psychological and mental labyrinth is possible. The novel, then, cannot simply be read as an allegory. It is as much a denotative map as it is a connotative parable. An analogy here might help: if I produce the sign = on the written page, the reader immediately transforms that sign into its verbal coefficient: "equals." Through the use of geometric forms and their representation in language, both = and "equals" are possible in the novel.

Yet, while such descriptions depersonalize that which is described (maintaining their focus on contour and surface form while ignoring individualized body or depth), they are, nevertheless, very personal, in that, as is the case for all of these structures, they "tell" as much about the narrator-observer as about the thing observed.

These descriptions employing geometry must also be read cross-referentially as in a poem, for, while they are denotatively specific and precisely actualized, they are also generic, abstract, and thus not restricted. Consequently, they too reinforce the _mise-en-abime_ quality of the labyrinth. In other words, scenes with very disparate thematic content merge through their form (geometric): the street becomes the apartment of the narrator-observer which becomes the tableau of "La Défaite de Reichenfels," which becomes the cafe which becomes the apartment of the woman, invalid and boy, and so on. Structures of geometric configurations thus become aligned with structures of repetition.

(3) Structures of Depersonalization

Structures of depersonalization represent a further attack on anthropomorphism; like the geometric configurations, they are denotatively specific and connotatively imprecise. They are generic and thus non-restrictive, as is evidenced in the following description:

> Un peu plus haut, une hanche, un bras, une épaule s'appuient contre le fût du réverbère. . . . Les paupières sont grises, comme le reste; elles sont baissées. La tête est inclinée en avant. Le regard se trouve dirigé vers le sol. . . . (p. 17)

Through minute observation (close-ups), the narrator-observer analyzes the body parts of the soldier with the same intensity (precision) and detachment (no value judgments assigned to that precision) employed in the analysis of the fly spot. Contrary to the novels of Balzac or Flaubert, a reliable census is impossible in a Robbe-Grillet novel. Characters have no names per se. Often they are designated by letter (A...in _La Jalousie_, N., A., and X. in _L'Année dernière à Marienbad_, N. in _L'Immortelle_). More often they are designated generically, that is, by occupation or function, by abnormality or eccentricity, often by gender alone: the soldier, the doctor, the serving-girl, the invalid, the woman, the child. As such, they are representative forms whose generic names conceal the individualized body beneath. Because of this, both doubling of character and negation of character are possible, which further complicate denotation/connotation and envisioning/seeing. The "soldier" is specific enough as a type but illusory and phantasmic as a concrete individual through (1) doubling ("soldier" refers to the soldier most often observed, to him and two companions in flashback, to him and to two other soldiers in the cafe, to the three soldiers in the painting, to the soldier of the photograph, to the soldiers in the pseudo-infirmary. This doubling is further enhanced by the fact that the vision of the main soldier and the narrator-observer are equally unreliable): and through (2) negation: denotative referents like serial number (regiment), insignia (rank), and accoutrements (boots, weapons, knapsacks, etc.) prove illusory; the main soldier wears a uniform which does not belong to him, so that all attempts at character identity fail; the lieutenant is a pseudo-lieutenant; the corporal is not really a corporal; the doctor is a doctor by function, although he has no license and does not practice medicine; the invalid becomes a false invalid; the boy(s) are all alike, yet he/they has/have the voice of an adult, etc.

These generic types derive their concreteness, their "presence" from the fragmentary (description of body parts instead of whole bodies) yet complete (precise and extended analysis of those body parts from all possible angles) observations of the narrator. Even here the generic cloaks the specific: the indefinite article ("une hanche, un bras, une épaule") or the definite article ("les paupières, la tête, le regard") are much more frequent than the more traditional (more anthropomorphic, more connotative) possessive adjectives ("son épaule, ses paupières"). Where the individualized possessive adjectives would emphasize the character viewed, the generic indefinite and definite articles emphasize the observing narrator and the act of vision like that in film (all objects and people within the film frame are immediate, interrelated and yet anonymous: a house depicted within the frame is interrelated with a character we may see inside the house without necessarily belonging to him , so that the "possessive" is almost impossible in film, since the house remains autonomous, whether there is any character present or not.) In the same way, the ensemble of soldat is fragmented and depersonalized in the novel. The eyebrows, the head and the stars, described generically, become autonomous, independent of the possessive body. Consequently, characters do not dominate their landscape as they might in the traditional novel. The organic and inorganic worlds are reintegrated in Robbe-Grillet's novels through the discriminating (physically) but non-discriminatory (mentally) vision of the narrator-observer.

Paradoxically, although an observer's vision may be distorted either internally (the soldier's fatigue, fever, wound, delirium, sleep-walking) or externally (the lack of sufficient light, the change-ability of a fixed scene), the resultant perceived and described vision is neither deformed nor less real. Thus, another means of depersonalization stems from false perspective, whether internal or external. A recurrent example of this false perspective (hallucination vraie) occurs in the narrator-observer's filtered perceptions of the little boy through the soldier, especially evident either at the boy's arrival or at his departure:

> C'est l'enfant cette fois qui vient à sa rencontre. Il n'est d'abord qu'une silhouette indistincte, une tache noire irrégulière qui se rapproche, assez vite, en suivant l'extrême bord du trottoir. (p. 44)

> Lorsque le fuyard traverse le zone éclairée par un lampadaire, on aperçoit la pélerine sombre qui flotte largement autour de lui, pendant quelques secondes, une fois, deux fois, trois fois, plus réduite et moins nette à chaque apparition, jusqu'à n'être plus là-bas qu'un douteux tourbillon de neige. (p. 40)

Again, such examples of false perspective indicate more about the observer and observation than about the thing observed. Consequently, even false perspectives (boy as black spot, boy as snowball) are real perspectives. Robbe-Grillet's highly stylized universe is one in which linear potentialities are replaced by contradictory probabilities, forever contradictory, forever probable.

(4) Structures of Negation and Immobility

From these fragmented descriptions which are often tempered with false perspectives proceed the structures of negation and immobility. Since Robbe-Grillet's narration is so predominantly based on spatial description, it is not surprising that a trait common to all of his narrators is the desire to immobilize, the need to freeze-frame their observations, the need to stop action (horizontal) in order to explore the arrested moment, the inbetween step, the half-gesture (vertical). And since all scenes are mirrored or duplicated in one way or another by all other scenes, the *mise-en-abime* interweaves mobility and immobility. Always from the angle of vision of the narrator's stare, characters are frozen, as if caught off-guard in a photograph, framed as in a painting. By contrast, representative objects like photographs, paintings and mirrors become animated through this same narrator's stare. It is interesting to note that in either case Robbe-Grillet manipulates both the image track and the sound track of the scene. For example:

> Ceux-là font des gestes démesurés et des contorsions violentes du visage, arrêtés net en plein dévéloppement, ce qui en rend la signification également tres incertaine; d'autant plus que les paroles qui jaillissent de toutes parts ont été comme absorbées par une épaisse paroi de verre. (p. 26)

Contrast this description with the following:

> Bien que le fond de leur désaccord ne soit pas facile à déméler, la violence en est indiquée suffisamment par le maintien des antagonistes, qui se livrent l'un comme l'autre à des gesticulations démonstratives, prennent des attitudes théâtrales, font des mimiques exagérées. (p. 219)

A clear parallel is established in both passages between vision and motion (or lack of it). More importantly, whether the passage is from mobility to immobility or from immobility to mobility, the key question in either case is that of signification or meaning. And where the narrator-eye freely freezes any scene before him (denotatively stripping action or stasis of actual meaning), he also freely projects several conflicting yet probable meanings (connotative hypotheses) onto the scene. We shall return to this point in the section on triadic structures.

While the freeze-frame device allows the narrator to edit action, to break it down into its component parts, expanding his descriptions, mixing them with hypotheses, it also animates objects by deanimating characters. Indeed, it provokes connotation by denying it (negation):

> et le patron derrière son comptoir, penché en avant vers les six hommes aux costumes bourgeois, formant un petit cercle aux attitudes emphatiques, figés ainsi que tous les autres au beau milieu de gestes auxquels cet arrêt arbitraire a enlevé tout naturel, comme ceux d'une compagnie qu'un photographe a voulu

> prendre en pleine vie, mais que des nécessités techniques ont contraint de garder trop longtemps la pose: "Et maintenant ne bougeons plus! . . ." Un bras reste à moitié levé, une bouche entrouverte, une tête penchée à la renverse; mais le tension a succédé au mouvement, les traits se sont crispés, les membres raidis, le sourire est devenu rictus, l'élan a perdu son intention et son sens. Il ne subsiste plus, à leur place, que la démesure, et l'étrangeté, et la mort. (p. 118)

Imbalance, strangeness, death. Immobility, in which the narrator-observer's descriptions are most precise, most active, most alive, paradoxically connotes paralysis, decay, _rigor_ _mortis_: "Leurs yeux sont creux, leurs lèvres serrées, leur peau est grisâtre." (p. 180) Whereas to see is to be able to immobilize for the narrator, to be immobilized often has to do with not being able to see for the characters observed:

> Tous sont parfaitement immobiles et silencieux. Sans doute, n'ont-ils pas sommeil: il est encore trop tôt; et le manque d'une lumière suffisante les empêche de rien faire d'autre que de rester là, les yeux grands ouverts, à regarder celui qui arrive, son aspect de statue et sa boîte à chaussures, ou les fausses fenêtres devant eux, ou le mur nu, ou le plafond, ou le vide. (p. 114)

Thus, immobility serves many purposes; while those purposes vary, one thing is constant: immobility provokes connotative reading by denying it. Immobility, to go one step further, may be a premonition of death (freeze-framed within the labyrinth):

> Il était dans une tranchée sinueuse, dont le haut lui arrivait juste à hauteur du front; il tenait à la main une sorte de grenade explosive, de forme allongée, un engin à retardement dont il venait de mettre le mécanisme en marche. Sans perdre une seconde, il devait lancer la chose hors de la tranchée. Il entendait son mouvement d'horlogerie, comme le tic-tac d'un gros réveil. Mais il restait là, avec la grenade à la main, le bras tendu dans son geste ébauché, figé de façon incompréhensible, et de plus en plus rigide, de moins en moins capable de bouger ne fût-ce qu'un doigt,

> à mesure que l'instant de l'explosion approchait. Il a dû pousser un hurlement, pour se tirer du cauchemar. (pp. 128-129)

Or it may be seen as a means to avoid death, immobility thus seen as preferable to any movement:

> Il sera nécessaire qu'elle sorte, afin d'aller voir au-dehors, qu'elle franchisse la porte restée entrouverte, qu'elle repasse par le vestibule où attend le parapluie noir, et par la longue succession des couloirs, des escaliers étroits, et encore des couloirs, obliquant à angles droits et se recoupant, où elle risque fort de se perdre avant d'avoir atteint la rue. (p. 213)

These structures of immobility are both related to, and made possible by, structures of negation. The role that negation plays in a Robbe-Grillet novel cannot be overestimated. As with the structures of repetition, structures of negation must be read cross-referentially. Where repetition implies similarity, negation implies difference. And, as Julia Kristeva has stated: "le texte poétique est produit dans le mouvement complexe d'une affirmation et d'une négation simultanées d'un autre texte."[10] Thus, structures of negation construct through destruction; they affirm through denial. They reinforce the denotative level of the text, because it is not possible to envision negation: it can only be experienced; that is, seen. It is in this context that negation and immobility are interrelated:

> Ils <u>n'ont</u> <u>rien</u> à faire. <u>Personne</u> <u>ne</u> les <u>regarde</u>, et eux n'ont rien à regarder non plus. L'orientation de leurs visages - l'un de face, l'autre de profil, le dernier de trois-quarts arrière - <u>n'indique</u> <u>aucun</u> sujet commun d'attention. Le premier, le seul dont les traits soient entièrement visibles, montre d'ailleurs des yeux fixes, vides, sans expression aucune. (p. 30)

Negation, then, is both the cause and the effect of immobility. From a semiological standpoint, negation must be viewed as the positing of both A and non-A, rather than positing A because one negates non-A. Where this is most evident in the text is at the level of the narrator-observer's discourse. See, for example, the imcomplete erasures within an _hallucination vraie_, the negation of affirmation in the following example:

> porte, couloir, porte, vestibule, porte, puis enfin une pièce éclairée, et une table avec un verre vide dont le fond contient encore un cercle de liquide rouge sombre, et un infirme qui s'appuie sur sa béquille, penché en avant dans un équilibre précaire. _Non_. Porte entrebaillée. Couloir. Escalier. Femme qui monte en courant d'étage en étage, tout au long de l'étroit colimaçon où son tablier gris tournoie en spirale. Porte. Et enfin une pièce éclairée: lit, commode, cheminée, bureau avec une lampe posée dans son coin gauche, cercle blanc. _Non_. Au-dessus de la commode une gravure encadrée de bois noir est fixée. . . . _Non_. _Non_. _Non_. (p. 103)

Negation in this example does not destroy the descriptive images which precede it (thus, we can speak of incomplete erasures), but rather it serves as complement or counterpoint to those affirmative descriptions: in other words, it posits both A and non-A:

> Cet _extra-parole_, ce _hors-logique_ s'objective dans l'énoncé dit artistique. C'est dans le "simulacre," le "modelage," l'"image" que Platon va chercher la réalisation de ce type de négation qui ne suit pas la logique de la parole lorsque cette "négation" affirme ce qui est nié dans un geste non plus de jugement (tel est le geste de la parole), mais de mise à jour de la production signifiante, ce geste qui réunit simultanément le positif et le négatif, ce qui existe pour la parole et ce qui est non-existant pour elle.[11]

Thus, negation is as necessary to the Robbe-Crillet labyrinth structure as mirror images, interior duplications, repetitions and geometric forms are. Without it, the labyrinth would become linear, and escape would be possible. We will return to negation at the level of the artist-as-_gommeur_ later. For now, we can affirm that all oppositions and contradictions and conflicting probabilities within the text--real-imaginary, true-false, construction-destruction--could not exist without these structures of negation. As Kristeva has pointed out, negation is the index _par excellence_ "de _l'exclusion_, de la _fausseté_, de la _mort_, de la _fiction_, de la _folie_."[12]

(5) _Dialogue_

One particular application of these structures of immobility and negation occurs in the novel's dialogue, which is singularly repetitive, monotonous, circular and negative. After having read several exchanges, one becomes aware of several patterns emerging. For one thing, dialogue is difficult, one might even say impossible, in _Dans le labyrinthe_. Even the simplest sentences are problematic for the characters, who either do not genuinely understand or choose not to understand; thus, characters conduct monologues instead of dialogues:

> -Qu'est-ce que tu regardes?
> -Qu'est-ce qu'il y a dans ton paquet?" répète l'enfant au lieu de répondre. (p. 48)

Questions go unanswered and are instead replaced by other unrelated questions. These questions come from the mind and not the mouth; consequently, it is often impossible for the listener to read any meaning into the question, the phrase or the sentence. In other words, language becomes pure denotation, and the listener cannot read any connotation into the language, so that it becomes pure form, not unlike the geometric forms discussed earlier. This explains the malaise felt by the characters who cannot interpret and thus prefer to remain laconic, taciturn, silent:

> Mais, sitôt la phrase achevée, et le silence revenu, il devient impossible de retrouver l'intonation qui paraissait à l'instant avoir un sens - crainte, ennui, doute, solicitude, intérêt quelconque - et seule demeure la constatation: "Vous n'avez pas mangé," prononcée d'une voix neutre. L'homme répète son geste évasif. (p. 68)

Stripped of meaning, voices are interpreted by their tenor, which is equally illusory, equally false (which brings us back to affirmation-negation):

> "Oui," dit-il, de sa voix redevenue calme, lointaine elle-même, comme absente. (the soldier) (p. 40)
>
> ....
>
> La voix était grave, et ne ressemblait pourtant pas à une voix d'homme. . . . Une jeune femme à la voix très grave, cela se rencontre parfois; mais le souvenir est trop fugitif: il ne reste déjà plus qu'un timbre neutre, sans qualité, pouvant appartenir aussi bien à n'importe qui, faisant même douter qu'il s'agisse à coup sûr d'une voix humaine. (the woman) (p. 57)
>
> ....
>
> et, comme s'il avait attendu ce moment avec impatience pour éclaircir un point qui le préoccupe, il demande de sa voix sérieuse, qui n'est pas celle d'un enfant. . . . (the child) (p. 214)

This depersonalization of the voice is related to structures of immobility and to the whole <u>mise-en-abime</u> structure of the novel, in that characters portrayed in the painting are -as if- speaking, whereas characters who should be speaking are not:

> Mais les autres en face de lui demeuraient figés, la bouche fermée, les lèvres immobiles; et la phrase, sans personne pour l'avoir prononcée, semblait être une légende au bas d'un dessin. (p. 159)

Again, we can repeat that, once stripped of connotative meaning (communication), voices can only assert (express themselves to themselves). What remains is the tenor, the size of the voice, the shape of the voice, the texture, the distance. To grasp even this much, characters are forced to repeat and repeat; each time repeated, the language becomes more labyrinthine, more abstract, impossible to decipher:

> la voix d'homme reprend sa même phrase pour la troisième fois, mais avec moins de force, ce qui empêche de nouveau d'y reconnaitre autre chose que des ébauches de sons, privés de sens. (p. 88)

Just as description can fragment body parts in close-ups and can thus render them autonomous, independent of the whole, so too language, when abstracted, cannot be possessed, even by him who uses it:

> Le soldat essaye maintenant de se rappeler les termes exacts qu'il vient d'employer. Il y avait le mot "caserne," mais il ne parvient pas à se souvenir de la phrase bizarre qu'il a prononcée. (p. 78)

> Sa phrase est si peu distincte qu'elle se désagrège avant d'être achevée; il doute même ensuite de l'avoir prononcée vraiment. (p. 142)

Denotation to repetition to depersonalization to abstraction to negation to doubt and forgetfulness: all attempts to possess and manipulate language fail.

It is interesting to note that by stripping language of its connotation, by leaving only form (meta-language), the novel's sound-track is actually converted into a visual track. As forms, language can be visualized and spatialized. This visualization of dialogue in particular and language in general (emphasis on seeing rather than on envisioning) is suggested by the soldier, who, unsure that his words have even been voiced, suggests that the woman may have heard him by reading his lips:

> Il répète encore sa question. Cette fois, des sons, faibles mais distincts, sortent de sa bouche, comme si la voix aux intonations trop basses lui rendait l'usage de sa propre parole; à moins que la femme n'ait deviné les mots en lisant sur ses lèvres. (p. 142)

Repetition leads not only to differences but also to negation (implying further differences). If formalization of language has for its purpose the creation of a total ambiguity or uncertainty of meaning, it has for its effect the creation of a visualized and spatialized sound track. Even here, characters are often uncertain from where a sound comes, how far away it is, whose it is, etc. This visual or spatial uncertainty becomes a repeated motif in the scenes in the street involving the soldier and the child. The child is like a poltergeist for the soldier who would like to immobilize him, freeze-frame him: the child visually appears, disappears, reappears. But the same holds true for his voice, which is spatialized by the soldier:

> "Qu'est-ce que tu attends?" Puis, sur le même ton, comme en écho au bout d'une dizaine de secondes: "Qu'est-ce que tu attends là?"
>
> La voix est bien celle du gamin, une voix réfléchie, tranquille, sans bienveillance, un peu trop grave pour un garçon de dix ou douze ans. Mais elle parait très proche, deux ou trois mètres à peine, alors que le coin de l'immeuble est au moins situé à huit. L'homme a envie de se retourner pour contrôler cette distance, et voir si l'enfant ne s'est pas de nouveau rapproché. (p. 54)

With these observations in mind, we can now analyze the infrequent but important exchanges of dialogue, the non-conversations in the novel. They usually begin with a question, most often posed by someone to the soldier; they usually end with the soldier's most frequently repeated remark: "Je ne sais pas." The following are examples of this stylized dialogue: (Emphasis mine)

(1) Qu'est-ce que vous allez faire, demande enfin la femme, puisque vous avez perdu le nom de cette rue?
-_Je ne sais pas, dit le soldat._
-C'était pour une chose importante?
-Oui . . . Non . . . Probablement.
-Qu'est-ce que c'était?
-_Je ne sais pas_, dit le soldat. (pp. 66-67)

(2) C'est quel régiment? dit-elle à la fin . . .
Je ne sais pas, dit le soldat.
Vous avez oublié, aussi, le nom de votre régiment?
-Non, ce n'est pas ça . . . Mais cette capote-là n'est pas la mienne.
Et à qui appartenait-elle?
Je ne sais pas, dit le soldat. (pp. 75-76)

(3) Ça fait longtemps? demande l'infirmier en chapeau de feutre.
-Longtemps que je suis là?
-Non: que vous avez la fièvre.
-_Je ne sais pas_, dit le soldat. (p. 141)

(4) Qu'est-ce qu'il y a, dedans? dit-il de sa voix trop grave, qui n'est pas celle d'un gamin.
Je ne sais pas. Du verre, aussi, probablement.
-C'est noir.
-Oui. C'est du verre noir.
. . . .
Pourquoi? Et, comme le soldat ne répond pas, il répète: Pourquoi c'est là-dedans?
-_Je ne sais pas_, dit le soldat. (p. 154)

(5) C'est vrai que tu me la donnes?
-Oui, je t'ai dit.
-D'où elle vient?
-De ma poche.
-Et avant?
-Avant? Avant, _je ne sais pas_, dit le soldat. (p. 155)

It would be wrong to think that this pattern applied only to the soldier, for the soldier has merely learned the ritual from the child. The first time that the two met in the street, the roles were reversed:

> Eh bien, tu as peur que je te mange?
> -Non, dit l'enfant, j'ai pas peur.
> -Alors, dis-moi où je vais, par-là?
> -Je ne sais pas, dit l'enfant. (p. 37)

This negation is what holds the labyrinth together as a structure. Beyond negation (denotation), it implies uncertainty, restraint, indecision. It is this indecision which dooms the soldier who loses himself inside the labyrinth whose only avenue of escape is in the room (the mind) of the narrator, the one described room in the novel in which the soldier never enters.

(6) Echo Structures and Metaphor

What creates the labyrinth is point of view, a point of view which bends and shapes objective reality into a serialized, circular, repeated or fixed subjective reality. Echo structures, like repetition, reinforce the labyrinth. The "je ne sais pas" is echoed throughout the novel. The child's quick and frequent rejoinder to the soldier, "Tu sais pas rouler tes molletières," is another. Thus, each time that molletières are mentioned, often in different contexts than in conversation with the child, the repetition shapes the context surrounding it, becoming symbol or leitmotif. Herein lies the function of metaphor. Traditional similes or metaphors are scarce in Robbe-Grillet's visualized and spatialized novels, so that when they do occur they deserve our attention. They are most often related to the echo structures. For example, a fairly simple (almost cliché) simile like "comme par un coup de chiffon," through repetition, becomes a leitmotif for scene erasures, for blinking, for coming out of the hallucinations vraies. This simile functions, then, as a blur or wipe dissolve would function in film (pp. 10, 14, 43, 122 in the novel).

In a traditional simile or analogy (A is like B), the B factor serves to clarify or explain the A factor. Let us take an example:

> like spiders in that crumbly manor house, perched like jumped-up jackdaws on the roof, watching out over drives and fields like German generals from the tops of tanks.
>
> (from Allan Sillitoe's The Loneliness of a Long-Distance Runner)

The description refers to the borstal authorities; it depends for its effect upon three similes (like spiders, like jumped-up jackdaws, like German generals), each of which carries the comparison into a different connotative realm. Significantly, the B factor in each simile has very weak denotative value and very strong connotative value. We do not see the spider, the jackdaw or the German general actualized independently of the authorities: that is, we envision them, but we do not literally see them, since they are never really "present"; only the authorities remain present. It's as if "authorities" represented a naked conceptual symbol to the reader, and the author clothed that symbol with three garments that, in so doing, lose their autonomy and very existence, becoming part of "the authorities."

The cinema cannot portray a simile in which the B factor is figurative clothing for the A factor. A cinematic attempt might include: shot of the authorities, shot of the spider, shot of the authorities, shot of jumped-up jackdaw, shot of authorities, shot of

German general from the top of a tank. In such a configuration no simile exists. Because of the strong denotative value of the cinematographic image, the shots of the spider, jackdaw and general would take on a reality all their own: they would exist as concrete entities, independent of the shots of the authorities. With Sillitoe we envision the B factors of the simile as superimposed on the A factor; they do not exist independently. With the hypothetical filmic equivalent, the shots are not superimposed, but rather juxtaposed: they co-exist, the one next to the other.

> The proper end of 'language' is to communicate the meaning of a being which is other than the thing signified. In film, contrariwise, significance and the thing signified are one: the thing conveys its meaning in itself, without mediation.

As in the cinema, both factors co-exist in Robbe-Grillet's novels. As such, similes are never arbitrarily chosen in his novels. Indeed, they can be read as belonging to the _mise-en-abime_ ensemble. In other words, where similes in Sillitoe expand, those in Robbe-Grillet contract, since they must be read cross-referentially. Robbe-Grillet's similes are equations in disguise: A is like B means A equals B in Robbe-Grillet. And while they are equal connotatively, they retain their "presence" and their independence denotatively.

> Il se trouve bientôt au centre d'un cercle, qui s'aggrandit progressivement à mesure que les silhouettes reculent, seules leurs faces blêmes demeurant encore visibles, espacées de plus en plus, à intervalles égaux, _comme une succession de lampadaires_ le long d'une rue rectiligne. (p. 177) (emphasis mine)

Here again Robbe-Grillet forces the reader to participate in the creation of meaning by stripping the simile of its envisionary or connotative powers. The B factor here denotatively exists and is in in fact more concrete than the A factor (the silhouettes). While retaining their independence denotatively (their form, in other words) they also equate. Yet, even in such an obvious equation, there is always a difference. Here the difference lies in the fact that, within the juxtaposition of the two factors, the form has changed: from a circle to a rectangle. This change can of course be explained in the point of view of the observing narrator.

(7) Associative Editing

Associative editing in *Dans le labyrinthe* is always related to the *mise-en-abime* ensemble, that is, to the vision of the observer who sees similarities in differences and independent entities in repetitions. Since the novel is completely spatialized, temporality breaks down, so that a linear, chronological (B comes after A), cause-and-effect (B is the result of A) narrative is impossible. Transitions between scenes not temporally or spatially related are effected, then, through association: one element in one scene provides the link with the following scene. For example:

> Ensuite, assis sur le lit et courbé en avant, il commence à enlever ses molletières, avec lenteur, enroulant au fur et à mesure la bande d'étoffe sur elle-même, en la tournant autour de la jambe.
>
> "Tu sais même pas rouler tes molletières." Au pied du réverbère, sur le bord du trottoir, le gamin considère fixément les chevilles du soldat. Puis, remontant le long des jambes, il détaille tout le costume des pieds à la tête, arrêtant à la fin son regard sur les joues creuses, noires de barbe:
>
> "Où tu as dormi, cette nuit?" (p. 115)

It should be clear that *molletières* provides the visual link between scenes which are unrelated both in time and in space. The passage forward is relatively simple compared to the passage backward. Where Robbe-Grillet excels is in the way that he associatively weaves back to the first scene. The child stares at the soldier from feet to the beard on his face. When the child asks, "Where did you sleep last night?" the two scenes are interlinked again. In the same way, the act of lying on the bed associatively links the observer-narrator in his room with the soldier lying on his bed in the pseudo-infirmary (p. 136); the sounds of an approaching motorcar trigger a "present-lived flashback" for the soldier: that is, the sounds of the motorcar are like the shooting of guns. The circle is completed when the men on the motorcar begin shooting their guns (p. 174), which in turn precipitates a further association between the wounded soldier of the flashback (or is it a flash-forward?) and the wounded soldier of the present (p. 228). The frequency of associative editing is proportionate to the deterioration in the soldier. From fatigue and fever to forgetfulness, delirium and sleep-walking, the soldier's final moment is prefigured by the almost blinding rapidity with which he changes scenes and confuses them (he confuses the invalid and his crutch with the doctor and his umbrella-cane; he sees the child in the street with the umbrella-cane; he prophetically confuses all of the characters in the novel in his answer to the question: who was at Reichenfels). There are of course other novelists who have used associative editing to link two unrelated scenes. But there are very few who, like Robbe-Grillet, can solidify that linkage with a second association, so that "scene A is like scene B" comes to mean "scene A equals scene B."

(8) Triadic Structures of Description and Hypotheses

If there is a patterned numerology at work in Dans le labyrinthe, then the predominant number, the number which structures the entire text, is the number three. At the thematic level, this predominance is fairly obvious: there are three soldiers in the painting; there are three people in the room where the soldier dies; there are three soldiers in the flashback; there are three different and yet similar women; questions and answers are repeated three times; "halt" is cried three times; there are three shots to be given the soldier by the doctor (the soldier dies before the problematic third one can be given), etc.

What is perhaps more subtly concealed, on a first reading of the text is that triads structure the language of the novel also. When these triads are purely descriptive (denotative), they are usually spatial indicators, which, by filling up the "space" of the scene, encircle the observing narrator and pinpoint his point of view: (emphasis mine)

(1) et la fine poussière se dépose en couche uniforme, sur le plancher, sur le couvre-lit, sur les meubles . . . Sur le plancher ciré, les chaussons de feutre ont dessiné des chemins luisants, du lit à la commode, de la commode à la cheminée, de la cheminée à la table. (p. 12)

(2) La platitude de tout ce décor ferait croire, d'ailleurs, qu'il n'y a rien derrière ces carreaux, derrière ces portes, derrière ces façades. (p. 25)

Indeed, the second example is one of filling up negative space, that is, giving negation full form and body. There are numerous examples of descriptive triads that while not involving directional prepositions nevertheless spatialize object-referents:

(1) La voix de l'homme n'intervient que par phrases brèves, ou même par monosyllables, sinon par des grognements. (p. 88)

(2) Il ne subsiste plus à leur place, que la démesure, et l'étrangeté, et la mort. (p. 118)

(3) Leurs yeux sont creux, leurs lèvres serrées, leur peau est grisâtre. (p. 180)

(4) Elle projette au plafond une ombre déformée, où ne se reconnait plus aucun élément de l'insecte initial: ni ailes, ni corps, ni pattes. (p. 15)

These triads not only create the rhythm or souffle of the poetic text--not only do they "fill" the frame spatially,--but also, in the case of conjecture or hypothesis, they create a labyrinth of probabilities, a pluridimensionality of meaning. Thus, at one point in the opening descriptions of the narrator's room, an object (poignard) is not immediately named; rather, it is given three possible forms: On dirait une fleur. . . . Ou bien ce serait une figurine vaguement humaine . . . Ce pourrait être aussi un poignard . . . (pp. 13-14). And, even though it is eventually named, the other two probabilities do not disappear; they continue throughout the text. Triadic hypotheses still involve the vision of the observing narrator, but they introduce connotation into the scene they describe. For instance, in the following passages:

(1) Il a tiré sa main droite de sa poche et l'avance en crispant les doigts, comme celui qui craindrait de laisser échapper quelque détail dont il se croit sur le point de fixer le souvenir, ou comme celui qui veut obtenir un encouragement, ou qui ne parvient pas à convaincre. (p. 163)

(2) Le soldat a pensé, un instant, que ce personnage faisait exprès de garder le silence: qui'il était en effet le destinataire en question mais qu'il refusait de se faire connaitre, qu'ayant appris ce qu'il desirait lui-même savoir il se dérobait . . . C'était absurde, évidemment. Ou bien l'affaire ne le concernait en aucune facon, ou bien il ne s'était pas encore aperçu de ce qu'on s'efforcait de lui dire et qui l'intéressait au premier chef. (p. 165)

We have already seen how the simile ("Comme . . .") functions as an equation in Robbe-Grillet. We could affirm here that the "ou bien" which provides the parallel construction in the second example functions linguistically, not as "or else" but rather as "and" since all three probabilities are true. In other words, where triadic hypotheses are concerned, there are at least three ways of reading the text. The elements of the triad are not exclusive; rather, they parallel each other and as such they belong to the mise-en-abime ensemble. What translates as either-or in these triads should instead be read as and-and . . . (pluridimensionality of meaning).

The triad is that structure which best fits the labyrinth. If it were a question of either-or, that is, if there were only two alternatives possible in each hypothesis, the labyrinth would collapse, because there would always be the possibility of a clear choice, both empirical. The introduction of the third element (and the suggestion of an endless series) makes any choice problematic, since no choice is definitive or empirical; makes characters repeat their steps; makes characters hesitate; immobilizes them. For the labyrinth to exist, there must be a minimum of three elements or three choices possible, none of which is "right," all of which are probable and simultaneously actualized. Thus, even when there seem to be only two choices available (either-or), a third enters in (such as time) and creates a triad (the either-or plus the probability of choosing neither):

> le soldat devait choisir entre deux solutions: parler plus franchement, ou faire aussitôt machine arrière. Mais il n'avait pas eu le temps d'opter pour l'une ou l'autre, et il s'était obstiné dans les deux directions à la fois, ce qui risquait par surcroît de décourager son interlocuteur s'il avait été, malgre tout, etc. (p. 165)

Kristeva and the Russian semiologists (Todorov, Syrkin, Lotman) have pointed out that triads usually comprise mytho-ethical signifying systems and are, if "open" triads, less stable than tetradic structures, which are usually the basis for speculative signifying systems. Their discoveries are of great use in reading _Dans le labyrinthe_: thus, where there is mobility (instability), we could expect to find triadic structures; and where there is complete immobility (stability), we could expect to find tetradic structures. Indeed, it is these tetradic structures or elements that completely immobilize (stabilize) the novel's conclusion (I have numbered the elements in parentheses for the sake of clarification):

> Ici la pluie n'entre pas (1), ni la neige (2), ni le vent (3); et (4) la seule fine poussière qui ternit le brillant des surfaces horizontales, (1) le bois verni de la table, (2) le plancher ciré à chevrons, (3) le marbre de la cheminée, (4) celui, fêlé, de la commode, la seule poussière provient de

> la chambre elle-même, (1) des raies du plancher peut-être, (2) ou bien du lit, (3) ou des cendres dans la cheminée, (4) ou des rideaux de velours dont les plis verticaux montent du sol jusqu'au plafond sur lequel l'ombre de la mouche. . . . passe maintenant à proximité de la mince ligne noire, qui, demeurant dans le pénombre hors du cercle de lumière et à une distance de quatre ou cinq mètres, est d'observation très aléatoire: un court segment de droite, d'abord-, long de moins d'un centimètre, les-mêmes festonnées . . . (1) mais la vue se brouille à vouloir en préciser les contours, de même que (2) pour le dessin trop fin qui orne le papier des murs, et (3) les limites trop incertaines des chemins luisants tracés dans la poussière par les chaussons de feutre, et, après la porte de la chambre, (4) le vestibule obscur où la canne-parapluie est appuyée obliquement contre le portemanteau, puis, la porte d'entrée une fois franchie, (1) la succession des longs corridors, (2) l'escalier en spirale, (3) la porte de l'immeuble avec sa marche de pierre, et (4) toute la ville derrière moi. (pp. 238-29)

Point of View and Temporality

We have been speaking all along, in every section of this study, of the curious je néant point of view in Dans le labyrinthe which justifies every cinematographic technique in the novel, even those techniques which stem from cinematographic practices but which could never be filmed, literally filmed. We have yet to speak of the relationship between point of view and time. As Peter Wollen, based on the work of Gerard Genette, points out, point of view and time are always inter-related.

We have said that in a visualized, spatialized novel, time breaks down. In other words, a linear, chronological or cause-and-effect narrative is no longer possible. Thus, where space is fixed (described, pinpointed), time is fluid, mobile, circular, indeterminant: "Dehors il neige. Dehors il a neigé, il neigeait, dehors il neige." (p. 15) This fluidity of time, as can be seen in this example, is translated into a fluidity of verb tenses. The usual temporal movement in a novel is one of sequence or succession. That in film is usually one of simultaneity (since all images, even flash-backs, are as if in the present tense, because they are spatial and involve movement). In other words, succession can only be implied in film. But Robbe-Grillet's mixture of (progressive) past-tense and present-tense verbs represents an attempt to transcend both succession and simultaneity: transcend simultaneity by transforming time (narration) into space (description); transcend succession or sequence by re-integrating wholly unrelated points in time and wholly unrelated points in space. In this respect, there is no temporality for the soldier ("Demain, ce soir déjà, ou même dans quelques heures, cela sera trop tard.") except the moment of death when time stops (solidifies, freezes) because space is fixed, immobilized, forever framed. Thus, all of the structures of spatial immobility are connotative premonitions of the soldier's death. The only moment in which the _vertige_ becomes _fixé_ is precisely at this moment of death.

Converge as they must, time and point of view intersect at the level of the individual reader of _Dans le labyrinthe_. The use of the _je-néant_ narrator is calculated to shuttle the reader back and forth between real time (the time of reading) and mental time, between the time of dreams and the time of false memories or unclear recollections, as that of the soldier "envisioning" the defeat at Reichenfels. The _je-néant_ narrator is also calculated to provide the spectator with a "frame" (as one would frame a painting) on the opening page and the concluding page of the novel, between which the reader is invited to become a spectator (as with a painting or in a film) and to travel freely the vertiginous spectrum of multiple and shifting points of view, made possible by the "camera-eye" of the narrator, whether it be the doctor's direct narration or the soldier's indirect narration. Thus, time and point of view are both related to perspective, since links between different time frames and between different points of view are spatialized. There is a very real comparison to be made between the Picasso of "Les Demoiselles d'Avignon" and the Robbe-Grillet of "La Défaite de Reichenfels." Both presume all possible angles of vision simultaneously and not successively.

Dans le labyrinthe represents a crisis in that it explores the limits of the cinematographic novel: the spatialization of time and the _je-néant_ point of view. The crisis stems from the fact that the level of creation is not always synonymous with the level of reading (for anyone but the author, that is). Indeed, it is upon the reader that the success or failure of a Robbe-Grillet novel must fall, for Robbe-Grillet has purposefully suppressed the _deus ex maquina_ powers of the traditional novelist to be omniscient, to oversee plot, to translate the feelings of his characters, and to drive the deterministic time of the traditional novel from start to finish, a little like poor Phaethon drove his father's chariot to usher in the dawn--and killed himself in the process.

As Robbe-Grillet has accurately perceived, characters in modern fiction do not thrive on control from the outside. Just as the reader must open himself up to the sensory filter of narrators who are "pure" vision, so too Robbe-Grillet limits his own creative tampering to those very same visions.

Dans le labyrinthe is undoubtedly Robbe-Grillet's most important novel to date, for it provides a *mise-en-abime* mirror of all of the techniques used in his earlier novels and it represents the closest that he could come to film without actually making a film. Not surprisingly, *L'Immortelle* (1962), Robbe-Grillet's first film as director after writing *Dans le labyrinthe*, should contain the same structures of repetition, structures of geometric configurations, structures of depersonalization, structures of negation and immobility, structures of description/dialogue, echo structures and metaphors, structures of associative editing, triadic structures of description/hypothesis, subjective point of view and multiple time frames that the novel contains.

In retrospect, then, the proper frame of reading for *Dans le labyrinthe* is that of a spectator in a film. If this is true, then the reader should see *Labyrinthe* in terms of "scenes" and not in terms of events. One could also read the novel cross-referentially, as one would read a poem. Film and poetry are not very far apart here, for each demands several "sittings" with a complete reading at each sitting.

In his preface to the published text of L'Immortelle, Robbe-Grillet explains the ciné-roman (film-novel) in terms of music. The analogy is especially revealing, in that music has always been meant to be listened to an infinite number of times, each time involving a complete listening to the whole work. One does not come and go at a symphony the way one picks up and puts down a book. Again, the burden of creation has been shifted from that of the sole creator to that of a shared authorship between the creator and the reader/spectator who must become a co-creator in order to fully appreciate the work. What Robbe-Grillet has recently stated for his films also concerns his fiction:

> De même que le seul temps qui importe est celui du film, le seul "personnage" important est le spectateur; c'est DANS SA TÈTE que se déroule toute l'histoire, qui est exactement IMAGINEE par lui.

Time being understood as "the time of the film" is not an authorial dodge for achronology in modern art. Rather, it reinforces the subjective nature of the narration involved, a narration which is incomplete without the spectator becoming a co-narrator. Ironically, then, the objective (the time of the film) becomes objective and is explained by the subjective state of the audience ("dans sa tête," "imaginée par lui").

To point out all the various structures at work in Dans le labyrinthe is to distort the complexity of their interrelationships. If we have done so in this discussion, it is so that the reader may go back to the novel and reintegrate them in his mind, as they are already integrated on the written page. Indeed, the structure of the labyrinth works both internally and externally. All of the structures pointed out in this discussion form a complex network of intersections, so that repetition must be understood in terms of negation and immobility, just as the geometric configurations relate to time and point of view. Thus, Robbe-Grillet's novels are practically inaccessible if interrupted. Like the film, the poem, or the musical symphony, they must be "read" from start to finish at one sitting. They must be re-read from start to finish at another. That is the meaning of the labyrinth at the level of reading: the reader is "caught" in the novel, and the only way out is to finish. Because of the unique way in which Robbe-Grillet denies "envisioning" for "seeing" and ambiguates connotation through denotation which is both abstract and obsessive, his novels cannot be read in any other way. A reader cannot interrupt the continuous time of reading, come back to the novel hours or days later and expect to remember all the complex associations conjured up each time he sees the word "molletières," for example. *Dans le labyrinthe* is an exercise in hypnosis, an exercise in memory rather than one in cognition. That is why the novel must be read cross-referentially and continuously. With a novel like *La Jalousie*, which is really a long short story, there seems to be little problem. But having personally taught *Dans le labyrinthe* in the classroom, I seriously question how many readers are willing to expend either the time or the energy required to read it from start to finish without interruption. Robbe-Grillet seems to have solved this problem by making films.

Notes

[1] I am referring here to the excellent analysis of cinematographic techniques in *La Jalousie* in Richard Mitchell Blumenberg's *The Manipulation of Time and Space in the Novels of Alain Robbe-Grillet and in the Narrative Films of Alain Resnais, With Particular Reference to Last Year at Marienbad* (Ohio University, Ph.D. dissertation, 1969).

[2] This passage from James Joyce's *Ulysses* is the opening paragraph of the second "section" of the novel and is the first description of Bloom.

[3] Laurence Perrine, *Sound and Sense* (New York: Harcourt, Brace and World, 1956), p. 38.

[4] Alain Robbe-Grillet, *Dans le labyrinthe* (Paris: Editions de Minuit, 1959)(Collection 10/18), p. 1. All subsequent page references will be to this edition and will follow the quotations immediately in the text.

[5] Julia Kristeva, *Sēmeiōtikē: Recherches pour une sémanalyse* (Paris: Editions du Seuil, 1969), p. 259.

[6] Kristeva, p. 259.

[7] Blumenberg, p. 36.

[8] A more detailed discussion of Maya Deren's theories can be found in P. Adams Sitney's *Film Culture Reader* (New York: Praeger, 1970). This quote is from page 178 of that book. The reader is encouraged to read Deren's *An Anagram of Ideas on Art, Form and Film* (Yonkers: The Alicat Bookshop Press, 1946).

[9] Blumenberg, p. 133.

[10] Kristeva, p. 257.

[11] Kristeva, p. 251.

[12] Kristeva, p. 249.

[13] Jean Mitry, *Les Structures* (Paris: Editions Universitaires, 1963), p. 102.

V

Explorations and Innovations of the *Cinéma des Auteurs*

A. The "Subjective" Documentary

> "I was surprised to find that many people automatically assume that any DOCUMENTARY film would inevitably be objective. Perhaps the term is unsatisfactory, but for me the distinction between the words DOCUMENT and DOCUMENTARY is quite clear."
>
> -Joris Ivens

The making of *ciné-romans* or film-novels by the directors of the literary new wave was not just a simple transposition of themes and techniques explored and developed by Armand Gatti, Jean Cayrol, Marguerite Duras and Alain Robbe-Grillet in their fiction or in that of the *nouveau roman* generally. There was a filtering process in which these novelists began as apprentices to Alain Resnais, whose apprenticeship, along with that of Agnes Varda, Chris Marker and Henri Colpi concerns us here, for everything that was to appear in the feature-length films had already appeared in the shorts or *courts métrages* that Resnais, Varda and Marker made their specialty. Thus, any thorough discussion of the film-novels of the literary new wave should rightly include a discussion of their documentary shorts. I propose to discuss here in some detail the "subjective" (here synonymous with "personal," "poetic," "ironic," and "imaginary-objective") documentaries of four directors: Alain Resnais, Jean Cayrol, Agnes Varda and Chris Marker. In the course of my discussion, I shall draw parallels between their shorts and also distinguish between their documentaries and more traditional documentaries. I will also be paying special attention to the written texts of these documentaries, for it is in the text that these directors developed their highly "literary" dialogue that would be so characteristic of their later *ciné-romans*.

Alain Resnais made eight documentary shorts for which there are published texts available.[1] Only four will concern us here: Van Gogh (1948), Guernica (1950), Nuit et brouillard (1955) and Le Chant du styrène (1958).

Van Gogh was for Resnais the culmination of, and a departure from, the series of "visit" films about painters done from 1945 to 1947 (Lucien Coutard, Felix Labisse, Hans Hartung, Cesar Domela, Oscar Dominguez and Max Ernst). It was a very important film for the cinéma des auteurs, for it marked the path that directors like Marker and Varda would take in using literature or painting as a metaphor for social or political concerns. Van Gogh was a radical, even sacrilegious treatment of the painter; its purpose, clearly, was not to catalogue Van Gogh's work, as one might expect to see it in a museum, but rather to dissect the works (through a rapid, fragmented editing style and through continuous penetrating forward pans by the camera), to make them come to life, through this camera movement and through this continuous cutting, and to see in them the interior life of Van Gogh's frenetic mind. All reality, thus, was reconstructed along the lines of the paintings. The sun was Van Gogh's sun, the sea was Van Gogh's, the room in Arles was Van Gogh's. In a sense, the experiment for Resnais was to see if the paintings could replace photography in creating a new reality.

> Il s'agissait de savoir si des arbres peints, des personnages peints, des maisons peintes, pouvaient, grace au montage, remplir dans un récit, le rôle d'objets réels, et si, dans ce cas, il était possible de substituer pour le spectateur, et presque à son insu, le monde intérieur d'un artiste au monde réel tel que le révèle la photographie.

Resnais made two critical decisions at the outset: (1) he would not simply catalogue the works of the artist in their totality, their frames and their chronology, as one would expect from a museum; and (2) he would not remain "objective"; that is, he would not keep a respectful distance from the painter, either in terms of theme or in terms of technique. These decisions in turn brought others. He would trace, through the juxtaposition of very disparate paintings, the steps leading to Van Gogh's madness, that madness being shown either through the paintings themselves, with their brighter colors and more obsessive imagery, or through even more convulsive camera movements forward into the paintings and even more rapid editing. Because he knew that he would want to juxtapose very different paintings (that is, with no respect for chronology or for "periods") and because he knew that he would want to use an active camera and rapid editing, Resnais decided to film _Van Gogh_ in black-and-white, not in color. The choice of black-and-white was a crucial one, for Van Gogh's sense of color was so important to understanding his works. Filming in black-and-white instead of color represented for Resnais a distortion of Van Gogh from the reality of the paintings as art objects to the symbol of Van Gogh as artist. Filming in black-and-white also allowed Resnais to capture a fluid time sense: black-and-white makes the paintings themselves seem less fixed in time, while the mobile camera traversing the fixed art work makes the artist (and viewer) seem somehow present in the work.

One might momentarily compare Resnais's _Van Gogh_ with Vincent Minnelli's fictional treatment of Van Gogh in _Lust for Life_ (1956). Even an excellent colorist like Minnelli could not excape the trap of simulated color in the latter film, for, not only was he committed to using colors that most closely approximated the paintings of Van Gogh (while falsifying them), but he was also committed to a chronology that was both fatalistic and predictable. Lewis Jacobs has commented on the use of color in Minnelli's film:

> Failure to merge color with the elasticity and dramatic flow of the subject accounts for the weakness of Moulin Rouge (1953) and Lust for Life (1956), whose color design stemmed from the palettes of Toulouse Lautrec and Vincent Van Gogh. Because the directors of these movies failed to realize that, on the screen, color can be structured in time and not just in space as in painting, they neglected to use color for more than its emblematic associations.[3]

Jacobs goes on to point out how Minnelli was most effective at the end of the film, where color coordinated theme with technique.

> Yellows, oranges, reds, and black keyed the visual style of Lust for Life. But only toward the end of the film was the color pattern extended beyond individual shots to a succession that underlined the dramatic situation. As Van Gogh's mind begins to falter and he becomes increasingly mad, the color progressively changes from shot to shot; the reds and browns appear less and less until there is only the pale yellow of a wheat field, which provokes an uncanny sense of foreboding and approaching death. When the artist finally dies, the yellow of the field is suddenly torn apart by the swift inundation of a flock of black crows. The impact of the abrupt contrast between yellow and black was striking and both dramatically and psychologically expressive. The scene gained an added overtone from the fact that the color scheme and composition which inspired it came from the artist's own painting of a wheat field and crows, made at the very time of his own approaching madness and death.[4]

But what Jacobs admired in the Minnelli film was already present as a given in the Resnais short: the use of paintings to enliven symbolically the artist's life. And the effective condensation of color in the Minnelli film, until there is only the yellow and black, is none other than the black and white of Resnais's film which are extended throughout the film, in terms of time as well as space. Resnais has commented on his choice of black and white over color in the film:

> Si nous avons choisi le noir et le blanc de préférence à la couleur, ce ne fut pas seulement en raison de difficultés techniques. Nous esperions qu'ainsi apparaîtrait mieux l'architecture tragique de la peinture de Van Gogh. Le noir et blanc m'intéressait parce qu'il me permettait de créer des liens entre des toiles extrêmement disparates.[5]

At the same time that Resnais juxtaposes paintings from different periods of Van Gogh's career, he also uses the same painting for different periods in Van Gogh's personal life: thus, "L'Homme à l'oreille coupée" becomes a kind of self-portrait, once for the hospital, three times for the sanatarium, and twice more for Van Gogh's last hours. The progression of Resnais is clear, from the use of self-portraits and still lifes to denote the exterior of Van Gogh to a juxtaposition of self-portraits with luminous objects, which denote Van Gogh's progressive madness: "L'apparition proprement dite de la folie est traduite par une alternance au rythme de plus en plus rapide d'auto-portraits et d'objets lumineux: les étoiles, bec de gaz, lumière, soleil et surtout monstrueux tournesols (montrés cinq fois) se heurtent violemment à un visage filmé de plus en plus près jusqu'à se résoudre seulement à deux yeux exorbités."[6] At the same time that Resnais progressively closes in on the face of the artist in the self-portraits, and in particular on the eyes, he also closes in on the opposite of those eyes in the still lifes, the ever-deepening and accusatory shadows, to signify the closeness of the artist's death.

> "Les couleurs vibrent dans l'air surchauffé"; la musique hausse le ton, les zooms se multiplient et les paysages filmés en larges panoramiques sont rapidement mitraillés de plans de coupe: oliviers, fleurs...Resnais souligne la force des contrastes de ses peintures, faisant alterner les ombres et les lumières soumises à la loi du soleil. Ainsi, montrant un arbre baigné de clarté, le cinéaste nous projette sèchement par un court panoramique latéral sur son ombre durement accusée par le peintre. Mais l'apparition de plus en plus fréquente de fondus au noir, assez discrets au début du film, vient étendre peu à peu le voile de la mort...[7]

Resnais tried to capture the rhythm of Van Gogh's madness and death, not only through the machine-gun camera and editing (panoramiques mitraillés), but also through Jacques Besse's music which would punctuate the camera movements and the cuts between shots. Thus, as Van Gogh's death approaches, the music becomes more strident, louder and less harmonious. Significantly, Resnais had not yet found the personal-poetic text in Van Gogh, the kind of text that would become his trademark. If there is anything in the film which encumbers its development and its impact, it is the text, which all too often duplicates what is already evident in the visuals. Yet, the conclusion of the film text attains a level of poetry worthy of Resnais's later films. Resnais relates Van Gogh's madness to his paintings, that is, to the proliferation of sunflowers and suns in the paintings, as if to say that the artist had looked too long and too much into the sun. In addition, Resnais makes of Van Gogh a mythical artist, a kind of Prometheus, a player of fire. Thus, the concluding lines of the commentary are:

> On ne joue pas impunément avec le feu...et ce n'est pas pour rien que les tournesols s'appellent des soleils. Arrivé au sommet de son art, Van Gogh, vainqueur, s'arrête..., saisi de vertige.

It is not so much Van Gogh but the camera which stops suddenly, seized by vertigo. For the first time in the film, the camera pulls back to reveal, also for the first time, a full painting, enclosed in its frame: the painting is that of Van Gogh's last and incomplete work. René Prédal has commented on the effectiveness of this camera pulling back to reveal the framed work, thus, revealing the death of the artist:

> Mais au moment où la mort saisit le peintre en train d'achever une dernière toile, sur laquelle il essaye de retrouver aux fins fonds des Caraibes sa Bretagne neigeuse (tableau resté inachevé), la caméra opère un lent mouvement vers l'arrière découvrant, pour la première fois, le cadre autour du tableau: le peintre est mort; son oeuvre jusqu'ici vivante se trouve desormais figée dans un musée. Un artiste n'est plus.[8]

With Guernica (1950) Resnais moved from the personal, interiorized life-force of the artist to the multiplicity of meaning so characteristic of his later ciné-romans, for Guernica is at one and the same time a historical reality, a painting by Picasso and a poem by Eluard. Just as the sense of madness through creative energies being burned out was more important to *Van Gogh* than a detailed and objective presentation of the painter's life, so too the works of Picasso are important to *Guernica*, only in that they reveal the horrors of the historical reality, and not because they reveal anything in depth about the personality of Picasso. With *Guernica* Resnais began the process of using art at the service of life, mixing different levels of reality surrounding the same event. Resnais is one of the few artists capable of blending the political with the aesthetic, and *Guernica* was his first attempt to deal with politics through aethetics, just as he would explore the effects of the bombing at Hiroshima through the private love story in *Hiroshima mon amour*, just as he would explore the political situation in Spain through the private meanderings and meditations of Diego in *La Guerre est finie*. *Guernica* was also Resnais's first attempt at literary collaboration, and it is significant for the understanding of the *ciné-roman* that Resnais chose to work with poets (Paul Eluard on *Guernica*, Jean Cayrol on *Nuit et brouillard*, Raymond Queneau on *Le Chant du styrène*) for the shorts before he chose to work with novelists for the feature films (Marguerite Duras for *Hiroshima*, Alain Robbe-Grillet for *L'Année dernière à Marienbad*, Cayrol for *Muriel*, Jorge Semprun for *La Guerre est finie* and Jacques Sternberg for *Je t'aime je t'aime*).

Everything has been reconstructed in *Guernica* for the total effect of the film. Thus, Paul Eluard wrote an elaborated version of his previously published poem. Thus, not just that mural of Picasso entitled "Guernica," but also paintings from before "Guernica" and paintings from after "Guernica," in addition to collages and sculptures, are used in the film. In fact, the actual mural of Picasso bearing the title of the film is used in very restricted terms: as the visual counterpoint of the leitmotiv of the electric lamp, a leitmotiv used so effectively by Orson Welles to show the mental breakdown and suicide attempt of Susan Alexander in _Citizen Kane_. In _Guernica_, the unshaded electric lamp corresponds to the explosions of bombs, and the intermittent flashes of lightness and darkness recreate very effectively for the spectator the sense of being under attack. As in _Van Gogh_, Resnais is not concerned with showing the work of art in its framed totality, that is, in its museum state; rather, he is concerned with transforming the work of art from a finished work that is closed and immobile to a work of art whose very fragmentation brings life back and recreates the historical moment. Thus, Resnais uses Picasso and Eluard as _image-témoins_ (eye-witnesses), internal spectators who, by expanding their works of art, comment directly (as if in progress) upon the historical situation. For Resnais, Guernica was not 1936; it re-occurs every time the film is shown. If _Van Gogh_ rose gradually to a violent crescendo of light, cutting, text and music, _Guernica_ assaults the viewer from the very first images: in effect, the spectator is machine-gunned by the work of art. René Prédal has commented on the severity of Resnais's film:

> Cette dureté est traduite cinématographiquement par un montage très rapide, véritable mitraillage de visions restreintes mais édifiantes; certaines images ne sont aperçues que le temps d'un éclair (celui des explosions) rappelant le motif de la lampe. Par deux fois, un montage très serré fait alterner le mur à graffiti, des gros plans de journaux (sur quoi certains des mots ont été tracés en plus: _Guernica_, _Fascism_ Resistencia...) et des portraits peints par Picasso, mais criblés de balles qui laissent des traces sur le mur placé derrière eux, pendant que chaque peinture disparait progressivement pour laisser place à la suivante; le réel et l'art, la vie et la mort, l'information et le mensonge sont alors étroitement mêlés, indissociables.[9]

Resnais's Guernica (13 minutes) is only one minute longer than Robert Flaherty's Guernica (1949) in actual time, but because of Resnais's use of a poetic text, his rapid montage and his expansion of the art work from one mural to many paintings and sculptures of Picasso and to newspaper headings and pictures, the film of Resnais seems far more detailed and emotionally draining than the Flaherty film. Flaherty, consistent with his romantic vision of the world and his dislike for too much editing, never leaves the actual mural of "Guernica" and he rarely cuts the painting into the fragments that Resnais does. Flaherty's statement is correspondingly less political than Resnais's and his film is less harsh; Flaherty laments the historical reality of Guernica, seemingly more so than Resnais, and he also projects much more hope than does Resnais. Both the lament and the hope in Flaherty seem exaggerated and somehow unfounded, when they are compared with the document brought back to life of Resnais; Flaherty's Guernica is a document of innocence lost in the past, and his film never leaves that Eden in the past; by contrast, Resnais's Guernica forces the document back into the present, reveals the document unfolding, and constantly draws parallels between the past and the present, as he would do in his later feature films. If Resnais is less faithful than Flaherty to the Picasso mural, he can surely be excused on the grounds that his distortions of the art works and his recreation of a historical reality are ultimately more "authentic" than the Flaherty film.

Visually speaking, Resnais sets out to burn the spectator's eyes with his film. His visuals are always interesting but also hard to sustain for the spectator. Resnais seems less concerned that the spectator capture the individual image's impact (many of the shots are shown so rapidly that they are as if unseen by the spectator) than that the spectator capture the totality of the images. His montage of explosions only softens at the very end of the film when his camera ceases the almost epileptic zooms and begins to move laterally along the mural of Picasso, as if the mural were a text in images reading from left to right, showing the vast expanse of dead beasts and humans. In the midst of this lateral movement, without breaking the continuity of the movement itself, Resnais cuts to show the total destruction in three-dimensional horror, moving from painting to sculpture. At the same time that the sculptures of Picasso give more weight, depth and "life" to the corpses than the mural could, they also accentuate the feeling of death, the feeling of full-bodied things without life. This softening of the editing pace and the lateral movement of the camera, progressing from paintings to sculptures, is the equivalent of the backward movement of the camera and the revelation of the framed painting in _Van Gogh_. Having distorted the work of art for almost the entirety of both films, Resnais very effectively restores both Van Gogh's painting and Picasso's mural to their museum stasis.

Where _Van Gogh_ is perhaps more lyrical but also more artificial, because of the weakness of the spoken text, _Guernica_ seems to hold together more, because the text not only works in its own right, but it also provides pace and pauses, reins in the machine-gun images and gives them texture and meaning. For the first time, Resnais, as Prédal has pointed out, has found the image-text counterpoint that would characterize his later _ciné-romans_.

> Une bande "son" très travaillée, joue généralement en contrepoint de l'image; la voix _off_ est d'abord celle, neutre et objective, d'un homme semblant commenter un banal documentaire. Puis Maria Casarès

> commence la lecture du texte d'Eluard de cette manière déclamatoire, à la limite d'une théâtralité excessive, qui restera une des caracteristiques des films de Resnais. Des sons stridents, tour à tour très réalistes puis artificiellement récréées, accompagnent les passages où l'horreur est à son comble. Les synchronismes sont rares (par exemple la voix prononce le mot de "bête" sur l'image d'un taureau); le plus souvent, au contraire, Maria Casarès parle des habitants de Guernica alors que l'on ne voit que le mur couvert de graffiti, seuls restes de ceux qui furent vivants, où les sèches nouvelles brèves aperçues sur un journal sont denoncées par la voix parlant de mourants achevés. L'horreur véritable est dans le texte, mieux à meme d'évoquer le drame que les "preuves" refroidies du "fait divers".[10]

Resnais is one of the first filmmakers to place so much importance on the text, giving it equal importance with the images; in this, he differs from most documentary filmmakers and from most filmmakers in general. One need only compare the text of Resnais's shorts with those of Flaherty's documentary films to see how really incidental the texts of Nanook of the North (1920-21) or Louisiana Story (1946-48) really are. Flaherty simply was not as concerned with the text as he was with the images. If his films are preserved, it is for their visual beauty, not for their spoken texts. With Resnais, the preservation is for both the sound track and the image track. And, if Prédal is right in saying that the real horror of Guernica is in its text, we would do well to look at the text with an analytical eye.

Actually, there are two texts in Guernica: the one spoken with restraint and apparent indifference by a male voice and which describes rather than evokes the feeling of a Guernica once more inhabited for the recreation of its disastrous annihilation, the other chanted by Maria Casarès in a voice that projects as one would in the theatre, a voice that vibrates with emotion, a voice that trills the words and seems always about to crack, a voice that restricts itself to the poem of Eluard and to the most destructive moments of the film. When Resnais wishes to convey the utter horror of the historical event, he switches from the male narrator to the poetry of Eluard and the strident solo of Casarès. The poem of Eluard, already moving at a silent reading, is doubly effective when given this operatic orchestration. It reminds me of Eisenstein's observations on the Kabuki theatre, in which the culmination of a character's emotional outburst is expressed, not by the voice of the character, but by the sound of the samisen or the flute.

Yet the two texts do complement each other and, thus, have certain points of similarity. If they differ in tone, that is, in the way they are delivered, they are nonetheless similar in composition.

Resnais's film texts are never prosaic, even though the monotone of certain narrators' deliveries suggest them to be so and reinforce the sense of little emotion or that indifference that so pervade the voices of Marienbad or Muriel. The male narrator's lines in Guernica are delivered in hushed restraint and thus, they counterbalance the hysteria of Casarès. But they are in themselves poetic and surprisingly similar to the construction of Eluard's poem. For example, at one point the male narrator "describes" the life of the people in Guernica while the visuals flit here and there across the Picasso mural. The description is as follows:

> Les gens de Guernica sont de petites gens. Ils vivent dans leur ville depuis longtemps. Leur vie est composée d'une goutte de richesse et d'un flot de misère. Ils aiment leurs enfants. Leur vie est composée de tout petits bonheurs et d'un très grand souci; celui du lendemain. Demain il faut manger et demain il faut vivre. Aujourd'hui, l'on espère. Aujourd'hui, l'on travaille.

The apparent banality of the text comes from the accentuation of small details: they've lived there a long time, they love their children, they worry about tomorrow, and tomorrow means eating (concrete) and living (vague) while today means hoping (vague) and working (concrete). The banality is further reinforced by the insistence upon smallness: "petites gens," "goutte de richesse," "petits bonheurs." Yet, as poetry, the text has rhythm and it works on the basis of repetition. If we underlined the repeated elements of the description, without regard for their meaning, we would have the following:

> Les gens de Guernica sont de petites gens. Ils vivent dans leur ville depuis bien longtemps. Leur vie est composée d'une goutte de richesse et d'un flot de misère. Ils aiment leurs enfants. Leur vie est composée de tout petits bonheurs et d'un très grand souci: celui du lendemain. Demain il faut manger et demain il faut vivre. Aujourd'hui, l'on espère. Aujourd'hui, l'on travaille.

Gramatically speaking, what we have here are simple sentences. But, in terms of their meaning and in terms of the way that such lines easily "slide" into the lines of the Eluard poem, their simplicity is deceiving.

The Eluard poem is agrammatical in the sense that there are few verbs (the moving camera and the rapid cuts provide the verbs for the text); it is composed of fragmented descriptions whose disparate elements are held together by both rhythm and repetition of key words:

> Visages bons au feu visages bons au froid
> Aux refus à la nuit aux injures aux coups
>
> Visages bons à tout

In addition, the Eluard poem, chanted by a "hysterical" woman, accuses the seeming indifference of the male narrator, since it accuses men for crimes perpetrated on women and children:

> Les femmes les enfants ont le même trésor
> Dans les yeux.
>
> Les hommes le défendent comme ils peuvent.

The two voices, while retaining their idiosyncracies of tone and delivery, ultimately merge when the male narrator "accepts" the guilt of Guernica, saying with characteristic repetition of several words:

> Allez donc retenir une bête qui sent la mort. Allez donc expliquer à une mère la mort de son enfant! Allez donc inspirer confiance dans les flammes!

But, if there is one line in the text that sums up the entire movement and rhythm of the work, it is a line from the Eluard poem: "Et la Mort a rompu l'équilibre du temps." That broken equilibrium between the past and the present is evident in the switching back and forth visually, with no respect for chronology or for medium, the "periods" of Picasso giving way to the graffiti and the newspaper headlines, the paintings of Picasso giving way to the collages and sculptures. The line of Eluard equally applies to all of Resnais's later films, both shorts and features.

For _Nuit et brouillard_, Resnais chose another poet - Jean Cayrol. This was the writer of _Poèmes de la nuit et du brouillard_ more than the author whose novel _La Noire_ Resnais wanted to adapt for the screen. With Cayrol's poetic text, Resnais was to make his most artistic and most successful documentary.

For _Nuit et brouillard_, Resnais juxtaposed newsreel footage and photographs of the camps and their victims in black-and-white with a measured and constantly moving camera in color. Camera movement with the black-and-white stills and newsreel footage effectively evoked the horrors of the past, just as black-and-white photographs, rather than actual film footage, effectively evoked the nostalgia of the past in Chris Marker's _La Jetée_ (1963). The real horror of Resnais's film, however, comes from the peaceful, almost innocuous images of the present in color.

Nuit et brouillard represents the same slowing down of camera pace and decrease in editing pace from Van Gogh and Guernica that there is between Marienbad and Muriel. The reasons for this change are strikingly similar in both cases. The rapid editing in Guernica and Marienbad corresponds with the broken equilibrium of time in both films. The electric lamp in Guernica is replaced by alternating overexposed and underexposed images in Marienbad. With Guernica Resnais had focused on a specific historical reality; with Nuit et brouillard, his focus was more on a socio-political phenomenon rather than on a specific event in time, and his intent was correspondingly to universalize that phenomenon, where his intent in Guernica had been to give life again to a specific tragedy. The passage from Marienbad to Muriel, like that from Guernica to Nuit et brouillard, is the passage from black-and-white to color, the passage from machine-gun editing to longer takes and quieter cuts, the passage from a time-oriented film to a space-oriented film. Resnais's mobile camera in the colored images of an eternal present in Nuit et brouillard, along with the text of Cayrol, is an attempt to "rebuild" the physical space that was once a concentration camp and to plant the spectator inside, just as Resnais's muted colors which distinguish the old Boulogne before the war with that reconstructed after the war in Muriel, again in conjunction with the text of Cayrol, are an attempt to depict a realistic and claustrophobic space which oppresses the characters (they cannot remember or have difficulty recapturing the memories of the past) and the spectator, for whom the use of color represents a "locking in" to a banal present which is the sole relic of an emotional past.

Resnais's Nuit et brouillard differs from all other films about the concentration camps, in that it does not fictionalize the horrors of the past. It depicts that historical past through documents (films, stills), not through actors or story. And while it brings that past back to life through the mobile camera, it keeps the past as past by the contrast between black-and-white and color. Resnais's intent seems not to be to invoke the emotional horrors of the past so much as to question the undetermined present (and implied future). Resnais allows no actors in his colored images of the present. The camps have changed only through decay, it seems. The train tracks are unused, the grass is untended, the barbed wire hangs loose and broken. Resnais's appeal to the conscience of the spectator is ultimately more effective than other films' appeal to the emotions, for Resnais's film does not let go of the spectator, and his colored images of an untrespassed but still chilling present offer an unanswered question, whose premise seems to be: to remember is to assume guilt or responsibility. Nothing is quite so chilling as the thought that the film leaves the spectator with: that the whole phenomenon of the camps could happen again, does happen again, day after day, and that we've already forgotten (and continue to forget) the horror of those camps.

The true horror of the film is in the vacant present with its lush colors, a present whose solidity (the colors) and whose vacancy (the lack of visual icons, except those from the past) invite the spectator in, even insist that he come in. The true horror of _Nuit et brouillard_ is also in its _image-témoin_ or eye-witness text.

It is a tribute to Resnais's artistic power that such disparate literary styles, as those of Eluard, Cayrol and Queneau in the shorts or those of Duras, Robbe-Grillet, Semprun and Sternberg in the features, seem to resemble each other very strikingly when transposed to a Resnais film. Thus, the stylistic elements already mentioned with the Eluard poem in Guernica reappear in large measure in Cayrol's text for Nuit et brouillard. The poems in Cayrol's anthology bearing the same name seem melodramatic and trite at the same time, when compared with the original text that Resnais elicited from him for the film.

To Cayrol's credit, the text for Nuit et brouillard stands alone much better than the Eluard poem does from Guernica. The Eluard poem is effective on its own, but it is quite a different poem from that delivered by the chanting Maria Casarès and from that juxtaposed with Resnais's images. By contrast, the effect of Cayrol's text for Nuit et brouillard is a highly provocative poetic text when read separately from the film; in juxtaposition with Resnais's images, the poetic text acquires the solidity and authenticity of prose.

Also to Cayrol's credit is the fact that the two voices, the two narrators in Guernica, have been combined into one voice, one narrator, who, with seemingly little fluctuation in tone but with a wide range in volume and in speed of delivery, arrives at both the male narrator's apparently detached monotone and the female narrator's hysterical chant in Guernica. In addition to this economy in voices, there is also more control over the visuals, more poetry in the repetition and accumulation of details and more irony in the distance between the narrator and the subject. If the Eluard poem in Guernica is the equivalent of Eisenstein's observation of the substitution of music for voice in the Kabuki theatre, then Cayrol's narrator's voice in Nuit et brouillard is analogous to the detached yet scathing voice of the narrator in Buñuel's Las Hurdes

(_Land Without Bread_, 1932). There is the same irony of appraisal and the same close attention to grotesque detail in both, in conjunction with the same "distancing" of irony through music in both: Bunuel's use of Brahms' romantic music in _Las Hurdes_ seems totally out of place in the abject poverty depicted, at the same time that it is an indictment of a society which is cultured enough to produce a Brahms while socially and politically negligent enough to tolerate such poverty, ignorance and disease; Resnais's use of the original score by Hans Eisler for _Nuit et brouillard_ is also a deliberate attempt to produce contrast: that between the lightness of the music and the weight of the film's theme.

Cayrol's text begins with irony and distance. The entrance into the film, as it concerns the text, is not that into a concentration camp at first, but rather that into a travelogue film: we are clearly treated as tourists, and the text seems to universalize the horrors of the camps by universalizing their landscape, as if to say that we are here, but here could be anywhere. At the same time, the voice hypnotizes us through repetition, through gathering up more speed and more words. The opening of the text is as follows:

> Même un paysage tranquille.
>
> Même une prairie avec des vols de corbeaux, des moissons et des feux d'herbe.
>
> Même une route où passent des voitures, des paysans, des couples.
>
> Même un village pour vacances avec une foire et un clocher peuvent conduire tout simplement à un camp de concentration.

The opening sentence fragments, held together by their repetition at first, are finally held together by the completion of the verb and its predicate: "peuvent conduire tout simplement à un camp de concentration." The effect, in terms of poetry, is that of an enjambement: that is, prolonging the completion of a grammatical cluster from one line to the next. Cayrol very deftly holds the spectator's breath throughout the film with such _enjambements_. In terms of meaning, the opening of the text reminds me of the opening of Shirley Jackson's short story, "The Lottery," in which the shock of the conclusion is prepared by the seemingly pervasive peace and banality of the opening. In terms of its form, the opening of _Nuit et brouillard_, with its recitative tone and its rolling delivery, has much in common with W.H. Auden's poetic text for John Grierson's and Basil Wright's _Night Mail_ (1936) and Pare Lorentz's Whitmanesque recitative of repetitions that build upon each other in _The River_ (1937).

Resnais would solicit the same kind of musical text of repetitions, of accumulated details, and of modulated rhythms, usually increasing in detail and volume to a crescendo and then stopping suddenly, in both _Hiroshima mon amour_ and in _L'Année dernière à Marienbad_, his first two _ciné-romans_.

Cayrol's text continues its highly effective ironic distancing by citing the names of the various camps as if reading them from a map and by listing the different architectural styles of the camps, as a tour guide might mechanically read them to a group of tourists:

> Le Struthof, Oranienbourg, Auschwitz, Neuengamme, Belsen, Ravensbrück, Dachau furent des noms comme les autres sur les cartes et sur les guides.
>
> Un camp de concentration se construit comme un stade, ou un grand hotel, avec des entrepreneurs, des devis, de la concurrence, sans doute des pots de vin. Pas de style imposé.

> Style alpin, style garage, style japonais, sans style.

The narrator establishes this style of accumulating details, all inanimate, while continuing the form of the preceding lines; then he abruptly shocks the spectator by anticipating the horrors to come, even when they are already past, by listing a random sampling of the camp's future victims:

> Pendant ce temps, Burger communiste allemand, Stern étudiant juif d'Amsterdam, Schmulzski marchand de Cracovie, Annette lycéenne de Bordeaux vivent leur vie de tous les jours, sans savoir qu'ils ont déjà, à mille kilomètres de chez eux, une place assignée.

Within that list, Cayrol effectively plays upon the sentiments of a French audience: one name stands out from all the rest and it is the last name listed... "Annette lycéenne de Bordeaux." It's the only first name mentioned in the group, the only woman, the only one without an occupation, the youngest one ("lycéenne" seeming younger than "étudiant") and the one closest to home for a French audience.

What follows this preliminary accumulation of details is a denial of ultimate meaning through a Proustian sentence which builds upon itself and upon repetitions:

> Cette réalité des camps, méprisée par ceux qui la fabriquent, insaisissable pour ceux qui la subissent, c'est bien en vain qu'à notre tour nous essayons d'en découvrir les restes. Ces blocks en bois, ces chalits où l'on dormait à trois, ces terriers où l'on se cachait, où l'on mangeait à la sauvette, où le sommeil même était une ménace, aucune description, aucune image ne peuvent leur rendre leur vraie dimension, celle d'une peur ininterrompue.

This uninterrupted fear is, thus, reinforced by the uninterrupted flow of details, flow of items in a series, flow of clauses in a series.

But it is Cayrol's almost surrealistic grasp of grotesque details that makes Resnais's film closer to Buñuel than to Grierson or to Lorentz.

At times, this grasp of detail is a juxtaposition of culture and barbarism, as Buñuel's use of Brahms was in Las Hurdes:

> Chaque camp réserve des surprises: un orchestre symphonique. Un zoo. Des serres où Himmler entretient des plantes fragiles. Le chène de Goethe à Buchenwald. On a construit le champ autour, mais on a respecté le chène.

At other times, it is a small detail involving the victims, in which the evocation of their utter misery is more effective than the evocation of their ultimate destruction:

> Les médicaments sont dérisoires, les pansements sont en papier. La même pommade sert pour toutes les maladies, pour toutes les plaies. Quelquefois le malade affamé mange son pansement.

At still other moments, the text indicts the spectator directly, along with every tourist who has ever visited a concentration camp, when the tourist guide suddenly turns on his tourists and accuses them:

> Un crématoire, cela pouvait prendre, à l'occasion, un petit air carte postale. Plus tard - aujourd'hui-, des touristes s'y font photographier.

Just as Resnais and Cayrol, in a voice and camera called by some critics "style objectif, plat d'horreur," emphasize suffering over death, they also emphasize decomposition over death. Rather than shock the spectator with image after image of the victims' bodies, they effectively create total disgust in the spectator by listing the uses made by the Nazis of the various body parts of their victims:

> Le seul signe, mais il faut le savoir, c'est ce plafond labouré par les ongles. Même le béton se déchirait.
>
> Voici les réserves des nazis en guerre,
> leurs greniers,
> rien que des cheveux de femme...
>
> A quinze pfennigs le kilo...
> On en fait du tissu,

> Avec les os...
> des engrais. Tout au moins on essaie.
>
> Avec les corps...mais on ne peut plus rien dire...
>
> Avec les corps, on veut fabriquer...
> du savon.

In the last couple of years, there have been several documentaries about the wholesale slaughter of whales by the Russians and the Japanese. That they are slaughtered or that they are endangered as a species is not nearly as effective, in terms of stimulating consumer protest, as a cold listing of the numerous ways in which the whale is hacked up and reused by us - without knowing it. How much more effective, then, is the horror inspired by Resnais and Cayrol by the mere suggestion that everyday articles were made from the slaughtered bodies of the Nazis' victims.

The open ending of Nuit et brouillard, in which Resnais's camera pulls back in the present and in which Cayrol's text steps back and speaks directly to the spectator, for the first time including itself among the spectators, is also characteristic of Resnais's later eye-witness documentaries on socio-political subjects:

> Et il y a nous qui regardons sincèrement ces ruines comme si le vieux monstre concentrationnaire était mort sous les décombres, qui feignons de reprendre espoir devant cette image qui s'éloigne, comme si on guerissait de la peste concentrationnaire, nous qui feignons de croire que tout cela est d'un seul temps et d'un seul pays, et qui ne pensons pas à regarder autour de nous, et qui n'entendons pas qu'on crie sans fin.

The "sans fin" effectively negates "cette image qui s'éloigne," so that the film's ending does not bring release or reprieve for the spectator.

Resnais, himself, seemed to be in need of some reprieve after making Nuit et brouillard. His next short, Le Chant du styrène, is the most fanciful and least political of all Resnais's documentaries. The visuals of Resnais consist of endless, vertiginous travelling shots by which Resnais constructs a veritable ballet around the making of polystyrene in the factory. This ballet would seem to be an update of Fernand Leger's _Ballet mécanique_ (1924), were it not for the burlesque text by Raymond Queneau, which has more to do with mathematical word games and with exercises in style than with explaining the product. Even the title is ironic, "styrène" being substituted for "sirène." Queneau begins his exaggeratedly grandiloquent poem in alexandrines... by parodying Victor Hugo: "O temps, suspends ton bol" (instead of "O temps, suspends ton vol..."). Later in the poem-text, Queneau says of the process of refining polystyrene:

> On lave et on distille et puis on redistille
> Et ce ne sont pas là exercices de style

Queneau again is talking as much about language as about polystyrene, making humorous reference, in retrospect, to his own _Exercices de style_.

Resnais lightly dismisses _Le Chant du styrène_, saying that he thought it would be interesting to combine the form of the alexandrine (large-scale poetry) with cinemascope (large-scale film), but that he saw the error in his thinking. Yet, the mobile camera is too lyrical and the text too farcical for the film not to be seen as satirizing the very people who commissioned the film: the creators of polystyrene. The film remains important, too, for its indication of the way in which Resnais could apply poetry to the most unpoetic of subjects.

For Jean Cayrol, Nuit et brouillard was an apprenticeship. In working with Resnais, he came to believe that the text in counterpoint with the image was what gave the image its impact, its "life," especially when that image was one of the horrors of a war that most spectators would rather forget. For Cayrol, the commentary in a documentary is a constant reminder:

> Même si la guerre n'est plus de ce monde, si l'image décrit des faits qui lui sont déjà différents, le commentaire, parce qu'il exprime une mémoire individuelle, actualise l'image, la rend dénonciatrice, et en même temps la replace dans l'éternité.[11]

Cayrol insists upon the fact that the filmmaker's personal experience is not enough if that experience cannot be transferred to the spectator. He proposes that the spectator participate in the images by way of a poetic text, as opposed to what he sees as the traditional documentary's bombardment of images which try to overwhelm the spectator into a belief of fatigue or passivity:

> Aussi bien un fait vécu ne peut-il être restitué, rendu actuel que si on donne aux autres, aux spectateurs, la possibilité de l'inventer. Le documentaire, avec ses preuves surabondantes, veut que l'événement soit plus riche qu'il n'a été SUR LE MOMENT.[12]

Cayrol collaborated with Claude Durand on his first four documentary shorts after Nuit et brouillard,[13] the first three of which stem directly from Cayrol's concentration camp experiences: On vous parle (1960), La Frontière (1961), Madame se meurt (1961) and De Tout Pour Faire un Monde (1963).

The text for On vous parle begins with the following indication for the images:

> Images qui affleurent au sortir d'un mauvais sommeil, cendres de cauchemars, ou présages d'un avenir déjà consumé: eau derrière des

> barreaux, lampes clignotantes comme on peut en regarder dans les gares, enseignes de l'attente.

Juxtaposed with these somber and impressionistic images of short duration are the poetic words of a witness to the camps:

> Licht aus, licht aus, faites la nuit, rentrez vos ombres, rentrez dans vos ombres; c'est dans le sommeil qu'on met à jour un lendemain facile; laissez passer le matin comme une eau qui coule par-dessus les ponts; licht aus, licht aus, défaites la nuit, défoncez-la, crochetez-la comme une porte de prison dont vos amis n'ont pas trouvé les clefs. Vous ne m'avez laissé que des mots.

The only thing in common between the images and the text is water, which is actualized in the images but which is used as a simile in the text: "laissez passer le matin comme une eau qui coule par-dessus les ponts." What holds the images of the film together is this poetic text which approximates the subjective feelings of a witness who has physically lived through the experience of the camps but whose mind still inhabits the past of the camps. As the scenario indicates:

> tandis qu'au bord du promontoire le personnage s'étire, toujours vu de dos et que les images de rêve, les documents de son passé, les visages de son espoir, vont devenir présents à l'appel d'un monologue conjugué en dépit du temps.

The impact of both the commentary and the images stems also from the juxtaposition of the narrator's childhood experiences with those of the camps. As the text indicates:

> La vie était en avance sur mon horaire. Alors je me suis dit que mes parents n'étaient pas les vrais. Mon père était un prince de Java. Il possédait des cavernes pleines de pierres. Il habitait dans un palais avec des cygnes et ma mère était une femme qui apprivoisait les singes en jouant sur un violon, et la mer se calmait, et les murailles s'effondraient au pincement des cordes.
>
> "Tu ne peux pas être un enfant comme tout le monde?"
>
> Alors, j'étais condamné au pain sec.

The same punishments given to the child by the parents become magnified when given to the adult by the Nazis: "le pain sec." As the child-adult narrator indicates:

> Je mangeais mon pain, le coeur sec. Dans le camp, on pesait le pain avec une petite balance très primitive; je surveillais la pesée; je devais faire vite, car c'était défendu. Non, je ne trichais pas, je n'ai jamais pris plus que ma part, et si Jeanne m'a fait une scène après le repas...pour un rien, parce que je ne savais pas manger mon pain. Ce n'est pas moi qui ai commencé.

The logical conclusion to such a merger of childhood and adulthood is the scene of recognition, in which the man returns from the camps a skeleton and is not recognized by Jeanne, who has become fat and inert during his absence:

> Elle portait une bague; sa coiffure avait changé; tu aurais pu rester la même; est-ce que tu ne crois pas que j'ai caressé tes cheveux toutes les nuits, là-bas? on ne peut s'aimer quand on est terrifié l'un par l'autre. Elle était devenue grosse, bouffie, et moi, squeléttique. Je n'avais plus assez de toute mon existence pour connaitre, jour après jour, ce qu'elle avait vécu sans moi. Alors je fermai les yeux, at je la voyais douce, svelte, ses cheveux tirés, ses petites mains agiles, sa poitrine...

The image for this part of the text is that of a man, still seen from the back, walking furtively into an empty house. With <u>On vous parle</u>, Cayrol merges the witness-narrator (all those sections in which Jeanne is referred to as "elle" and the man as "il") and the dialogue-participant ("tu aurais pu rester le même"), a merger which characterizes all of the later <u>ciné-romans</u>.

Memory is again the leitmotiv of <u>La Frontière</u>. The images are of a countryside which has covered over all traces of the war. The only people present are children. The adult narrator remembers his childhood at the same time that he remembers his experiences in the camps. As in <u>On vous parle</u>, the longing of the camps becomes fused with the longings of the child:

> Qui est chez moi? Qui a pris ma place? Qui marche sur mes pas?... Un pays qu'on a quitté, c'est comme un costume: il se démode, il s'abime dans ses plis. Alors il faut l'imaginer, mais comment faire remuer un feuillage, une lèvre, un regard, comment faire qu'un visage se retourne, s'inquiète de notre absence? J'étais un enfant triste.
>
> Je suis toujours en guerre. Je n'ai pas désarmé, mais je n'ai plus d'armes. Ma mère dort à présent toute mangée comme un chapiteau dans l'herbe.

Juxtaposed with the images of an empty church and its stained-glass windows and cold lifeless statues is the text which indicates that one must lose one's memory in order to live.

> Mon enfant, pour vivre, il suffit de perdre la mémoire. Même les saints ont de drôles de pensées, les évangélistes, les rois défunts, les disparus illustres, les disciples. Donne-moi la liberté.

The incurable pain of this Lazarus resurrected from the dead of the camps is that he cannot but remember, and, remembering, he cannot live. His eye is the camera eye: passive, inert. He never appears on the screen. His voice remains a disturbing echo on the sound track.

Already in Madame se meurt Cayrol had found the images of decay that he would use for Muriel:

> monde des urnes, des bronzes, des volets scellés par le lierre, des balcons en bois découpé des bas-reliefs de chevaux, des fontaines de céramique, des kiosques, des médaillons et des statuettes, monde où la joie n'est plus qu'en effigie.

Here, as in all his other shorts, Cayrol fuses the surrealistic with the banal, telling the story of the vagabond Valence against a backdrop of dry, somber images. It is the character of Valence, depicted in the text that brings meaning to these lifeless images of short duration:

> Elle ne rêvait jamais; elle se laissa endormir par un inconnu parce

> qu'il avait les mains douces. Elle partait le long des plages sur un vieux cheval de course. Sa chevelure était célèbre. Valence disparaissait comme par enchantement. Parfois, on la croyait morte.

The images unfold as though they were the faded pictures in a photograph album. The conclusion of the film is the acknowledgement of Valence's death, precipitated by the death of her lover in the war. Cayrol's text at this point breakes into rhymed and rhythmic poetry to denote the voice of Valence beyond the grave, while on the image track there is only the sight of a setting sun.

More than Resnais and Cayrol, it was Agnes Varda who first gave substance to the term: "subjective" documentary. In her first feature, _La Pointe courte_, she fused _cinéma vérité_ shots of the fishermen in a small village with the love story of a young couple whose theatrical acting and highly literary dialogue set them apart from their documentary surroundings. This obliteration of the boundaries between fiction and documentary would characterize all of Varda's films.

Her films can be divided into two categories, both of which are "subjective": the personal-poetic shorts and the ironic or satirical shorts. _L'Opéra mouffe_ (1958) and _Salut les cubains_ (1963) would fall in the first category, while _O saisons ô chateaux_ (1957) and _Du côté de la Côte_ (1958) would fall in the second.

O saisons ô chateaux was a film commissioned for television. Presumably, Varda had little choice over her material. Yet, it is obvious that she had a large degree of choice in her approach toward her subject. Somewhat less vituperative than Buñuel and less scathingly satirical than Jean Vigo, she nevertheless shows herself to be the inheritor of a surrealistic tradition of documentaries in the

1930's, a tradition characterized by "false" travelogues (Buñuel's Las Hurdes or Vigo's A propos de Nice). Where Buñuel used the travelogue format to show the abject poverty and ignorance of a small Spanish village, Vigo used the travelogue format to satirize the idle rich in Nice. Varda seems to combine the two approaches in her film. Of the film, she said:

> Il dure 22 minutes, on voit 7 minutes de chateaux et 15 minutes d'amuseries, de citrouilles, de chapeaux et d'autres choses.[14]

She cuts in the middle of her film from a collage of shots of different castles to a fashion show, conducted in semi-serious pomp and circumstance amidst the castle turrets. At another point, after showing a baroque castle built by Francis the First, Varda's narrator comments: "The rooms were scarcely built before his death and never lived in. Francis could hardly have known that three generations of caretakers would live in them." But the conclusion of the film is even more typical of Varda's stance of irony and ridicule. She saves the most exaggerated castle for last. This castle even has Chinese ideograms engraved on the walls. The commentary which ends the film is the following:

> Monsieur Sifflet bought a plot of ground in order to build---some ruins. He only succeeded in ruining himself. See the steps that lead nowhere. The house is known to one and all as--Sifflet's folly.

With Du Côté de la Côte, Varda becomes more political in her irony. Her portrayal of the Riviera is that of an Eden despoiled by tourists and, in particular, by foreign tourists.

Thus, she notes the "invasion" of England and America on the Riviera, an invasion which she has already stated as having begun with the landing of the Allies in 1944:

> Une côte mal taillée et l'azur font "la Côte d'Azur" appelée aussi "le Côte d'Azur" en hommage aux Anglais qui ont inventé quelques succès de cette côte:
> -la promenade des Anglais (Nice)
> -l'hôtel des Anglais (Menton)
> -l'église anglaise, qui se nomme aussi "English Church."
> -la pharmacie anglaise, ou "British pharmacy."
>
> Notre propos n'est pas d'étudier les indigènes.

After using the image-témoin technique so characteristic of the "subjective" documentary in which she cites the words of Apollinaire, Zola, Colette, Nietzsche, Giraudoux, Flaubert, Fitzgerald, Sagan and Dante on the Riviera, and, after having shown several clips from films whose locale was the Riviera, she concludes that "la côte d'Azur, c'est le plus beau cimetière de la France." What is supposed to be a travelogue encouraging more tourists for the Riviera is, in reality, an ecology film and a political film: it traces the gradual but complete destruction of the natural landscape by foreign invaders, until the Riviera becomes a cemetary, inhabited by foreign zombies.

Varda concludes on the mythical. The Eden that the Riviera was supposed to be is no more. With a text that evokes the garden of Eden, she negates all the pretty images she has given by negating the authenticity of this transplanted Eden:

> Mais la nostalgie de l'Eden, c'est un jardin. Ce n'est plus la Côte d'Azur, c'est un jardin transplanté.
>
> Et ce sont de fausses Eves, de faux Adams, de faux amours, de trompeuses Vénus, de fausses grottes et de fausses nymphes.

Alain Robbe-Grillet would use the same contrapuntal negation of the post-card images of Turkey in L'Immortelle (1962) by a similarly mytho-poetic text, which renders all images suspect. At the same time that Lâle evokes the mythology of Byzantium, she denies its very existence by pointing out the falseness of everything, the reconstruction of everything, the false appearances of everything.

> Qu'est-ce que ca peut faire...Ce sont de faux bateaux, aussi, vous voyez bien, qui ramènent les prisonnières...
>
> C'est comme cette construction, vous croyez surement que c'est une mosquée...Eh bien, ce n'est pas une vraie mosquée, c'est le musée de la marine!

With L'Opéra mouffe and Salut les cubains, Varda enters more directly into her material, and the ironic distance gives way to the poetic proximity of a double vision. L'Opéra mouffe is at one and the same time a documentary film about the Mouffetard district of Paris and the "subjective" vision of that district by a woman whose eyes have been "changed" by the knowledge that she is pregnant. Thus, shots of children wearing masks for a holiday and a shot of a sign on a wall saying "Peace in Algeria" become transformed in her mind: they become metaphors for the anxieties she feels about her still unborn child. The chapter headings which begin each section of the film "reappear" again in Varda's Cléo de 5 à 7, in which the vision is doubled, this time to portray a Paris changed by the eyes of a singer who thinks she is about to die.

With Salut les cubains, Varda composes a personal film about the Castro revolution and the Cuba which followed it. The film is comprised totally of photo-stills. Her politics here is the opposite of that in

Du Côté de la Côte, in which she deplored the colonialism of foreign countries in France. Here she applauds the restoration of self-government with Castro and the expulsion of America's colonial influence. Resnais, Cayrol, Varda and Marker would all attack the invasion of foreigners upon a country's independence at the same time that they would laud any country which regained that independence.

I have saved Chris Marker for last, because he has remained more in the documentary tradition than the others, and he has also done more than the others to renovate that tradition. For anyone who has seen even one of Marker's films, documentaries will never be the same. Chris Marker is both the most politically engagé and the most ironically humorous of all the "subjective" documentarists.

His point of departure, like that of Varda, is also the travelogue format. His travelogues can hardly be called objective, however; Marker's idiosyncratic eye transforms everything he sees. Thus, in Dimanche à Pékin[15] (1955), he states that his trip to China was a trip from his childhood dreams: "Je rêvais de Pékin depuis trente ans, sans le savoir...C'est plutôt rare de pouvoir se promener dans une image d'enfance." His adult vision is, thus, tainted with the child's way of seeing double. At one point, the spectator sees a Chinese wearing a white mask around his mouth. Marker's comment is the following: "Non, ce n'est pas un chirurgien distrait. C'est un citoyen qui se protège contre la poussière..."

In Lettre de Sibérie (1957), Marker's eye is even more idiosyncratic and his wit even more acerbic. His subjective description of Siberia begins with a bit of personal folklore, in which a Yakut legend becomes the basis for an attack on the two "super-powers":

> Le proverbe sibérien dit que la forêt vient du Diable. Le Diable fait bien les choses. Sa forêt au total est aussi vaste que les Etats-Unis. Il est vrai qu'il a peut-être aussi fait les Etats-Unis.

Later in the film, Marker admits to juxtaposing shots of Russian fire planes with shots of fires taking place in Montana. His ironic and political comment on his falsification of documentary reality is the following:

> Etant un peu, ici, à court d'image, et jugeant que tous les incendies de forêts se ressemblent, je n'ai pas cru trahir la réalité documentaire en insérant quelques plans fournis par les Actualités Pathé-Journal. Mais comme ces plans proviennent du Montana, peut-être faut-il signaler que voici le seul film à ce jour où l'on voit, préfiguration de la coexistence, des pompiers soviétiques éteindre un feu américain.

Marker's most bitingly political comments, however, are masked in the animal imagery used in the film. Thus, all animals are personalized and made symbols for their human counterparts, just as they had been in Eisenstein's Strike (1924):

> J'ai rencontré ce matin un kolkhoze de canards. Le canard est un animal naturellement collectiviste, point de canards-koulaks.
>
> Assez étrangement, le seul animal auquel Sibériens et Chinois trouvaient un air de famille avec le mammouth était - la taupe. Ils étaient persuadés que c'en était la variété géante, creusant sa galerie et bosselant de son front la surface de la terre.
>
> Toute l'économie des peuples du Nord repose sur le renne. Il leur est tour à tour le blé, le lin, la barque, l'arbre de Noël, l'armoire à pharmacie et le sacristain. Castré, il sert de cheval, et gagne en prime de conserver les beaux bois soyeux que les mâles imbéciles se découpent en lamelles.
>
> Des autocars volants mais qui ont, du moins, le privilège de vous déposer dans les endroits intéressants, où il est conseillé de se déguiser en ours pour passer inaperçu.

In addition to making fun of the Russians, the Chinese and the Americans, Marker also pokes fun at the documentary form itself. At one point, he cuts away from a discussion of reindeer to present a television commercial that carries the reindeer's "utilitarian" value to the absurd. At another point, Marker shows the same sequence three different times, each time with a different commentary and different music, to point out the way in which the filmmaker interprets his material and, thus, distorts it. At still another point, Marker's narrator announces that the camera is about to show the classic documentary shot: the juxtaposition of past and present:

> Et voici juste l'image que j'attendais, que tout le monde attendait, sans laquelle il n'y aurait pas de film sérieux sur un pays qui se transforme: l'opposition du passé et de l'avenir. A ma droite, le camion, 40 tonnes. A ma gauche, la télègue, 400 kilos. L'Ancien et le Nouveau, la Tradition et le Progrès, le Tibre et l'Oronte, Philémon et Chloé, regardez-les bien, je ne vous les montrerai plus.

Marker's compilation of collage scenes is at best surrealistic. Yet, no Surrealist ever dreamed of filming in the way Marker does. His comment on the colonial invasion of Russia by France (and the Russian peoples' ignorance of what is really French) is both humorous and absurd:

> Nous retrouvions là les composantes de l'incroyable et assez émouvant prestige de la France en URSS: un quart de 89, un quart de Zola, un quart de Comédie-Francaise, un quart de Paris by Night inavoué, et quatre quarts d'Yves Montand...

Everything but Yves Montand, of course, predates the Russian Revolution when Russia was in effect "closed" to the West.

Marker effectively undercuts the images both visually and verbally. He mixes the factual with the imaginary, cutting away from "straight" shots of Siberia to show a simulation of a television commercial or an "imaginary" documentary that begins with a look-alike of Nanook and ends with Sputnik. Images, thus, contradict each other; at the same time, his commentary is always wry and ironic, ridiculing the technological advances of Siberia, lamenting the loss of poetry and folklore, and along with them, the loss of individuality.

L'Amérique rêve (1959) is undoubtedly Marker's most fanciful short and perhaps his best, since the admission of the "imaginary" permits him the freedom to juxtapose totally disparate shots of America with strikingly similar comments. As Marker's text states, with his typical tongue-in-cheek tone:

> L'Amérique rêve, Tout ce que vous avez vu dans ce film, c'est du rêve. Du bon rêve américain, lavable, incassable, garanti un an.

With the tone of a television commercial, Marker's implication is that the American dream can be bought ("one year guarantee"). As usual, Marker's format is that of a travelogue, and his underlying assumption is that his viewer will not know the country first-hand. An American will, of course, be startled by what he sees in Marker's film: startled by its apparent distortions, startled equally by the creativity of the distortions.

For Marker, the loss of a culture is always indicated by a decline in the arts and a rise in technology. The reason that America has always remained a "dream," according to Marker, is that America never had a culture. In other words, America never had a past. Lacking that past, Americans consume culture in the same way that they consume objects. As the text of Marker indicates:

> Dans ce pays, où l'on jette les voitures (et les livres) après usage, même le passé est tout neuf. Ce qui s'est passé AVANT le passé, personne ne s'y intéresse.

The two major themes in all of Marker's films - colonialism and cultural stupidity - are given free expression in L'Amérique rêve.

Juxtaposed at the beginning of the film are images taken from photographs of the "old" West (empty landscapes of hills and forests and panoramic shots of the desert) and those of the "new" West (cars, skyscrapers, urban civilization). The commentary of Marker makes it perfectly clear that this civilization of dreams was founded on the invasion of the Indians. Marker notes that the expropriation of the Indians' lands could not, however, achieve an expropriation of their culture. For Marker, the stealing of land meant the sacrifice of cultural memory:

> La conquête du territoire opposait aux Indiens des Européens fraichement débarqués. Les Indiens y ont perdu la vie, et les Européens la mémoire.

The political colonialism leads to a culture based on newness and sameness. The metaphor that Marker chooses to show this progression is, significantly for the whole film, that of photography:

> Peu importe alors si nous sommes 150 sur le même sujet, lequel est reproduit en excellentes cartes postales à deux pas d'ici. Permettre à tout le monde de prendre la même photo, c'est peut-être une définition de la démocratie. Et d'ailleurs pour 150 pécheurs, il y a toujours un juste qui les sauve.

Marker is indirectly indicting Hollywood with such a statement. It is no coincidence that his film begins and ends in California, centering on the "American Dream" (L'Amérique rêve) that Hollywood has engendered. In Marker's view, American photography and American films are overwhelmingly competent technically and, because of that emphasis on technology, they're just as overwhelmingly devoid of content.

If the price for colonializing America was the sacrifice of a cultural memory that linked America with Europe, then an added result of that colonial "rape" is the cultural isolation in which Americans find themselves cut off from the rest of the world. Again, the metaphor chosen by Marker to express this isolation is that of the media. According to Marker, Americans do not trust what they see, unless it can be reproduced by Kodak. He furthers his twin themes of colonialism and cultural ignorance by relating the rise in technology with the mechanistic way that Americans travel:

> Mais la vraie raison, c'est que les Américains se méfient du monde. Aucun pays n'est tout à fait vrai, aucun moment n'est tout à fait vécu tant que l'image n'en est pas fixée. Et pour beaucoup d'Américains, la réalité n'est que l'antichambre de la photographie. Ne vous étonnez donc pas de les voir courir le monde sans le regarder, se servant de leur Kodak comme d'un Colt pour couvrir leur retraite. Une fois de retour, dans leur fauteuil, en face d'un album ou d'un appareil stéréoscopique, ils se détendront, ils se mettront à aimer le monde, ils commenceront à voyager.

Marker elaborates on this point of mechanistic travel by relating it to what he sees as an American hatred of nature. His metaphor again is that of film: the proof for Marker that Americans hate the natural world is Walt Disney!

> C'est que la nature a toujours été l'ennemie qu'il fallait vaincre. On lui en garde un peu rancune. Sur une boite de crème, sur un paquet de bonbons, l'Américain exige la garantie "parfum artificiel." Il était normal qu'au Dieu créateur de la Nature s'ajoutât un Dieu créateur de l'artifice. Il est venu.

> Il s'appelle Walt Disney. Et son royaume est venu. Il s'appelle Disneyland. Ici les vrais Indiens, qui ne scalpent pas, le vrai feu, qui ne brûle pas, le vrai monde rassemblé dans un parc, un jardin d'Eden gardé par les hippopotames, symboles de la pureté-dont les fruits ont le goût délicieux du refus de comprendre, comme un second péché originel qui efface le premier.

Here as in other parts of the film, Marker purposefully distorts what he sees in two ways: (1) he personifies the natural world and all objects, including billboards, comic strips and photographs; and (2) he dehumanizes all the human beings. He personalizes the objects through a mobile camera and through quick cutting. He dehumanizes the people by presenting them in static images or by juxtaposing shots of people with photos or ads which approximate the movements of those people. The result, of course, is always ironic. For example, Marker "visits" Ghost Town, only to show that Americans revere what is dead or immobilized (like the Kodak pictures), at the same time that they become the inhabitants of Ghost Town by visiting it.

> Ghost Town est si l'on veut un carnaval permanent, une espèce de Musée Grévin en mouvement. L'intéressant, c'est que les visiteurs y deviennent personnages. Comme si la nature à la longue secrétait son propre maquillage, les visages réels finissent par ressembler à ceux des dessins animés, des comic strips. Les dessinateurs n'ont plus rien à inventer.

Those areas of the imaginary in other countries are not needed in America, for America is one giant imaginary dream: "les dessinateurs n'ont plus rien à inventer."

Another juxtaposition of the animate with the inanimate, in which Marker reverses the roles of each, is in a discussion of American beaches and the emphasis in America on the body and grooming.

> Et comme les aveugles lisent avec leurs mains, les jeunes Americains pensent avec leurs corps...Nous baptisons nos plages Tahiti,

> Ecuador, Eldorado-la grande plage de Los Angeles s'appelle Muscle Beach, la plage du Muscle. Toute la différence entre Valéry et Hemingway.

The visuals for this commentary are shots of Muscle Beach (perhaps a reference to Joseph Strick's Muscle Beach - 1950), mixed with billboards for products like Coppertone and comic book ads for body-building along the lines of the Charles Atlas method. The mention of the French beaches, with their emphasis on far-away countries or on imaginary places, and the mention of Valéry, as contrasted with Hemingway, is clearly an indication that this "travelogue" is for a French audience. It says in effect: if you've read Hemingway, you can understand the emphasis on brute force, on machismo and on the body as an object in America.

If Marker has a weakness as an artist, it is his own sense of humor. He cannot keep himself from digressing from the most serious of discussions to make a wryly humorous point. Yet, even when he gives way to his own wit in L'Amérique rêve, it seems to further the development of his themes. For instance, Marker opposes Werner von Braun (technology) with the process of having a baby (natural). Although the text states an absurdity, it makes a point:

> Car, selon la forte parole du Dr. von Braun à propos du temps nécessaire aux essais astronautiques, c'est une erreur de croire qu'avec neuf femmes enceintes, on peut obtenir un bébé en un seul mois.

At another point in the film, Marker creates a bilingual pun on the word "nickel" to contrast the lack of creative art in America (which would not be based on money) and the emphasis in America on earning money:

> Mais tout de suite après l'Age d'Or vient l'Age du Nickel. Celui où l'enfant américain doit apprendre que la vie se gagne.

Thus, Marker ends where he began: the American dream can be bought. The added barb here is that the dream is devaluated in proportion to the currency (the golden age to the nickel age).

Americans could lightly dismiss Marker's film as an outright fantasy, were it not for the "oddities" that Marker has found in America: that is, where the "truth is stranger than fiction." Thus, Marker cites the prevalence of twins in America just after the passage about everyone taking the same photos. Even when the process is natural, like that of having babies, Americans seem to exert enough control to get the desired degree of conformity and sameness. Marker produces photos of a twins' convention in San Francisco as proof. Within the collage of photos, he quietly introduces a book drawing of twins, a drawing for what looks like Dr. Jekyll and Mr. Hyde.

Another example follows the discussion on body-building and beaches. Marker notes that America is a sports-oriented society, an observation which seems harmless enough and accurate enough. He goes on to say that Americans, because of the glorified past of cowboys and Indians, like the rodeo. He then notes that at a certain prison farm in Texas there is a rodeo consisting of prisoner-contestants performing in order to get lightened sentences or visits from their wives. Here is Marker's description of this "model prison":

> C'est une prison modèle. Le premier prix du rodéo a gagné un an de réduction de peine. Le second prix, une semaine auprès de sa femme. Le clown n'a rien gagné, sinon de retrouver son vrai visage.

It would be difficult to verify Marker's eye-witness report. Supposing that such a prison does indeed exist in Huntsville, Texas, one wonders how Marker ever found out about it. Marker's method, however, should be clear. Either he picks famous landmarks like Ghost Town or Disneyland and then superimposes his own ironic point of view on those landmarks through the text, or else he picks "oddities" like the twins' contest or the prison farm rodeo, for which less distortion is needed in the text.

The emphasis throughout is on the text. For my own satisfaction, I made a list of the "topics" covered by the images in Marker's travelogue. They are as follows:

- San Francisco (with quotes from Jean Cocteau)
- The cult of youth in America
- Art and advertising
- Ghost Town and Disneyland
- Huntsville prison farm and its rodeo
- The role of eating in America
- The psychology of parents in bringing up children
- The importance of newspapers in America
- Auto-racing (with stills from racing films and comments on method acting)
- Husband-catching by women (with stills from a Miss America contest)
- Discussion of Americans as being either cats or dogs, as belonging either to "la race chien" or "la race chat" (with quotes from Cocteau)
- Mardis gras in New Orleans with a discussion of the use of masks (juxtaposed with images from a police line-up)
- The Holy Rollers and how emotions are chanelled in America
- Gambling at Las Vegas
- Skyscrapers in eastern cities like Chicago and New York

One can easily see from this list that Marker's documentary is hardly typical of the usual travelogue. Further, one can see that the images jump without transitions from one testament to another. The text is the film, since the film was never made (beyond the photo-essay stage). It is the text which provides those needed transitions.

Were the "film" run silently, the viewer would not understand a thing.

With Description d'un combat (1960), that relationship between image and text changes. Some of the humor remains, as in the following transposition of an Oscar Wilde gag:

> -Pourquoi êtes-vous en Israel?
> -Pour oublier.
> -Pour oublier quoi?
> -J'ai oublié...

In addition, Marker still uses art works to describe people, just as he had done with Valéry and Hemingway in L'Amérique rêve:

> Ils sont beaux. La légende veut qu'ils soient tous grands et blonds. En fait, la grace orientale corrige quelquefois le modèle européen, et parmi ces Rubens, il reste des Chagall.

But Marker's tone and whole approach toward the subject have fundamentally changed in Description d'un combat. The text is much more factual, more straight-forward than in the earlier films. As such, they become subservient to the images, which here are straight photography: no collages, no billboards, no comic strips. The effect of those images derives from their candid nature. Description d'un combat is the beginning of cinéma vérité in Marker. Candid shots appear in the earlier films, but they are always modified or distorted by the ironic narrator. Here, they make the film. The text, when it is not factual or straight-forward, is mythical or poetic, straining to create an aura of legend or myth around the subject.

These differences in style are due to differences in subject. When Marker is dealing with a super-power (the Russia of Lettre de Sibérie, the China of Dimanche à Pékin, the America of L'Amérique rêve), he depicts those countries in a wry and personal way, rendering them somehow smaller, more easily assimilated. He concentrates on their lack of culture, on their political colonialism, on their eccentricities and stupidities. By contrast, when Marker is dealing with an under-developed country, the Israel of _Description d'un combat_, the Cuba of _Cuba si_ (1961), the Mexico of _Soy Mexico_ (1965), Marker wishes to stress the authenticity of the people: their struggle, their dignity, their grandeur. In this latter type of film, Marker lets the people of the country move about more; that is, his camera becomes much more an observer. The images strive for candor. The text in turn becomes more educational, because it is more historical, more factual. The text also sacrifices satire for poetry, the kind of accumulation of details, repetitions and recurrent rhythms which characterized _Nuit et brouillard_ or those which would characterize Marker's _ciné-roman_, _La Jetee_ (1963).

Cuba si (1961) is perhaps Marker's most successful juxtaposition of candid-camera images with a poetic text. Marker's text begins as though it were a Christmas tale or a folklore text. It ends on militancy:

> C'était l'année dernière, à la Havane. On se préparait à célébrer dans l'ordre: le ler janvier, qui est le ler janvier, le 2 janvier, qui est l'anniversiare de la Révolution, et le jour des Rois, qui est Noël - le vrai Noël, le jour des cadeaux, où l'on offre aux enfants des bébés-chiens, qui grandiront, des bébés-lapins, qui grandiront, des perruches baptisées poissons, des ours et des poupées, et aussi des bébés-mitraillettes - qui grandiront.

When Marker's text attacks, it attacks the American influence which the Castro revolution has tried to erase. On the one hand, Marker lists a litany of nationalized industries, in order to show that a more authentic Cuba has been born; on the other hand, he notes that abroad there is a mythology to deal with this nationalization:

> ...jusqu'à une façon cubaine de boire l'eau fraiche, ou le coca-cola nationalisé.
>
> Mais pour le reste du monde, et particulièrement pour les Américains, il est plus commode de ressuciter les mythes. Fidel Castro, c'est Robin des Bois.

Cuba si is structurally divided into two parts: Marker's Cuba and Castro's Cuba. The first half of the film belongs to Marker and consists of his observations or recitations on the new Cuba. Significantly, this section has musical indications like "scherzo" or "andante" for the recitation of the text. It is also significant that his section ends on a litany, a poetic recitation that places Cuba in its historical perspective:

> De quoi parlait-on dans le monde, à cette époque?
> de gens, de pays, d'animaux fabuleux,
> de l'Algérie,
> de la France,
> de l'Amérique,
> de l'espace,
> du temps,
> du Congo,
> du Laos,
> de l'Afrique,
> et des formes qu'y prendraient, dans la deuxième moitié de ce siècle, la violence et la prière.
> On écrivait aussi l'Apocalypse. C'était le livre le plus cher du monde.
> C'est alors qu'on s'est mis à parler dans le monde, également, de Cuba.

It is against this poetic backdrop, in which the revolutions and acquired independences of small nations like Cuba are related to the Apocalypse, that the long section on Castro is introduced. In this second section, the images show an angry Castro, a humorous Castro, a dedicated Castro, an authentic Castro. He is clearly not Robin Hood. For its part, the text supports the images. The text consists solely of Castro's speeches: the word of the Apocalypse.

Similarly, A Valparaiso (1963), the film of Joris Ivens with a text by Marker, is also divided into two parts. The first part is deliberately ironic. Marker's text traces the residue of colonialism in Valparaiso:

> Cette forgée, peuplée par les marins. Ici les traces sont anglaises: la Banque de Londres, les Arcs de Triomphe, l'Armée du Salut et peut-être une qualité inférieure de whisky. La France a offert au Nouveau Monde la galanterie de ses corsaires et la dernière des sociétés secrètes, l'Alliance Francaise.
>
> Les Espagnols ont baptisé la ville. Ils l'ont convertie, adoptée, épousée. Elle les a trompées avec les Hollondais. Elle continue.

This enumeration of foreign traces in the country reminds one of the same enumeration in Agnes Varda's Du Côté de la Côte. The contrast is not only that between what is foreign and what is indigenous, but also between what is anachronistic and dead (the foreign element) and what is the real pulse of the country (its people).

The second part of A Valparaiso, for which Ivens abruptly changes the film from black-and-white to a monochromatic red tint to signify blood, is more poetic, more incantatory, more historical. Marker simulates the entire history of Valparaiso in a litany which is strikingly similar to that employed by Cayrol in Nuit et brouillard:

> Tel est le quatrième élément de Valparaiso: le sang.
>
> Et c'est sa mémoire.
>
> Mémoire des corsaires: Hawkins, Drake, Joris de Spilbergen. Tortures et pillages.
>
> Mémoire des Espagnols. Tortures et pillages, et l'oppression coloniale pour des siècles.
>
> Mémoire des incendies. Les éléments relèvent les hommes. Après le feu, la mer.

> Mémoire des tempêtes. Des bateaux de Jules Verne jettent au rivage des naufragés de Gavarni.
>
> Et la ronde continue.

The text justifies the switch from black-and-white to color in the images by its biblical tone: the repetition of key words, the accumulation of details, as well as the progressive lengthening of each phrase.

For all intents and purposes, there is practically no text at all for _Le Joli Mai_ (1962-64), the film which raised Marker to the level of Jean Rouch in France and the film which established Marker as a master of _cinéma vérité_. In _Le Joli Mai_, Marker is no longer an observer; instead, he is an actual participant in the film, conducting interviews throughout. His back is always to the camera when he is in the frame at all. His questions are as brief and as elusive as his physical presence. Because of the interviews, Marker lets his camera run; thus, _Le Joli Mai_ is the least edited of any Marker film. His intent in the film seems to have been to capture the pulse of Paris through its inhabitants. That intent is also political, for Marker clearly shows that the young are unconcerned about world affairs and naive about their own future. An interview of a young couple about to be married brings blank stares and vague answers to Marker's pointedly political questions. An interview with three intellectuals, by contrast, reveals that they have a rational or theoretical grasp of the problems surrounding them, but that they are isolated by their intelligence. Their elitist responses to problems like unemployment or the war in Algeria have little to do with the concrete realities that the working class faces.

The real poetic power of *Le Joli Mai*, however, comes, not from the string of unrelated interviews, but from the film's final images and text. Those images are of a prison, in which no people are shown (just as in Resnais's and Cayrol's *Nuit et brouillard* no living people are shown). The text switches from the voice of Marker to the voice of an inmate released from the prison. It is still Marker's voice, but now it is from the point of view of the prisoner. With a gradual shock, the spectator realizes how all of the interviews hold together. The whole film can be interpreted from the point of view of the inmate: what the world looks like to a newly liberated man. The metaphor of the prison is doubly effective because of this double vision, for Marker has clearly revealed that Paris is full of prisons, even though the walls are not always visible and the uniforms are not always gray or striped. The introduction of the inmate's point of view makes *Le Joli Mai* a film similar to Varda's *L'Opéra mouffe:* both are simultaneously objective and subjective.

It is ironic that what is often called *cinéma vérité* involves people speaking directly to the camera. As I see it, the problem is double-edged. If one makes a documentary film of a performance, that film is no more authentic than the performance itself. To film a performance of Bob Dylan or the Rolling Stones singing is to capture the performance, not the people: they "act" as much for the camera as they do for an audience. The same is true of interviews in which the person being interviewed is aware of the camera. Using non-professional actors, longer takes, natural sound and unrehearsed dialogue cannot mask this problem. Marker seems to have sensed this when he added the point of view of the inmate.

Language itself is the subject of Le Mystère Koumiko (1965). Ostensibly a film about the Olympics in Japan, Le Mystère Koumiko is in reality an image-témoin film in which the sense of Japan and all its contradictions is achieved through the very personal interview that Marker conducts with a young woman named Koumiko. The sense of authenticity in the dialogue is heightened by the fact that Koumiko often makes very charming mistakes with her French, such as her difficulty in hearing and understanding the word "plis" because of the problems Japanese have distinguishing between "r's" and "l's". As the text of Marker indicates:

> Entre les prises de vues, nous parlons, Kumiko et moi. Dialogue quelquefois difficile, quelquefois désaccordé, ne serait-ce que par la façon charmante, mais un peu personnelle avec laquelle Kumiko manie la langue de Robbe-Grillet.
>
> Mais nous parlons.

Again, the direction of Marker is perfectly clear to anyone who has seen one of his films. He begins with the historical event of an Olympics in Japan, making a political statement about the Emperor's attending the games. He moves to Koumiko and establishes her as a personality. She and Marker discuss the fact that all the mannequins in Japan are facsimiles of western women. They discuss animals and what certain animals mean to Koumiko. They discuss the differences between Japanese children and western children. They discuss religion and sex. Gradually, Marker leads Koumiko from the strictly personal and concrete to the conceptual and political. Koumiko is no more aware of the world's political crises (the Kruschev-crisis, the war in Vietnam, De Gaulle's situation in France) than the young couple about to be married in Le Joli Mai were. Yet, Koumiko does profess to understand the violence which produced Hiroshima and Nagasaki. The film rejoins itself and the past rejoins the present as Koumiko explains what World War Two was like for her as a child. Quite effectively, it's the first time that she is visibly absent from the screen since the opening shots of the Olympic games. The closing images are of highways and bridges in modern Japan, taken from a camera tied to a moving vehicle. The counterpoint between the mobile camera on an inanimate landscape and the highly personal and poetic voice of Koumiko relating Hiroshima is quite similar to that of the voice of Emanuelle Riva's voice telling what Hiroshima meant for her as a young woman in Paris while the images are of shops and streets in modern Hiroshima in Resnais's and Marguerite Duras's Hiroshima mon amour (1959). Both the Resnais film and the Marker film involve a personal-poetic image-témoin (camera eye-witness) of a historical event: the Resnais film is from the point of view of a French woman, the Marker film is from the point of view of a Japanese woman. Were I a film distributor, I would suggest that the films be shown together.

With Yo Soy Mexico (1965), Marker returns to the mixture of historical reportage and legend-folklore that he had begun in Description d'un combat. The difference between the two films is that with Yo Soy Mexico, there is only a brief section (about five minutes) which involves a Mexico in progress or a Mexico that a tourist would likely encounter. Marker is more concerned with the "myth" of Mexico. If I could so express it, there is more poetic connotation than factual denotation in *Yo Soy Mexico*. The title ("I am Mexico") refers to the *image-témoin* format by which the film is structured and held together. Significantly, there is only one "witness" who pertains to present-day Mexico. The others are either historical figures (all dead) who "speak" through the Marker text or artists (all dead) who speak via Mexico. The reason for using mythical witnesses again refers to the fact that Marker is more interested in Mexico's poetry than in its actual pulse. If the project sounds familiar, it is no coincidence. Marker's film picks up where Eisenstein's unfinished *Que Viva Mexico* (1931) was forced to leave off. Indeed, Eisenstein, himself, is the last and most effective "witness" in a list that includes Cortez, an anonymous worker, Maximillian, and Emiliano Zapata. By concluding with Eisenstein, Marker effectively raises historical reality to the level of poetic reality, for while Cortez, Maximillian and Zapata actually wreaked violence in Mexico, Eisenstein abstracted it and tried to find its poetic roots in the culture.

Because Marker has continued to make "subjective" documentaries, which are usually not long enough for commercial distribution, he has not acquired the fame or critical attention of Resnais or Varda (Jean Cayrol is in a similar situation, being known mostly for the two films he made with Resnais and having made only one feature as opposed to five shorts on his own). Yet, while it was Resnais and Varda who laid the groundwork for the "subjective" documentary, it is Marker who has explored the form and continues to refine it. Marker seems destined for obscurity on the part of mass audiences and appreciation by only a select initiate. It is a shame. There are very few filmmakers today with the technical competence (Marker has worked as a professional photographer) and creative verve that Marker applies to his images. There are also very few filmmakers working today who can attain Marker's wit or poetry in the text. Ultimately, it is Marker's emphasis on poetic commentaries that makes him so important to the _cinéma des auteurs_, even though he made only one _ciné-roman_ (_La Jetée_). As André Bazin noted:

> Chris Marker est de cette nouvelle génération d'écrivains qui estime que le temps de l'image est venu, mais ne dit pas qu'il faille pour autant lui sacrifier les pouvoirs et les vertus d'un langage qui demeure tout de même l'interprète privilégié de l'intelligence. Cela signifie que pour Chris Marker le COMMENTAIRE d'un film n'est pas ce qu'on ajoute aux images préalablement choises et montées, mais presque l'élément premier, fondamental...[16]

In conclusion, we can now enumerate several characteristics which make a documentary "subjective," characteristics which are shared by Resnai, Varda, Cayrol and Marker. A subjective documentary may begin with a historical event as a point of departure, bringing that event "back to life" through unobjective and poetic narrators, through a mobile camera and through associative editing (_Guernica_, _Cuba si_). They may also involve the use of _image-témoins_, whether real or imaginary, whether visible or invisible, who speak directly to the spectator, who address the spectator with a language of poetry rather than one of ordinary conversation (_Nuit et brouillard_, _On vous parle_, _Yo Soy Mexico_). They strive to achieve objectivity through documentary images, at the same time that they attempt to personalize those images with a subjective point of view (_Van Gogh_, _L'Opéra mouffe_, _La Frontière_, _Le Joli Mai_). They strive for counterpoint between the images and the text, and they use music contrapuntally in addition (_Nuit et brouillard_, _L'Opéra mouffe_, _On vous parle_, _Lettre de Sibérie_). And stemming from a tradition of documentaries in France that is most exemplified by Buñuel and Vigo, the "subjective" documentary may present a false travelogue or convert the everyday into the surrealistic (Resnais's _Le Chant du styrène_, Cayrol's and Durand's _De Tout Pour Faire un Monde_ (1965), which juxtaposes children with blind men in a museum, or Marker's _Si j'avais quatre dromadaires_ (1966), which is a fantasy trip in "four voices" through all of Marker's photographs not used in previous films). More often, they are highly political documentaries, in which colonialism and cultural stupidity are subjected to satire (_Du Côté de la Côte_, _Lettre de Sibérie_) or in which the struggle of developing nations is raised to the level of myth or poetry (_Cuba si_, _Salut les cubains_). What saves these political films from being mechanistically propagandistic are the poetic texts, which, while committed to a political ideology, do not sound like a manifesto or an ideological party line. And it is precisely in the poetry of the texts that these "subjective" documentaries lead very easily into the _ciné-romans_ of their feature films, the distinction between documentary and fiction being dispensed with for the sake of realism.

B. The Use of Color

> "Color: clean, bright, resounding, ringing. When did I fall in love with it? Where?"
>
> -Sergei Eisenstein

The literary New Wave filmmakers approached color films cautiously at first, but when they did use color in their films, it was always in a highly stylized, anti-naturalistic and innovative way. Probably the biggest reason for their initial reticence to use color was the added cost in production. That added cost could not be matched with any anticipated addition in spectator success when Resnais, Varda, Marker and the other filmmakers of the literary New Wave had already demonstrated that their films were seldom commercially profitable. A possible aesthetic reason for their reticence might be the highly stylized way in which these filmmakers used black-and-white film stock to give the symbolic nuances, if not the actual tints, of color stock. Alain Resnais, who shot his documentary film of the paintings of Van Gogh (Van Gogh, 1948) in black-and-white, attests to having received letters from viewers who swore that they saw the film in color. They expressed admiration of Resnais's brilliant color contrasts and of his faithful recapturing of the Van Gogh originals.

It seems that the spectator can adapt black-and-white to color easily enough, but when the film is already in color, this same spectator becomes highly conscious of the artificiality of such color. One possible reason for our sense of the "unnaturalness" of film color is that we view it from a perspective of black-and-white: that is, from the darkness of the movie theater. We don't view it from the street or from inside the home where available sunlight or electric lighting contribute to our psychic definition of color. Black-and-white films are chromatically relevant and in keeping with the darkness of the movie theater, but when color is viewed in such darkness, it often seems too harsh, too obstrusive: an excess.

The literary New Wave directors recognized the inherent plastic artifice in the use of color in film, and, far from trying to hide this artifice, as if it were a flaw, they vaunted their colors, just as a Van Gogh or a Munch distorted their objects and transformed a room in Arles or a bridge in Norway into a yellow nightmare, an exteriorization of an interior state. In other words, these directors exploited the anti-naturalness of color to arrive at heightened states of subjectivity or of forced audience awareness. Color does not simply fill in a landscape or cover an object: it emphasizes the landscape; it gives the object another dimension, another visuality.

Color is defined, thus, not by what it hides, but by what it shows, as if in addition to itself. These directors do not use color descriptively in the sense that prose describes; they use it dramatically and expressively in the sense that poetry expresses itself: by suggestion. Color as dislocation need not be a disadvantage for the filmmaker. In fact, these filmmakers have exploited this dislocation, insisting upon the difference between film color and the color of the real world, a difference ironically much greater than that between black-and-white film and the color of the real world.

> Lorsque le cinéma en couleurs s'éloigne du réel, il s'en écarte plus que le film en noir, gris et blanc pour la simple raison que nous imposant des couleurs, et avec elles une vision faussement concrète, il ne laisse plus à notre imagination aucune latitude de reconstitution mentale du réel.[17]

Insisting upon anti-naturalistic color sets the film apart from the real world. It also emphasizes the structural quality of the film image, forcing the Spectator, by the device of dislocation already mentioned, to react critically (mentally) rather than emotionally. Forcing the spectator to become aware of colors instead of simply being aware of sizes and shapes emphasizes the subjectivity of the image, the temporality of the image and the montage between images.

One of the most obvious ways to distort color and emphasize subjective dislocation is to juxtapose images in color with images in black-and-white. Part II of Eisenstein's Ivan the Terrible (1944-46), Resnais's and Jean Cayrol's Nuit et brouillard (1955), Marker's and Joris Ivens's A Valparaiso (1963), and Agnes Varda's Les Creatures (1965) are examples of this type of juxtaposition. It is interesting to note that in all but the Resnais film color is brought into an otherwise black-and-white film. In these films, the effect is that of heightened emotion or intensified dramatic or subjective impact; on the contrary, in Nuit et brouillard, the effect of using black and white in an otherwise color film is that of playing down emotions, encouraging critical thought, dedramatizing an otherwise all-too-dramatic subject. More will be said about these examples later in the discussion.

A second way to use a color anti-naturalistically is to distort the color scheme by reorganizing all colors on the basis of a monochromatic system. Thus, some films can be said to be one-color conscious. Hiroshii Teshigahara's The Ruined Map (1968) is such a film. Teshigahara explains the reordering of all colors in the film to a monochromatic system based on the color yellow.

> La couleur, pour moi, est un moyen pour symboliser et mettre en relief le sujet du film. Dans mes films précédents, je voulais

> condenser dans le noir et blanc les couleurs complexes de la réalité. Pour L'Homme sans Carte, le principe est le même; il s'agit de sublimer les couleurs dans une dimension MONOCHROME. C'est pour cela que le jaune est la couleur de base dans mon film. Je veux rendre les couleurs non pas réalistes, mais plutôt surréalistes, une sensation de couleurs.[18]

Godard's Le Mépris (Contempt, 1964) is another example, based on the color red. Such a monochromatic color system is at once abstract and empirical, for it distorts objective space and renders it psychically or subjectively. In addition, a monochromatic color system can be used to represent emotions or sentiments, not as they are manifested by individual personalities, but rather as they are manifested by personality types. The difference here between the film in black and white and the film in color is the degree of nuance, lessened in the latter, and the degree of abstraction or universalization, heightened in the latter.

> La recherche stylistique qui, de Bresson à Resnais, soumet la présentation de l'espace au rythme d'une aventure intérieure, calquant le déroulement d'un paysage sur les mouvements d'une âme dont il devient le reflet subjectif, trouvait encore dans l'image grise la marge d'imprécision nécessaire à cette expression nuancée et changeante. Avec la couleur, la racine même d'un sentiment se voit mise au jour, et non plus sa durée vécue: l'action effective des couleurs rejoint une symbolique des sentiments, éclairant moins les variations individuelles que la nature élémentaire et la signification universelle d'un état.[19]

More precisely, this use of a monochromatic color system is a psychological use, replacing traditional psychological motivation in the acting or on the sound track. Just as Rimbaud had found equivalents for certain emotions among the various colors of the spectrum and the various tones of the musical scale, so too these filmmakers have often painted their characters expressionistically; that is, they have assigned certain emotions to certain colors which accompany or surround the characters of a film. For Agnes Varda, in films like Cléo de 5 à 7 (1962) and Les Créatures (1966), the predominant color is white (both of these films are essentially black-and-white films, but the whites are used structurally, in this case monochromatically). Varda explains her use of the color white:

> Tout ce qui est lié à l'amour se concrétise dans la blancheur-blancheur du sable, des draps, des murs ou du papier. Ou encore blancheur de la neige, de la lumière sur la pelouse, comme dans Cléo. Il existe une dissolution dans la blancheur qui est pour moi l'amour et la mort.[20]

Without resorting to a monochromatic color scheme in his Je t'aime je t'aime (1968), Alain Resnais has his characters discuss the emotions or sentiments behind various characters, and these discussions do reveal conflicts between characters. In an imagined scene (the scene seems "bleached" by the very whiteness of the image and stems from the mind of Claude Ridder), two secretaries are walking down a long and empty corridor. Their dialogue is as follows:

> Secretary A: La couleur de la psychose, c'est bien le rouge?
> Secretary B: Non, le rouge, c'est le futur.
> Secretary A: Et la psychose, alors?
> Secretary B: C'est le vert.
> Secretary A: Ah!...Je les confonds toujours!

This scene takes place in the corridor of a publicity bureau in the year 1962; it is later related to a scene involving Ridder and Catrine in the Gorges de Provence in 1966, in which Catrine delivers a long exchange on the color green (psychosis):

> Ridder: Et puis, ici la nature n'a pas ce vert écoeurant de la campagne.
> Catrine: Tu as raison...C'est un vert moins écoeurant que celui de la campagne. Et si l'homme était allergique à la couleur vert...? C'est peut-être le vert qui provoque l'usure des cellules, entrainant la vieillesse et la

mort. Ce serait drôle, non?...Des millions de savants qui s'acharnent à inventer des ouvre-boites, des bouchons...j'sais pas moi...et qui passeraient complètement à côté de cette idée qui changerait tout. Moi, je crois que le secret est là: tellement simple que personne ne l'a effleuré...On va rester un mois sans manger de la salade... pour voir.

Because of the predominance of one color and the lack of gradations or progressive tints between colors in the monochromatic system, the viewer tends to read the predominant color symbolically and to interpret images with varying colors as highly contrasted opposites, polarizing those images more in content than they actually are in form (the colors).

A third way to emphasize color stylistically is in the use of primary colors, colors which are not toned down: they clash for effect. Jean-Luc Godard often uses color in this way. In _Deux ou trois choses que je sais d'elle_ (1966), the Parisian backdrop is one of primary colors: orange cranes, red buildings, bluecars. Godard is careful not to use colors which are complementary, as Agnes Varda does when she juxtaposes warm colors (orange, gold) with cool colors (purple, blue) in _Le Bonheur_ (1965). Godard's intent is to jar the spectator loose from a purely emotional response to the images. His color-clashes become metaphors for the garishness and "prostitution" of the modern city, which in turn explains why the Marina Vlady character prostitutes herself. In addition, the Lichtenstein- or Warhol-like cartoon inserts are of the same variety: loud, primary colors which clash, which "offend" the eyes. These colors are used, not to heighten emotion, but to put distance between the spectator and the film image; that distance subdues emotional response and provokes thought.

Still a fourth way to use color stylistically is to strip it of its provocation; that is, to wash colors out until they achieve the nuances that middle gray's have in a black-and-white film. The two most prominent examples of this use of color are Resnais's Muriel (1963) and Antonioni's Red Desert (1964). This apparent barrenness of color is often used to show subjective states of characters, but it is also used to relate those characters to their psychic space and to their objective environment, both of which are usually wastelands. Lewis Jacobs describes this wasteland in Red Desert:

> A giant chemical plant with red and green condensers and the geometry of multicolored pipes and smokestacks ejecting billows of white steam and yellow smoke is made to look like some ominous technological monster. Streets and surroundings through which the woman wanders are weather-toned a ravaged, mineral gray that suggests a nightmarish fragment of a surreal world. An oppressive grayness also clouds the strange freighters and tankers that drift through a desolate canal flanked with barren pines trapped in a vise of petrified time and space. The foliage in a hotel lobby is modulated into a murky grayness to underline the barrenness of a mind drained of dreams and emotions.[21]

Color used in this way does not evoke the past as present, as the juxtaposition of black-and-white with color in Nuit et brouillard or A Valparaiso would. The somberness of the washed neutral colors insists upon time in a trapped present, a present which is analogous to, but not a duplication of, the world outside the film. The neutral colors, which best approximate the middle gray's of a black-and-white film, depict ambiguous emotional states (or else a bankruptcy of emotion), emphasizing an oppressive space rather than an individual personality whose free will or flights of fancy could cope with that space.

Both Hélène in Muriel and Giuliana in Red Desert are trapped by their past (memories) and by their spatial present (the drab and lifeless milieu they inhabit).

I propose to elaborate upon these four uses of color in film, specifically, in the films of the directors of the cinema des auteurs: Alain Resnais, Chris Marker and Agnes Varda.

Of the three, Agnes Varda is the most impressionistic. She uses color in the way a painter would. However, she does not attempt to transcend painting, as Marker and Resnais try to do.

In O saisons ô chateaux (1957), Varda presents a dialectical contrast between the old (the castles, the changing seasons) and the new (a fashion show). She tries to recapture the sense of the castles' beauty, a beauty made more striking by the passing of time. To introduce that temporal element, Varda brings out the "warm" quality of their colors: the reverent gold of the castles is juxtaposed with the soft browns of the autumn. The recitation of several medieval texts of Ronsard and Morot add to this effect. Through color, she denies the sense of the present in these castles, insisting that tourists are out of place in these monuments to the past. The endurance of architecture is then juxtaposed, in the very middle of the film, with the constantly changing caprices of fashion. Varda "dislocates" her documentary by presenting a quaint fashion show against the backdrop of the castles. All of the women who model for the fashion show are dressed in bright, primary colors. Varda is obviously aware of the fact that there is very little that so dates a film as dress codes. The fashions are, of course, outmoded today; Varda anticipated that. But, without the fashion show, there would be no metaphoric gauge for the actual venerability of the castles. With the fashion show inserted, the castles seem even older and their colors seem even more hushed, as if they had all been watered down and then shined.

The sense of the past still existing but in an irrevocably altered state is also the subject of Varda's second commissioned documentary, _Du Côté de la Côte_ (1958). There is an uneven monochromatic scale at work in the film, for the natural world is clearly painted in blue. For the published text of the film, in which many of the photos had to be reproduced in black and white, Varda explained: "Nous n'avons pas pu reproduire toutes les images en couleurs, puisse le lecteur n'y voir que du bleu."[22] Yet, the intrusion of the human element upon this natural landscape is portrayed through livid reds, greens and oranges. Varda likens the commercial pillage of this natural beauty by entrepreneurs and tourists to the despoiling of the beaches by the Allies when they landed there in 1944. The juxtaposition of soft cool colors with bright primary colors symbolizes the clash between the natural world of yesterday and the resort suburbia of today. As the film progresses, the cool colors (blue) of the natural world become progressively colder (browns, for example) to show the moribund state of what once was so majestic. The coloration of the film, then, is geared to render the sense of loss that Varda wished to convey in her film. Everything about the film points to this sense of loss, even the sound track, which is often made up of original poetry by Varda, like the following:

Palmier sauvage
tu perds tes palmes
tu perds ton calme

Ciseau volage
tu perds tes plumes
et du volume

Souffle sauvage
tu perds ton temps
tu perds ton vent

As the colors of the natural world gradually become harsher, the colors of the "invaders" become more palatable, less offensive. The colors of the natural world finally go to a contrasted black and white, and the melancholy of Varda's poetry is replaced by the venom of a Jacques Prévert poem:

Tout seul un olivier
jette désespérément
vers le ciel calciné
deux bras carbonisés
comme un nègre lynché

The Prévert poem, significantly, seems more "modern" than the Varda poem. The spectator gradually recognizes that the Varda poem, like the Ronsard text in _O saisons ô chateaux_, is meant to evoke the past, while the violence of the personification and metaphors in the Prévert poem ("ciel calciné," "deux bras carbonisés," "comme un nègre lynché") is perfectly in keeping with the present time and with the "rape" of the past by the present.

In both documentaries, Varda turned the outside world inward to reflect her private vision of a transformed world peopled by dying things, a world whose geographical locales reflect only a sense of loss, whereas the changing of the seasons, which also evokes a sense of loss, promises in return a sense of perpetual rebirth.

Marie-Claire Ropars-Willeumier has characterized Varda's subjective use of color in the following way:

> Ce que...Varda cherche dans la couleur, c'est d'abord un autre monde, différent de l'univers quotidien, un monde mystérieux, obsédant, névrotique, lugubre, imaginaire: alors que la réalité objective existe en couleurs, la création d'un univers coloré devient au cinéma un moyen d'expression subjective, orientant la vision extérieure selon les impératifs d'une signification interne.[23]

Varda carries the subjectification of color to formal extremes in Le Bonheur, in which the characters are not only not aware of the Mozart music which "colors" their transparent happiness but also not aware of the fact that they function as elements of an impressionistic painting by the very colors with which they are associated: their relationships form the basis of the color linkages, and, as such, the characters cannot exist apart from each other. Thus, the wife is associated with colors of gold or orange - more orange (warmer) in the beginning, more gold (cooler, fading) as the film progresses. Emilie Sevignac, the mistress, is associated with very cool colors - with very rich purples and with very soft blues. When she replaces the wife, she takes on the coloration of the wife. She begins to wear the orange and gold of the wife; because of this transformation, Emilie's hair appears to be less blonde than before, and she actually begins to look like the wife. The physical attractions and repulsions in the film can thus be explained, as Varda has explained them, in formal terms: that is, in terms of attractions and repulsions at the level of pure color.

> Vous me parliez du violet, c'est simple, le violet, c'est l'ombre de l'orange. C'est là une sensation qui ramène à l'idée de peinture. Les impressionistes ont découvert que les ombres étaient complémentaires, qu'un citron avait une ombre bleue et une orange une ombre

> mauve...Dans Le Bonheur, l'or appelle le violet, parce qu'il n'y a pas de couleur sans ombre.[24]

In effect, Varda is saying that there is no possibility of an individual personality ("il n'y a pas de couleur sans ombre") and that the characters are thus as abstracted objects: the lemon (yellow/the wife) has a blue shadow (Emilie) and the orange (the wife) has a purple shadow (Emilie). That the mistress should come to double the wife, without any apparent transformations in behavior (the children take to her immediately, as if she were their mother), is already evident in the coloration of the film. Thus, traditional psychological motivation of characters in a film is here replaced (or explained) by the impressionistic use of colors in a formal play of light and shadow which reinforces the feeling on the part of the spectator that the emotions of the characters are indeed transparent or hollow.

Varda said of her use of color in Le Bonheur: "J'ai utilisé la couleur parce que le bonheur ne peut pas s'illustrer en noir et blanc."[25] The underlying assumption of such a statement is, or course, that Varda's point of departure was as much the coloration of the film as the essay of emotions. Varda is, then, at the opposite extreme of those who would use color as an additive to black and white. This view of color as an additive has so pervaded American films that it is perhaps useful to put the situation back in its proper perspective, as William Johnson has admirably done:

> Probably the reddest of herrings that confronts a critic examining screen color is the fact that the history of photography runs back to front. If Niepce, Talbot, Daguerre, and the other pioneers of photography had found a chemical that distinguished among different wavelengths of light, they would surely not have rejected

> it in favor of silver salts that distinguish only between bright and dark. And in that case, black and white would have been the later and more sophisticated development - in both still and movie photography - that it is in the other visual arts. But because color came later, many people saw it as an additive to black and white instead of a medium in its own right. Those in favor of screen color welcomed it for its decorative value; those in opposition condemned it for painting the lily.[26]

Agnes Varda certainly uses color for its decorative value, but she has never "painted the lily." Far from using color as an additive, one could almost say, as Ropars-Willeumier has asserted, that Varda begins with color: the rest, in a sense, is an additive.

> Lorsque Agnes Varda explique la présence du violet dans Le Bonheur et le présente comme une ombre complémentaire de l'orange qui doit peu à peu se substituer à lui, c'est à la fois d'un succès technique qu'elle témoigne, et d'une vision nouvelle du langage cinématographique: car Le Bonheur est pensé en couleur et rythmé par elle, suivant les lois qui régissent les masses et les lignes colorées. Si bien qu'au lieu d'ajouter la couleur au récit, un certain cinéma contemporain part désormais de la couleur pour inventer le récit.[27]

It seems to have been on the basis of the dialectic between black-and-white and color that Varda composed Les Créatures, perhaps the most formal of her cinematographic experiments. The film involves a married couple. The husband is a writer working on a novel. The wife is pregnant. Due to his careless driving, the wife loses her speech. While she is thus muted and reduced to writing messages with chalk on a little portable blackboard, his novelistic "speech" proliferates: that is, he begins to imagine/write his novel. No doubt due to the guilt he feels over the wife's malady, he invents a fiction in which he plays chess against the diabolical Ducasse (who probably comes from the husband's reading of Lautreamont when he is not trying to write). In other words, the entire film, then, becomes the husband's hallucination *vraie*, in which the spectator is never sure whether the scenes are real, written or simply imagined by the husband. The stakes for this chess game, in which everyone on the island is a pawn (except the wife and the husband and Ducasse), is the speech and the very life of the wife (and the life of the child she carries inside). The one structural key left open to the spectator in this labyrinthine film is the play of colors.

As the "game" progresses, all characters, with the exception of the wife, dress more and more obviously in the checks of the chess-board. For her part, the wife is kept pure and spared these tribulations of the game. She is always dressed in white, which is as ever the beginning point of Varda's color vocabulary.

> Le blanc est une couleur fascinante, et là, mon propre vocabulaire persiste. De même que les écrivains ont des mots privilégiés, moi j'ai des mots images, dans tous mes films ils apparaissent.[28]

Contrasted with the checkered costumes of the characters-become-pawns, Varda inserts the red-tinted images, which signify that either the husband or Ducasse has plugged into a switchboard and given a character three minutes of free will. The red becomes the ambivalent color of both evil and salvation. When Ducasse plugs in, it is precisely at a moment when one character is suppressing violence or sexual passion towards another;when the husband plugs in, it is at a moment when an act of sacrifice or forgiveness (love without passion) could save a seemingly irredeemable situation. Ducasse seems certain to win, but at the moment when a lecher is about to rape a young girl (having already raped the girl's mother many years before - just as Maldoror had done in the Lautréamont "original"), the husband destroys the chess-board and wakes up. His dream has been his novel, and his greatest power has been that of creating his dream and then being able to leave it. Actually, he is saved by the wife's giving birth to a son. The anguish and apprehensions, as well as the dénouement, are quite similar to those expressed in Varda's earlier L'Opéra mouffe (1958) with the difference that L'Opéra mouffe was told from the point of view of the woman about to give birth, while Les Créatures is told from the point of view of the expectant and guilt-ridden father. As the husband thus "completes" his novel, Varda signifies the anti-climax by a complete whitewash of color: the film not only returns to black and white, it goes even further: it becomes all white, signifying the successful rite de passage from life to death to life again.

If Agnes Varda has turned to color, after having made successful films in black-and-white, it is precisely to convey heightened subjectivity. Since her colors are used so formally, the decoration being so formal that it replaces somewhat the object or character decorated, there is not the usual loss of nuance associated in the passage from black-and-white to color. The multiplicity of meaning so characteristic of the ciné-roman or film-novel created by Varda, Marker and Resnais stems not only from a use of music and literary dialogue that attain a value independent of the visual text but also from a use of color that transforms the usual time-space relationships in film and dislocates the color from the image it colors at the level of interpretation.

> De même que la musique, puis la parole, se sont trouvées peu à peu acquerir une valeur sonore, qui s'intègre dans le récit sans le doubler, par la couleur l'image libère sa propre tonalité pour en faire, suivant la qualité particulière de chaque teinte, un élément

indispensable dans une signification globale.[29]

More eclectic than Varda, Chris Marker seems to want to use the entire spectrum to add nuance to a particular scene or to create the transition between scenes. Indeed, Marker is one of the few documentary filmmakers to retain the authenticity of the black-and-white image found in most documentaries by a very subtle use of color. In Lettre de Sibérie (1957), for example, Marker depicts both the variety and the monotony of Siberia through color. For the actual footage of the film, Marker alternates between "day" and "night" color, both being carried to extremes. Thus. the shots of the workers in Irkutsk and the gold fields near Irkutsk both belong to the day sequences. Both are intentionally bleached, adding more light than was necessary to shoot them. The effect, of course, is that both the city workers and the gold field workers are potential slaves of the system under which they live. However, in the case of the gold fields, Marker goes from a basically monochromatic sense of color to one that is more varied and more authentic, precisely at the point where the text indicates that these workers have little need for the gold they mine and that they are perhaps the last individuals in a society of socialized automotons. By contrast, the shots of the Lena and the shots of the underground cave both belong to the night sequences. It is in these sequences that Marker becomes less satirical and more poetic, creating metaphors for both the ever-moving river and the frozen "jewels".

What makes this alternation between day and night coloring unobtrusive for the spectator are all the inserts. Lettre de Sibérie is in a sense a documentary about making documentaries, for it is full of so-called documentary inserts. And these inserts differ from each other both in terms of music and color. When Marker shows the same footage of Irkutsk workers paving a road three times, he is exposing the myth of the documentary as truth. By inserting the same sequence three times in succession, he reveals the importance of the filmmaker's eye and the way he distorts the objective reality before him. Marker does this by maintaining the color constant while changing the text from laudatory to attacking to eccentric-objective, with corresponding shifts in the music track.

When Marker breaks away from a shot of reindeer in Irkutsk, it is again to show the bias of the media; this time, it is commercial television. In cartoon form with quick animation, Marker constructs an imaginary television commercial on reindeer and their utilitarian exploitation by man. The music is a jingle. Corresponding to this jingle, Marker abruptly shifts colors, all primary, until their rhythm is also that of the movement of the animation. The music, the colors, the animation and the montage are all spritely, indicating a break from "real" imagery and underlining the rapidity with which all commercials must bombard their potential buyer-victims. As with most commercials, it makes little difference that the text is a random gathering of non-sequiturs. The important thing is the movement.

This kind of insert, of which Marker is fond, belies Marker's fondness for comic strips in particular and for animation in general. Conscious of the difficulty in manipulating the filmic image in color, Fellini once said: "La couleur, c'est l'immobilité."[30] And, indeed, for directors who use color as a decorative addition to the image, color does mean immobility in terms of montage, for the director is forced, not only to link images with images, but also to link colors with colors. The only way out of such an impasse is to use color stylistically, which means dislocation and a tendency toward discontinuous montage (where there is little or no linkage between scenes.) As Ropars-Willeumier has stated:

> C'est sans doute pour résoudre ces incompatibilités que le passage à la couleur s'accompagne d'un retour au montage discontinu.[31]

Marker inserts an imaginary documentary in his already fanciful documentary. His documentary begins with a Siberian who looks like Nanook and ends with the airplane. All shots in this imaginary documentary were originally black-and-white, it appears, and they are here tinted, usually light-sepia, to give them an ironic venerability. Significantly, as the inserts become more numerous, they also become more elaborated and closer to the color scheme of alternating dark and light. Thus, the exit from the real underground cave is to an imaginary football field. Shots of former reindeer hunters, now "civilized", which are day shots, are juxtaposed with "night" shots of the inserted Siberian theatre, whose savage mime dances with colorful costumes and make-up are the opposite of the "civilized" hunters. And the introduction to the monochromatic gold fields is an inserted slide show comparison of the American Yukon and Klondike strikes with those in Russia, in which all the shots are tinted gold and brown to symbolize the gold fever they portray.

Just as Fellini had done with Juliet of the Spirits, Marker merges fantasy with reality in Lettre de Sibérie by merging the colors of the inserts gradually with those of the larger documentary shots.

In _A Valparaiso_ (1963), Marker and Joris Ivens seem to have been inspired by the "explosion" of color (by holding back color, reserving it for a specific sequence) created by Eisenstein in _Ivan the Terrible_. The film, as long as it is in black-and-white, describes what Marker's text calls the "lie of Valparaiso" which is the sun which distorts the color of everything. But to convey the violence that seems both legendary and hereditary in Valparaiso, the filmmakers felt it necessary to bathe the images in blood: that is, they switch from black-and-white to a monochromatic red, which reinforces the abrupt shift from the casual and poetic evocation of the sun to the strident and incantatory evocation of violence in the text:

> Tel est le quatrième élément de Valparaiso: le sang.
> Et c'est sa mémoire.

Resnais also uses color for memory in _Nuit et brouillard_ but in a more subtle, and thus more rewarding way. The starkness of the fixed photographic images of the past, which convey in black-and-white the horrors of the concentration camps, are dialectically opposed with the mobile camera over colored shots of the empty camps of the present. But color here is not only a return from the past to the present nor a break between the two nor even memory itself. Rather, it functions as a cover-up of the past, as if the natural world had conspired to conceal the horrors: "De ce dortoir de brique, de ces sommeils ménacés, nous ne pouvons que vous montrer l'écorce, la couleur." Color symbolizes the hollow shell, the skeleton of what once housed bodies. Color, then, also symbolizes the loss of memory in the image, which the text on the sound track, with its persistent accumulation of grotesque detail, struggles to prevent.

Aware of the distinction between film color and the colors of everyday life, Resnais exploits that distinction to encourage a sharpened awareness and a heightened lucidity in the spectator. As Resnais has, himself, stated:

> On ressent les couleurs de manière beaucoup trop vive au cinéma, parce qu'elles sont entourées d'un cadre noir...mais quand on va au spectacle, on est bien là justement pour prendre conscience de ce qu'on ne voit pas dans la vie quotidienne: donc, le rôle de la couleur, c'est d'augmenter la lucidité du spectateur dans le spectacle de tous les jours.[32]

It is with Muriel (1963) that Resnais forces the spectator's lucidity to the limit. The malaise of the spectator watching Muriel is in part due to the coloration of effaced tones: colors meticulously "reconstructed" to more closely resemble those of post-war Boulogne-sur-Mer. Here the dialectic between past and present and that between film color and the colors of daily life has been transformed into a quasi-equation. In other words, Resnais is here insisting upon the weathered colors of daily life. What seems at first glance to be a bad print or simply a depressingly ugly film is in fact one of film's closest approximations of the modern city. Resnais prevents any emotive fascination with the colors in the film by stripping them of their brightness and their possibilities for harmony. By doing so, Ropars-Willeumier contends that Resnais has won a victory over painting, precisely by transforming the caprice of the technical in the medium into the will of the director's personal and artistic vision.

> C'est enfin vers une difficile lucidité que chemine Resnais, chez qui une véritable ascèse de la laideur vient refuser aux couleurs toute harmonie, et, arrachant le spectateur comme le personnage à la fascination ou à l'anéantissement, maintient entre l'homme

> et le monde un contrepoint rigoureux...Si cette volontaire désharmonie témoigne de la conscience dialectique de Resnais, elle représente aussi pour l'expression cinématographique une victoire sur la peinture. Resnais transforme en élément stylistique ce qui dépendait autrefois de vicissitudes techniques.[33]

There seems to be a definite structural key to the ugliness of color in _Muriel_: the old sections of Boulogne and the "old" moments, that is, those from the past, are painted in washed colors, often of a chestnut or sepia look; by contrast, the newer sections of Boulogne, those that have been reconstructed since the War, and the moments that are most rooted in the present, are done in brighter colors, which are, nonetheless, very displeasing to look at. Resnais has reacted against this assertion of ugliness on the part of most critics of the film by saying that the colors in _Muriel_ are also those in daily life and that film has merely made them visible to the spectator, where the spectator had not seen them quite so vividly in daily life.

> Les couleurs ne sont pas plus laides dans _Muriel_ que dans la vie réelle, mais dans la vie réelle on oublie de les voir; au cinéma l'obscurité les change, le "noir" les exalte en vous faisant voir plus nettement ces couleurs de la vie quotidienne.[34]

To attain this degree of realism, Resnais has bled the color from his colors, so that they do not attract the spectator for themselves. The color of _Muriel_, however, is thus enrichened aesthetically, for these colors contain the nuance of middle gray's in a black-and-white film at the same time that they trap the spectator, more than the black-and-white film could, and force him to contemplate the realistic physicality of Resnais's space in _Muriel_, the reality of which seems totally foreign to the spectator.

> ...et si _Muriel_ amorce, comme autrefois _Hiroshima_, une prise

> nouvelle du cinéma sur le monde, c'est que la couleur enlève au spectateur toute possibilité d'évasion, et force son regard à méditer sur une réalité qu'il ne reconnait pas comme sienne.[35]

Antonioni achieves the same apparent barrenness of color in Red Desert, in which almost every single object in the outdoor shots seems infected with fog, smog, dust or rust. Both Muriel and Red Desert subjectify space to reflect the interior lives of the characters who inhabit those spaces. The difference is the following: Antonioni's film seems the more forceful of the two, because his technique is foregrounded in the film; colors are cast so that they seem to jump out at the spectator, from the engulfing clouds of factory smoke to the yellows and ashen reds of the factories to the sickly algae-green dress that Giuliana wears. Since the colors are foregrounded, the spectator can easily perceive the relationship of the disturbed Giuliana to her nightmarish surroundings, especially when those surroundings are made transparently obvious, as is the case of the painted grass. Antonioni seems the more forceful of the two, then, because his technique is more accessible and his theme is more violent. With Red Desert Antonioni seems to have prefigured Godard's sense of colors as violent in Deux ou trois que je sais d'elle, with the difference that Antonioni wished to portray even violence as an interiorized state:

> Tout est couleur dans le monde moderne - agression des couleurs et du bruit. Du mouvement. Je serai plus violent, plus dur que je ne l'ai été jusqu'ici, la violence pouvant être d'ailleurs intérieure.[36]

The harshness of the colors (with Godard, because they are primary; with Antonioni, because they are willfully dirtied) is perfectly in keeping with the assault of noise. In daily life one is never so aware of noise pollution as one is while watching Deux ou trois choses... or Red Desert.

By contrast, Resnais seems less forceful than Antonioni, precisely because he uses color more subtly. Even in their neutral tones Antonioni's colors assault the spectator. Resnais's effaced tones just seem to fade quietly, for they are not foregrounded. Indeed, the emptiness of Hélène, Alphonse, Bernard and Françoise in the film is beautifully captured by this constantly dissolving color in Muriel, as if the film were a house whose paint were peeling. Characters become multiplied in the film without very much explanation for the spectator. One has the sense, in watching Muriel, of watching a television soap opera for the first time, in which all of the characters seem to know each other but do not properly introduce themselves to the viewer. That multiplication of characters, most evident in the eating scenes, ends abruptly with an empty apartment at the film's conclusion, an apartment made all the more hollow by the blandness of the color. Perhaps Resnais was too subtle with his colors in Muriel; many critics were perplexed by the open-ended conclusion and the constant coming and going of characters, while many spectators were just plain bored by the drab colors. In this respect, spectators seem to accept the colors that assault like those of Godard or colors that excite like those of Fellini. Unfortunately, they are much less able to accept colors that are not used in the most obvious way; consequently, they view Varda's Le Bonheur as too pretty, Resnais's Muriel as too ugly. They fail to see that a realism of vision, for Resnais or for Antonioni, goes hand in hand with the dissolution or obscuring of the traditional plot.

> En forçant le regard, en faussant des couleurs, en rompant l'habitude, c'est au seul véritable réalisme qu'aboutit ce nouveau cinéma, qui est de REALISATION. Parce qu'il réfléchit la réalité dans un miroir de coloration déformante, il fait réfléchir sur elle. Dans cette prise de conscience opérée sur le réel, le réalisme de la vision rejoint l'abstraction du récit: car il s'agit de dégager le sens de ce réel, et non plus d'en décrire les apparences.[37]

Color here is used, no longer to describe appearances, but to shape the development of characters' interior states and to punctuate subjective point of view or shifting point of view. In addition, if we return to Fellini's statement that color is immobility, we can see a new time-space relationship with this subjective use of color. Where Resnais and Antonioni had both explored the theme of time in their previous films by capitalizing upon the nuances possible in the black-and-white image and by playing with time through a manipulation of the camera (the soft focus and low depth of field at Nevers in *Hiroshima mon amour* of Resnais, for example) or a manipulation of light and shadow (the frames that seem too white in *Marienbad* show imagined scenes and mental time), they have become more concerned with space itself when they went to color. As Ropars-Willeumier has pointed out, space in a film like *Muriel* or *Red Desert* becomes a subject of enquiry in itself:

> Car ce n'est pas par hasard que le passage à la couleur s'accompagne, chez Resnais comme chez Antonioni, d'une rupture avec la recherche du temps et du développement d'un espace envahissant. Par la couleur, l'espace au cinéma devient son propre sujet au lieu de représenter le décor d'un drame ou le reflet d'un être.[38]

In effect, what she is saying is that space in these films, subjectified through color, becomes a proper subject of investigation for the artist, just as Alain Robbe-Grillet's *Dans le labyrinthe* (1959) investigates interiorized and imaginary spaces.

Agnes Varda, Chris Marker and Alain Resnais have gone a long way toward giving color in dramatic films the variety and flexibility that Disney had given to the animation film. They have reacted violently against the use of color as an additive or decoration of the black-and-white image, insisting that color have a functional purpose of its own, as the musical track and the text should stand ably on their own from the image track which they either complement or contradict but rarely duplicate. Color has generally been so misunderstood in films for so long that it will take more directors like Resnais, Varda and Marker. In their reaction against naturalistic screen color, they seem to have paid heed to Eisenstein who once wrote: "Irritation is an excellent creative stimulus."[39]

The _court métrage_ (short film) offered the literary New Wave filmmakers the chance to experiment with the soundtrack as well as with the images. From their very first shorts their use of music in films has always been highly original. As Jean Cayrol has stated:

> La musique n'est pas cette sauce qui sert à faire passer des images ou des mots "cuisinés"; elle n'est pas là pour faire vibrer une parole, la reprendre "en choeur," mettre le spectateur en hypnose par un accompagnement de chic ou de choc, annoncer comme par un roulement de battérie la prouesse technique d'une mise en scène, ou glisser encore sur une séquence équivoque, la litote d'un murmure musical prenant le relais des mots trop explicites et permettant notamment en amour de passer de la parole inachevée aux actes.[40]

In other words, music is not seen as being antithetical to the text in the _cinéma des auteurs_. It will not make up for a lack in the text. Its value lies precisely in its equivalency with the image and the text. As such, there are three languages being used simultaneously in the _cinéma des auteurs_: the language of the images, the language of the text, and the language of the music. Cayrol has commented on the affinities between film language and the language of music:

> A noter encore que parmi tous les arts qui utilisent le verbe "composer," le cinéma est celui qui par sa technique se rapproche le plus de la musique: il est modulation de plusieurs thèmes, il a une tonalité, une armature de clef dont les images sont au passage "altérées" (la valeur, la hauteur d'une image dépendant de cette contagion du montage qui développe entre elles interférences et métamorphoses, et des thèmes dont l'ambition nous a été dévoilée au départ...On peut dire au cinéma qu'il existe des brèves et des longues, qui ne sont pas données seulement par la durée des plans mais par une densité de lumière, à nombre d'images égal, plus ou moins rapide: un plan tres contrasté paraissant par exemple beaucoup plus bref qu'un plan dans les GAMMES du gris. Enfin plus se perfectionne la bande sonore du film (précision du synchronisme, mixage méticuleux donnant toutes les nuances de l'intensité, science des bruits, invention même de bruits irréels par le ralentissement ou l'accélération, primauté des partitions musicales dans le "conditionnement" du spectateur, développement de la stéréophonie), plus le montage du film ressemble à cette

> orchestration dont parle Eisenstein, polyphonie capable de nous rendre sensibles immédiatement les correspondances baudelairiennes entre la vue et l'ouie, et parfois les visions rimbaudiennes quand l'art des discordances parvient à DEREGLER nos sens. 41

It is no coincidence that Cayrol mentions Eisenstein, Baudelaire and Rimbaud in his discussion of the affinities between the two languages. Through the use of images and dialogues which are rhythmically related on the basis of music, the directors of the *cinéma des auteurs* strive for a "correspondence" between the arts, a *Gesamtkunstwerk* or "total work of art," as Eisenstein had also sought before them. The implication here is not just that of the total art work, but also that of the total art form, since film, for these directors, can accomodate painting, poetry and music without losing, in the process, properties unique to film. Thus, these directors are not concerned with raising film to the level of respectability that the other arts have attained. They have gone one step beyond. They are concerned with incorporating the other arts into film. It could be argued that such a film, assuming the incorporation to be successful, constitutes a new genre.

Through an extended analysis of several films in the *cinéma des auteurs*, I propose to show how Alain Resnais, Agnes Varda, Chris Marker, Jean Cayrol, Marguerite Duras, Henri Colpi and Alain Robbe-Grillet have consistently used music as an independent text to be "read" while viewing their films, and, further, how their films strive to be *ciné-opéras* (film-operas).

Even in his *courts métrages*, Alain Resnais searched for music with an eye to his subject. It would seem somewhat presumptuous for a filmmaker to seek out professional musicians for a film like

Guernica (1950), which lasts only thirteen minutes, but that is exactly what Resnais did. Just as he collaborated with established poets in the shorts (with Paul Eluard on Guernica, with Chris Marker on Les Statues meurent aussi, with Jean Cayrol on Nuit et brouillard, and with Raymond Queneau on Le Chant du styrène), so too he collaborated with professional composers: with Jacques Besse on Van Gogh (1948), with Darius Milhaud on Gauguin (1950), with Guy Bernard on Guernica (1950), with Hanns Eisler on Nuit et brouillard (1955), with Maurice Jarre on Toute la Mémoire du monde (1956), and with Pierre Barbaud on Le Mystère de l'Atelier Quinze (1957) and Le Chant du styrène (1958). And, because of the kind of close collaboration that Resnais demands of all his artists, he appreciates writing by working with writers, and he appreciates music by working with musicians. Just as he has demanded original scripts from the poets he has worked with,[42] so too he demands original scores from the composers he works with. But, whereas most of the poets were already established and approximately Resnais's contemporaries in age, the composers were relatively unknown and much younger than Resnais. They were chosen, however, for their interest in experimental music and their ability, not to adapt the classics, but to compose original scores based on what Resnais envisaged the music's role to be in relation to the images and the text.

For Resnais (as it had been for Eisenstein before him), music is particularly related to montage, especially the kind of rapid, discontinuous editing that Resnais perfected in the shorts. But the composer had to be sensitive, not only to the editing, as Resnais would explain it to him, but also to the subject. Thus, Resnais asked Maurice Jarre to compose a score based on _Lady in the Dark_, an opera of Kurt Weill. As Resnais has explained, the quick cuts and long travelling or tracking shots of the camera seemed to correspond very well to the baroque architecture of the National Library as well as to the Weill opera:

> _Toute la mémoire du monde_ est partie de quelques mesures d'une opérette de Kurt Weill, _Lady in the Dark_: cela a donné, séparés par des plans très brefs, de longs travellings, de grands mouvements qui correspondent aussi bien au baroque architectural de la Bibliothèque National qu'à la mesure de Kurt Weill.[43]

But it was the importance that Resnais placed on a rapid, almost blinding editing pace that forced him to compose his films in terms of the music. As he wrote of _Van Gogh_:

> La multiplicité des plans obligeait à donner à la musique une importance prépondérante. Elle n'était plus là pour "accompagner" les images, mais pour créer l'ossature du film. C'est à elle que revenait le rôle de souder les oeuvres entre elles et de rendre cohérent l'univers de Van Gogh.
>
> Il faut une musique précise, que le film d'art soit réalisé par des mouvements d'appareil ou par un montage de plans fixes. Elle donne au film rythme et même plus.[44]

Resnais juxtaposed paintings from several different periods in Van Gogh's life, with no respect for chronology. That juxtaposition works in the film, because the editing joins the various works, and, perhaps more importantly, because the music provides an alternate pace to the editing.

With _Nuit et brouillard_, Resnais began to think fully in terms of a musical "text" which would equal the spoken text and the visual text. To be their equal, Resnais and Eisler deliberately worked out an elaborate counterpoint system, in which the music would create distance between the spectator and the images. Marcel Martin has defined counterpoint in the following way:

> J'appelle "contrepoint" par analogie avec la musique la mise en parallèle de deux processus expressifs ayant le même contenu significatif mais dans deux régistres plastiques différents.[45]

Resnais's use of contrapuntal music slightly differs from the definition of Martin. While the images are, at one point in the film, of the heaps of bodies, hair, teeth and other grotesqueries, the music is light, even spritely. Similarly, the music is arranged contrapuntally in view of the text. Where Cayrol builds his text on repetitions, on accumulations of details and on longer and longer lines, Eisler's musical score does not repeat, remains deliberately short and almost staccato in contrast to Cayrol's text.[46] Yet, the musical score is more similar to the text than to the images, for, just as Cayrol's text often works by _enjambement_, that is, by prolonging the completion of a grammatical unit or an idea, so also Eisler's score builds tension by _enjambement_, that is, by introducing a musical theme at the beginning of the film which is not completed until the very end of the film. Henri Colpi has commented on the use of counterpoint in _Nuit et brouillard_:

> _Nuit et brouillard_ s'ouvrait sur le générique par une longue phrase mélodique, ample et émouvante, dont la résolution demeurait en suspens. Ce thème ne réapparaitra, encadrant l'"avant" et l'"après" de l'univers concentrationnaire, que sur le final pour, cette fois, merveilleusement se résoudre. Les autres motifs importants étaient le thème de la déportation dominé par un cuivre et le déchirant thème concentrationnaire. Par contraste avec l'imposante mise en scène des défilés hitlériens, Eisler utilisait de grêles pizzicati. Plus tard, les pizzicati accompagneront l'un des résultats du nazisme: les camps immenses, le typhus, les cadavres enfouis par bulldozer, les SS devenus prisonniers à leur tour.[47]

If there is a resolution to the musical theme begun and then cut off at the film's outset, that resolution is a false one: one of form, not of meaning. There is a similar false resolution in the camera movements. The camera ceases its constant tracking shots and pulls back gradually to a long-shot, creating visual distance, not critical distance. The music resolves itself, completes itself, "pulls back" to a distance. It is the text which attacks "la caméra qui s'éloigne" and raises questions which the arbitrary resolutions in the images and in the music cannot dispel or contradict.

It was with Hiroshima mon amour (1959) that critics first began to take notice of the importance of music in the films of Resnais. When asked about the role of music in his film, Resnais answered with characteristic modesty and then precision:

> J'ignore tout de la composition musicale, mais si c'est d'avoir un thème et de batir variations et contrepoints, alors c'est un peu vrai. Je crois que si l'on analysait Hiroshima par un diagramme sur du papier millimètre, on assisterait à quelque chose proche du quatuor. Thèmes, variations à partir du premier mot; d'où les répétitions, les retours en arrière que certains trouvent insupportables et qui peuvent l'être, du reste, pour ceux qui n'entrent pas dans le jeu. Le dernier mouvement du film est un mouvement lent: c'est un décrescendo.[48]

There seem to be approximately nine different musical themes in Hiroshima mon amour: oubli, corps, Musée, blessés, Ruines, tourisme, Fleuve, lyrique and Nevers. Of these nine themes, oubli, corps and Nevers are the most frequent and the most important.

The theme of forgetting (oubli) begins the film, establishing itself against the fixity of the visuals: two bodies interlocked, immobilized. It also ends the film, at which time the editing has all but come to a halt, the longer takes signifying a surrender to the present and a kind of forgetting-truce with the past. This theme consists of six identical notes repeated in a monotone. As Henri Colpi has pointed out, it is intimately related with the themes of "corps" and "Nevers," creating the bridge between physical love and memory:

> Il joue un rôle d'introduction au film en créant un climat étrange et désolé par sa répétition de groupes de six notes identiques. Quant au retour de ce thème Oubli, il se situe très loin, dans la séquence 51: le monologue intérieur est amené par le thème Nevers auquel se substitue le thème Corps pour l'ultime évocation de l'amour allemand, cet amour qui est déjà entré dans l'oubli, et alors reparait le thème Oubli, dont la monotonie inconsistante et désespérée domine la fin du film et l'achève dans un cri.[49]

The theme "corps" is equally fluid and polyvalent. It is first used in the three fixed dissolves of Riva and Okada at the beginning of the film. It thus follows the theme of forgetting and establishes the "presence" of the two lovers. It again follows the theme of forgetting in the Nevers sequences, as if to say that Riva's liaison is a fulfillment of a desire for the dead German lover, or perhaps that memory can be as carnal as sex in the present. Eventually, however, the theme of forgetting begins to reverse places with the theme of "body"; indeed, that reversal is also apparent in the second half of the film visually too. The irony is that Riva and Okada are almost like fixed statues in the first sections of the film, in which it is the camera and the editing which create the sense of movement. In the last sections of the film, Riva and Okada actually move about much more, but, because of the longer takes, the proliferation of the voice-over to convey Riva's increasing interior monologues and decreasing communication with the Japanese, we sense that the film gets slower and slower, until it ultimately stops suddenly and disconcertingly. Thus, the first sections can be characterized in the following way: (1) Riva and Okada don't move very much; (2) they "dialogue" in a kind of chant; (3) there is a great deal of cutting between Hiroshima and Nevers and, thus, between synchronous sound and voice-over. The last sections provide a dialectical opposite to those first sections: (1) Riva and Okada physically move about a great deal, the camera takes get longer and tracking shots seem to replace the editing of the earlier sections; (2) while the images present longer slices of Hiroshima and shorter ones of Nevers, Riva succumbs to the acceptance of her German lover's death and to a lyrical evocation of Nevers that resembles both a little girl's voice and a grown woman's voice, neither of which "remembers" the trauma of the love affair; (3) Riva ceases to dialogue in a communicative way with the Japanese, succumbing as well to her own _voix intérieure_ or interior monologue; (4) voice-over narration takes over the visuals of Hiroshima, whereas before they had pertained mostly to the images of Nevers, until the final exchanges. Whether the spectator is consciously aware of it or not, that reversal in the film is first introduced through the music: the reversal of the "oubli-corps" succession. That reversal predicates that the Riva-Okada relationship is no longer physical at the same time that the Riva-Nevers relationship is transformed.

Henri Colpi explains the function of the "corps" theme:

> Le thème Corps, lui, présente une chaleur et une profondeur qui font contraste. Il est associé aux amants du Prologue, mais il disparait dès l'apparition des visages et le début du dialogue proprement dit. Il ne réapparaitra qu'à la séquence 34 pour unir

> dans l'esprit l'amour actuel et l'amour de jeunesse. Cette connexion est encore fortement marquée dans le passage (séquence 49) où les images de Nevers et de Hiroshima s'entrecroisent. Dans la gare, le thème Corps s'appliquera seulement à l'amour allemand. Les jeux étant faits et l'oubli devant triompher, il fera une dernière, timide et fugitive apparition devant l'entrée du Casablanca. 50

Indeed, it is perhaps the visual icon of the "Casablanca" sign, conjuring up the conflict between past and present in the Michael Curtiz film, which falsely evokes the "corps" theme, even when that theme has already given way to the "oubli" theme. The "corps" theme is used contrapuntally at other times in the film too. For example, the first long tracking shots of the streets of Hiroshima are "personalized" or given body by the introduction of the "corps" theme. At still another point, it very briefly refers, not to Riva and her German lover nor to Riva and the Japanese lover, but to the Japanese and his wife. Riva asks the Japanese: "Ta femme, où elle est?" The response on the sound track is the "corps" theme. If the "corps" theme, necessarily brief in relation to the duration of the others, suggests a crescendo of memories and sensations that fuse Hiroshima with Nevers, then the "oubli" theme, progressively longer and more monotonous, suggests the cessation of struggle and the slow decrescendo which ambiguates the film's ending and raises several questions never to be answered: does Riva stay in Hiroshima or does she leave? Has she completely reconciled her past or not? Does the coming to terms with Nevers (forgetting) mean an equivalent forgetting of the Japanese?

The theme of "Nevers" follows a similar trajectory. It begins as a private evocation of the past for Riva, which then becomes a memory shared with the Japanese. The "game" is one of a simple transfer of identities. Okada accepts the role of the dead German lover in order to probe Riva's past. This is evident in the visuals when Resnais superimposes shots of Nevers containing the German lover's full silhouette with shots of Hiroshima containing a close-up in profile of the Japanese. The transfer is equally evident in the text when the personal pronouns become mixed: Riva alternates between "je" and "elle" in speaking of herself, just as she addresses her dead German lover through the medium of the Japanese by calling the Japanese "tu" when she is clearly not even aware of his presence. When the game gets to be too much for Riva (completely lost in the past) and for Okada (completely ignored), Okada slaps Riva and brings her abruptly back to a present in which the personal pronouns regain their normal place. This transfer is also evident, however, in the language of the music. The cuts between Hiroshima and Nevers accumulate to such an extent that Okada becomes "colored" with Nevers, and the musical theme of "Nevers" persists at times when Okada is present on the screen and the German lover is not. Gradually, however, the musical theme is dropped, only to be picked up again when Riva delivers her interior monologue to the German lover, to herself and to the mirror in her room. Thus, Nevers, which began as a solitary evocation and which then was made public through sharing, ends up as the theme of a new solitude: the solitude of a woman cut off from her past.

> Le thème Nevers cerne le souvenir heureux de la jeune femme. Il est allègre, primesautier. On remarquera que la première grande évocation de Nevers est soulignée par le thème Corps qui continue logiquement sur sa lancée (jusqu'à "et puis, il est mort"), mais

> que la deuxième partie de l'évocation appelle le nouveau motif: l'héroine a d'abord revécu sa vie antérieure à travers son amant japonais, à travers les instants où elle est amoureusement comblée, puis les heures de Nevers ont pris le dessus. Aussi bien le thème Nevers ne surgira-t-il à nouveau que lorsque la jeune Française se trouvera seule avec elle-même, avec son monologue intérieur (le lavabo 46, la gare 51). [51]

These three themes are interrelated very effectively in the film, especially in the opening sequences. The theme of "oubli" introduces a long evocation by Riva in the text of all that she has seen in Hiroshima, to which the Japanese responds: "Tu n'as rien vu à Hiroshima." Both are, of course, correct: when the musical theme is "corps," Riva is correct, and when the musical theme is "oubli," Okada is correct. The "corps" theme also introduces the hospital shots and serves as a transition between those shots and the shots in the museum. At the same time, this musical theme is a foreshadowing of what has already passed in Riva's life and of what is to be revealed in the film. For example, in both the hospital shots and the museum shots, mention is made of the hair of Japanese women falling out from the bombing. Later in the film we learn that Riva's punishment for having loved a German soldier was the public dishonoring of her and her family and the shaving of her head. The metaphor between the hair of the Japanese women and the hair of Riva is held together by the musical theme of "corps."

But perhaps the most striking fusion of the three themes is in the sequence where Riva and Okada sit separated by a quaint old woman and speak as if she weren't even there. The old woman is, however, a visual symbol for the fusion of the three musical themes: she has lived through the past, she has been devoured by the present, and she is destined for oblivion. As Colpi has stated:

> La séquence de la gare réunit les trois grands thèmes du film dans une troublante synthèse musicale: le passé (Nevers) est dévoré par le présent (Corps) et tous deux sont promis à l'Oubli.[52]

Colpi goes on to develop one more musical theme: that of the "Fleuve." This theme, in terms of the music employed, is somewhere between "oubli" and "lyrique." It is used in the opening sequences when Riva speaks of the river Ota, and it is used again in reference to the Loire at Nevers. Thus, it too corresponds to a simultaneous private-public echo system. As it relates to the river Ota, it evokes the passing of time and the trauma of memory surrounding the historical Hiroshima. As it relates to the Loire, it evokes the love-relationship between Riva and the German soldier. But this fusion of the rivers and love means that this musical theme is the structural opposite of the "corps" theme. Not surprisingly, then, the "Fleuve" theme gradually supplants the "corps" theme, being used in the long conversation between Riva and Okada in the cafe, at which time their love affair has effectively become non-sexual. As Colpi has noted:

> La belle phrase mélodique consacrée au Fleuve apparait dans le Prologue. Elle est liée aux vues de "l'estuaire en delta de la rivière Ota" et s'enchaine avec le thème Corps. Elle s'élève à nouveau au matin, lorsque la jeune femme fait quelque pas sur sa terrasse: le fleuve est en arrière-plan et c'est au Café du Fleuve que les amants se sont rencontrés. Le thème Fleuve se trouve donc rattaché à l'amour, ou mieux: il concerne à la fois un objet et un sentiment qui vont de pair, l'eau et l'amour non physique. Il relaie le thème Corps sur un mode plus affectif que charnel. Ainsi encadre-t-il, en débutant dans la maison du Japonais "après l'amour", les trente minutes de la séquence du café dont les deux seules interventions musicales sont "réalistes et justifiées" (disques).[53]

The playing of the juke box, at once assimilated by the spectator with the juke box visible in the images, announces and "sets off" the invisible "Fleuve" theme.

Indeed, none of these themes are alluded to or given names in the course of the film, and the spectator may very well see the film without distinguishing between these different musical "voices"; yet, he is surely aware of the fact that the music is strange or that the music is not very realistic. André Hodeir points out that Resnais's use of silences or "pedal points" is an attempt to make the spectator aware of the musical themes.[54] And Henri Colpi notes that Resnais's erasures of natural sounds for the full exploration of the musical themes is a similar attempt:

> Voilà un réalisateur qui n'hésite pas à supprimer au mixage tous les bruits lorsque la partition est la plus expressive. Dans la gare, conversations, rumeurs, trains, haut-parleur s'estompent au profit de la musique. Au sortir du café, grenouilles, clapotis, ville et pas disparaissent en faveur d'un piano soliste. Inversement, les deux grandes séquences de dialogue (l'hôtel 23 à 29, le café 40 à 43) ne sont dotées, chacune, que d'une seule incidence musicale, le Thème Lyrique.[55]

Colpi's conclusion of the ways in which the musical themes often "lead" the images and the spoken text seems very perceptive and especially revealing of Resnais's whole approach to the use of music in film:

> Resnais croit beaucoup, en effet, et à juste titre, à une fonction lyrique et dépaysante de la musique. La musique peut introduire un changement de style (monologue intérieur amené par elle à plusieurs reprises), justifier une modification de ton, ce qui est le cas des deux incidences citées; le Japonais devient lyrique, un thème special aide la transposition. De même, ce thème intervient dans l'intérieur nippon lorsque l'homme prononce trois phrases qui commencent également par "C'est là, m'a-t-il semblé": cette fonction lyrique de la musique apparait ici clairement et puisqu'elle permet de supprimer les enchainés visuels et de retrouver successivement le Japonais allongé, puis dressé, puis étendu.[56]

In other words, the lyrical and disturbing quality of the musical themes would perhaps not be worth mentioning, were it not for the images and spoken text which reinforce the musical structure of the film. Thus, the text of Marguerite Duras is constructed as a musical poem. It is musical because it involves a structural notion of related parts or "voices", it observes rhythm and tempo, and it plays upon themes and variations. Indeed, the opening lines of the text are unmistakably conceived in musical terms, specifically in terms of a _canto fermo_ or _plainchant_. The _canto fermo_ is a melody in long notes given to one voice while others accompany it with quicker counterpoints. Riva's insistence upon what she has seen, rendered in repetitions of key words and in an ever-increasing accumulation of details, is contrapuntally negated by the laconic response of the Japanese. Thus, the opening lines of Riva correspond to the long notes of the _canto fermo_ and the responses of Okada correspond to the quick counterpoints of the _canto fermo_:

Lui: Tu n'as rien vu a Hiroshima. Rien.
Elle: J'ai tout vu...Tout. Ainsi à l'hôpital, je l'ai vu...J'en suis sure. L'hôpital existe à Hiroshima. Comment aurais-je pu eviter de le voir?

Lui: Tu n'as pas vu d'hôpital à Hiroshima. Tu n'as rien vu à Hiroshima.

Elle: Quatre fois au musée...

Lui: Quel musée à Hiroshima?...

Elle: Quatre fois au musée à Hiroshima...J'ai vu les gens se promener. Les gens se promenent pensifs, à travers les photographies, les reconstitutions...,faute d'autre chose...les photographies ...,les photographies..., les reconstitutions, faute d'autre chose...les explications, faute d'autre chose...Quatre fois au musée à Hiroshima. J'ai regardé les gens. J'ai regardé, moi-même..., pensivement, le fer...le fer brûlé, le fer brisé, le fer devenu vulnérable, comme la chair...J'ai vu des capsules en bouquets. Qui y aurait pensé?...Des peaux humaines, flottantes, survivantes encore dans la fraicheur de leurs souffrances. Des pierres. Des pierres brûlées. Des pierres éclatées. Des chevelures anonymes que les femmes de Hiroshima retrouvaient tout entières tombées le matin, au réveil.

Elle: J'ai eu chaud place de la Paix. Dix mille degrès sur la place

Elle: de la Paix. Je le sais. La température du soleil sur la place de la Paix. Comment l'ignorer?...L'herbe...,c'est bien simple...

Lui: Tu n'as rien vu à Hiroshima. Rien.

Both Riva and Okada are chanting in these opening lines. Riva's plainchant builds upon repetitions ("quatre fois au musée," "faute d'autre chose," "le fer...," "des pierres,"), upon an increasing accumulation of details (corresponding to a longer souffle or rhythmic breath and upon an oneiric quality created by the increasing incidence of rhymed words ("fer-chair-pierres," "brûlé-bouquets-retrouvaient-réveil," "degrés-Paix-sais-soleil-Paix-ignorer"). Okada's part in the plainchant is that of negation: brief and repetitious negation. Riva continues her chant as if she hadn't heard the responses of Okada; and Okada continues to negate whatever Riva says. This is clearly not a conversation one could expect to hear in daily life. It is language raised to the level of music.

Thus, the text is used contrapuntally in the same way that the musical themes served as counterpoints to both the text and the images. André Hodeir has written the following observations on this text:

> In the non-realistic sequences-and frequently even in the realistic ones - the text is used in a contrapuntal spirit. There would be no novelty in this if it were a linear counterpoint, à la Hindemith, that was employed, but what is used instead is a kind of discontinuous virtually SERIAL counterpoint. Sometimes the text matches the images, sometimes it is ahead of them,or behind, sometimes it completely discards all visual support. The interior monologue declares its independence of the interior vision; the result is a dialectical language with which Resnais integrates the non-realistic use of the sound track. Everything is either foreshadowed or revealed later.[57]

Thus, for example, Riva looks pensively at Okada lying in bed in the morning, and, while she talks to him, we hear the faint sound of bells on the sound track. Later in the film, we discover that those bells come from Saint-Etienne in Nevers, not from any belltower in Hiroshima. This use of natural sounds for foreshadowing is explored to an even fuller degree in Resnais's La Guerre est finie (1965) and Robbe-Grillet's L'Homme qui ment (1968).

Hodeir notes the use of variations in the text of Duras by breaking up the text into four poems which go in pairs: one with three, two with four. One and three explore carnal love, the first juxtaposed with the daytime tracking shots of the streets of Hiroshima (Tu me tues, tu me fais du bien"), the third exploring the same subject via the night-time tracking shots of the Hiroshima streets ("Déforme-moi à ton image..."). This third poem also involves the assignation of people and places, naming one with the other ("Tu es Hi-ro-shi-ma," "Tu es Nevers-en-France"). The second poem is Riva's interior monologue in front of her mirror, while the fourth is the evocation of a peaceful Nevers ("poplars along the Nièvre, giving in to oblivion"). Yet one and two are related by tempo, as are three and four. As Hodeir has stated: "The tempo grows slower and slower after the parade...We proceed from andante to adagio to largo."[58]

Not only is the text composed in terms of music, but also that text is "arranged" musically with the images. As Duras has said: "Le texte est l'équivalent verbal des images, exaltant les images à venir."[59] And Marie-Claire Ropars-Willeumier has noted:

> Il s'agit là de correspondance et d'harmonie, non pas d'expression ou de traduction: l'image comme la parole ou plutôt la voix, constituent deux variations sur un même thème et ne peuvent exister l'une sans l'autre.[60]

The actors were positioned in terms of the musical structure: "Les personnages? Je les place là un peu comme le musicien plaque des accords."[61] And they were chosen for their voice projection more than for their experience in film acting. Okada had the right slightly-occidental face and the right slightly-foreign accent. Riva could deliver the lines with the right projection, the correct anti-realist and theatrical tone. Both were told that their lines were to be closer to a chant than to ordinary speech.

As Resnais, himself, has admitted:

> Je suis parti du récitatif et j'espère un jour aboutir à quelque chose de purement lyrique, voire au chant.[62]

Finally, Resnais's images are also composed along the lines of a musical poem. He has noted that his images often stem from a desire to write musically:

> Souvent dans un découpage, je pars d'une image autour de laquelle se développe un mouvement d'autres images qui doivent être solidaires de la première comme le sont les éléments d'une composition musicale.[63]

Thus, he controls the looks of his characters, so that very seldom do they meet; rather, they are projected off-screen, facilitating both the jumps in time and space and the passage from dialogue to interior monologue. When Riva asks the Japanese where his wife is, she does not face him. She looks off-screen, as if conscious of his eyes or the spectator's eyes or the past at Nevers. Significantly, that scene in the home of the Japanese leads directly into a return to Nevers which is mental for the characters but physical or actualized for the spectator. Similarly, Resnais controls the use of tracking shots to correspond with the use of interior monologue, just as he tries to approximate the "anarchy of memory" (Hodeir's words) in the editing. His camera movements and his editing are conceived both in terms of the text by Duras and the musical themes: an indication of his desire to compose films which are symphonies or operas. For Resnais, film should simultaneously speak three languages: the language of the images, the language of the text and the language of the musical score. As Colpi has pointed out:

> C'est dire que chez Resnais la musique ininterrompue n'est ni remplissage ni ameublement. Elle fait partie d'un ensemble esthétique à trois têtes: images-texte-notes. C'est dire aussi que chez Resnais les partitions sont travaillées, élaborées, finies.[64]

While not immediately grasping the significance of a film like _Hiroshima_, critics were quick to understand its musical structure. Thus, Jacques Rivette wrote: "Les problèmes que se pose Resnais à l'intérieur du cinéma sont parallèles à ceux que se pose Stravinsky en musique."[65] And Robert Benayoun added: "Il base sa conception de la durée sur les notions de contrepoint chères à Stravinsky et à Bartok."[66]

L'Année dernière à Marienbad (1961) was composed even more extensively on the basis of an opera, the whole film seeming to be conceived in terms of theme-and-variations. Ropars-Willeumier has commented on the use of serial counterpoint in the organ, violins and piano, as they relate to the voice-over narration, the immobility of secondary characters in a scene, the play of looks never returned directly and the recitative chant of the actors:

> Car on peut lire _Marienbad_ à travers la musique - orgue, violon, piano, orchestration classique ou invention sérielle - comme à travers les voix et leurs interférences - accent étranger du narrateur qui soudain se transforme en intonation théâtrale d'un acteur, dialogue d'un couple anonyme repris peu à peu par le couple présent, jeu subtil des voix OFF et des personnages en apparence

muets, des timbres naturels et des récitations d'opéra.[67]

Thus, Marienbad is a film of rhythm and tone more than one of plot and meaning. The organ music accompanies the long tracking shots of the walls and ceilings. With its repetitions and accumulations of details, the narrator's voice "plays" to both the organ and tracking camera. Resnais changed Robbe-Grillet's indications for modern serial music to include the Bach and Vivaldi pieces, because they more effectively conveyed the structure of a fugue with which Resnais composed his images. As René Prédal has pointed out:

> Resnais a appelé plusieurs fois L"Année dermière à Marienbad une comédie musicale sans chanson. Telle une fugue, le film développe un thème principal plusieurs fois repris et auquel s'ajoutent, au milieu de quelques diversions, ses contraires. L'harmonie entre les plans est d'ailleurs presque la seule justification du montage puisque le rhthme est plus important que les divers degrès de réalité des choses montrées.[68]

Thus, events in the film become musical moments: the breaking of the balustrade, A's tying her shoelace, the Nim game, the garden pose, the breaking of the glass in the big hall. All of these themes are conceived in musical terms, first suggested, then developed, then negated through counterpoint and developed again. And, in the text which conveys such moments, the speech always aspires to be a chant and not to faithfully reproduce the nuances of everyday speech:

> Il y a dans Marienbad une structure de poème musical, une valeur incantative du texte qui se répète, un ton de récitatif qui correspond à l'Opéra. A tout instant on a l'impression que les personnages pourraient s'arrêter de parler et continuer leur texte en chantant.[69]

Thus, the deliberate repetitions in the text, which both evoke the past ("une fois de plus...") and project the future ("demain je serai..."), are musically expressive more than they are linguistically communicative. The fusion of verb tenses between the past and the present, like the fusion of personal pronouns in Hiroshima, is not only an attempt at playing simultaneously with two different time frames, but also an attempt to fuse "voices" and to create a more fluid point of view. Resnais's use of poets and novelists whose texts are poetic enough to match the lyricism that he seeks in his imagery is a desire to convey music directly in the images. In other words, as Prédal has pointed out, Resnais seeks to transform music from the sound track to the image track.

> Chaque film, tout en renouvelant les références musicales, reste donc fidèle à un ton très particulier, Resnais tentant, si l'on peut dire, de faire passer la musique de la bande son à l'image elle-même.[70]

Resnais has continued his experiments with recitatives and his desire to make film as one would make opera in Muriel (1963), La Guerre est finie (1966) and Je t'aime je t'aime (1968). In Muriel, the use of music to convey strangeness or distance (the song of Ernest, the soprano solo of Ruth Streich, the harshness of the Henze score) are in direct contrast with the muted colors and faded emotions of the images and text. Ropars-Willeumier sees in Muriel an even stronger indication on the part of Resnais to de-emphasize the spoken word by emphasizing the role of voice and sound than he had achieved in either Hiroshima or Marienbad:

> Muriel se voit sans aucune participation affective, dans une gène qui ramène la passion au plan de l'esprit; non que tout lyrisme en soit absent, mais après l'avoir longtemps confié à la parole, Resnais le relègue maintenant, comme dans l'opéra, au seul support de la voix et de sons.[71]

The introduction of color in Muriel transforms the orientation of the film from that of time to that of space, and the lyrical recitatives produced in the spoken texts of Hiroshima and Marienbad are here produced by the use of natural and unnatural sounds (the traffic of the city versus Streich's soprano, for example). There is also a switch in aesthetic emphasis in Muriel. As Resnais has stated:

> J'espère que mon film se rattache un peu à un certain esprit du musichall...Si Hiroshima était du côté d'Edith Piaf, Muriel se rapprocherait, si j'ai réussi, de Jacques Brel.[72]

In Je t'aime je t'aime, after the opening choral from a Russian liturgical Mass, the musical score is geared to reproduce the mental sound track of Claude Ridder's mind. Natural sounds and unnatural sounds are fused in Je t'aime je t'aime, the former evoking certain memories for Ridder and the latter simulating the mechanism of memory itself. Indeed, the musical text is perhaps the only text with any continuity in the film. Where the visuals simultaneously reveal real scenes, relived scenes, remembered scenes and imagined scenes, the sound track provides the reader/viewer with the clues necessary to read those images. For example, Ridder seems to commit suicide twice. He shoots himself in Catrine's bedroom, but he falls to the ground at Crespel; however, the second suicide is reproduced with the sounds of underwater bubbles and water-breathing that characterized Ridder's entry into the past from the time machine, as if his suicide were a return to that moment and thus to the time machine. Critics and audiences alike were seemingly unable to adapt to this kind of aural text structuring the visual text, and, thus, Je t'aime je t'aime remains Resnais's most difficult and least appreciated film to date.

Yet, in his critcal pronouncements, Resnais has consistently pointed to the musical structuring of his film texts. Again, his aspirations have always been toward film-opera, the total art work and art form.

> I should like above all to react against the traditional structure of the theatre, against the tone of the so-called psychological drama. What I should like to discover is a certain lyrical tone, that is to say, in fact, to end up with opera.[73]

> Je suis fascine par le lyrique, l'Opéra.[74]

> Le cinéma fera des opéras.[75]

If Resnais's prophecy is ever realized, then film will have to admit new genres which are not based on content but on new techniques and on a fusion of other art forms.

Agnes Varda has also been interested in fusing the techniques of the other arts in film. For Varda, whether the music be that of original and popular songs with lyrics or that of classical music, the ultimate aspiration is one of juxtaposing painting, poetry and music. Thus, the use of chapter headings in L'Opéra mouffe (1958) is related to the language of music:

> Je procédais par têtes de chapitres: de la grossesse, des envies, de l'alcoolisme, etc. Suivant ce que je filmais, je savais dans quelle catégorie ça entrait, ou ca s'accrochait. C'était comme de grandes lignes mélodiques.[76]

At times, the lyrics of the song "L'Opéra Mouffe," which was composed especially for the film, provide an ironic comment on the emotions of the pregnant woman, as when the song reflects the banality of having a baby, while the visuals poeticize and exaggerate the importance of pregnancy through very striking metaphors: a sliced pumpkin, a tree bark, a sliced piece of fruit, a cabbage plant. At other times, the song becomes more subjective and seems to speak for the silent woman, as when the words of the song effectively convey the anguish that the woman feels toward the world surrounding her.

In _Cléo de 5 à 7_, Varda achieves an even more complex juxtaposition of painting and music. In terms of painting, Varda has asserted:

> Je voudrais...que cette histoire touche les gens comme me touche les peintures de Baldung Grien, où l'on voit de superbes femmes blondes et nues enlacées par des squelettes...Cléo, c'est une jeune femme nue qu'enlace un squelette et ensuite c'est le regard de cette femme.[77]

The majority of the images in _Cléo_ are of the streets and shops of Paris. The reconstruction of these outdoor shots toward an interior vision of Cléo is accomplished through the use of a violin and a metronome on the sound track.

> Il m'a paru intéressant de faire sentir ces mouvements vivants et inégaux, comme une respiration altérée, à l'intérieur d'un temps réel, dont les secondes se mesurent sans fantaisie.
>
> Je voudrais qu'on écoute en même temps les variations du violon et le métronome.[78]

The sound track, thus, approximates the body and mind (point of view) of Cléo. The fluctuations in the metronome are fluctuations in Cléo's heart and pulse, and the modulations in length and volume of the violin simulate the different rates of breathing or thinking of Cléo. This sound track is so unobtrusive, however, that the spectator who sees _Cléo_ for the first time may easily miss these associations. Such a spectator probably grasps the objective-subjective interplay only through the _placardage_, that is to say, the use of signs which refer both to objective reality ("pompes funèbres," for example) and to

Cléo's psychic state.

Both the painting and the music in Le Bonheur (1965) are outside of the film's characters; they are, in a sense, a secret shared between Varda and the audience. Just as Carol Reed and Graham Green had effectively imposed counterpoint from without in The Third Man (1949) (the diagonal camera angles on the image track, the musical themes for the main characters on the sound track), so also Varda injects counterpoint from without, perhaps even more formalistically than Reed and Greene. Francois and Emilie in Le Bonheur are not aware of the impressionistic colors with which Varda paints them. Emilie is not aware that she becomes an identical replacement for the dead wife when her colors go from blue and purple to orange and gold. Similarly, these characters are not aware of the Mozart sound track, which makes "light" of their easy happiness. Indeed, the sincerity of the characters is reinforced by the fact that subjectivity has been imposed from outside and not from within. Even the slightest hint that such characters might have more than one way to look at what is happening to them would destroy the thesis of the film. Le Bonheur is, thus, a companion piece to Cléo. Counterpoint in both is a sharing of privileged information between the author and the audience. The sharing in Cléo is more emotional, since it allows us to see the world from Cléo's eyes and to feel what she is going through. The sharing in Le Bonheur, by contrast, is more objective and critical, since we are given more keys to perceiving the characters (the impressionistic colors and the Mozart music) than the characters, themselves, have. Continually experimenting with forms and techniques transposed from the other arts, Varda seems as interested as Resnais in achieving the total art work and the total art form.

The virtuosity of the camera movements and editing of photo-stills in Chris Marker's La Jetée (1963) may blind the viewer to the very subtle sound track. But this sound track, like the images, is geared to documenting and bringing life to the poetic text recited by Jean Negroni. By itself, the text reads like a poem in prose. That poem acquires the density of a novel and justifies Marker's calling it a "photo-roman" through the images and the musical score. There were nearly 1200 photos taken for the film. The caesurae between past, present and future derive from the fact that the images are those of photo-stills, not of film footage per se. Those caesurae are mollified and made more fluid, for the purposes of the protagonist's time travel, through the camera zooms and the use of lap dissolves in the editing. Thus, the camera zooms in to build up a scene and to denote the protagonist's entry upon that scene, as in the zoom-in on the photos of a reconstructed Paris. The camera zooms out to create detachment and cut off a particular time frame, as when the text announces that the protagonist suddenly felt a barrier between him and the woman, the camera's zooming out effectively creating the impact of that barrier. The dissolves are even more audacious. For example, at one point the text says that the woman sometimes leaned on the protagonist, and a lap dissolve conveys this leaning. We see the woman's head tilted in the "past" and this image is superimposed with an image of the protagonist with blinders on in the underground camp, his head effectively where it would have been, were the woman really leaning on him in the past.

Less noticeable but just as effective are the manipulations of the sound track, both while the narrator recites and when he is silent. A religious choir both begins and ends the film, creating a sense of past-ness, which like the photo-stills is timeless. The narrator's voice fills up the body proper of the film, but Marker creates rhythm, not only in the voice itself, but also in the silences between narrations. During those silences or "pedal points," the spectator becomes especially aware of natural sounds or of the use of violins in the musical score of Trevor Duncan. Except for the open and closing "choir" passages, the most evident use of music is in the romantic theme developed in the museum sequence. Thus, the sounds of intermittent whispering or thumping heartbeats "punctuate" the film as much as the rhythmic cutting of the stills, and both are in contrapuntal contrast to the flow of the reciter's words. The sound of airplanes establishes the "presence" of the jetty at Orly. Similarly, the sound of crickets poetically parallels the woman's blinking eyes in the minute or so of actual film in _La Jetée_.

Thus, it would be a mistake to underestimate the importance of music in the films of Chris Marker. As one critic of Marker has written:

> Aime la radio beaucoup. Aime la littérature plus que la radio. Aime le cinéma plus que la littérature. Aime la musique plus que tout.[79]

But perhaps the most ambitious musician in the _cinéma des auteurs_, even more audacious than Resnais, has turned out to be Alain Robbe-Grillet. One might even postulate that the key to understanding all of Robbe-Grillet's so-called puzzle-films is a close "reading" of the musical text. It is not just that Robbe-Grillet extensively uses counterpoint between the images and the spoken text or that he builds his narrative on the basis of a theme with multiple variations (and multiple interpretations). It is also that he accords a predominant role to the entire sound track.

For example, L'Immortelle (1962) begins with a long tracking shot of the "ruins" and reconstructed buildings of Istanbul and the music of a popular Turkish song. Both the camera and the song give way abruptly to the sound of a woman's scream and the crashing of metal. The viewer later learns that the scream belongs to Lale and the metal crashing is the automobile accident. N, the narrator, experiences this accident at least once with L and perhaps several times, since both the images and the sounds of the accident are repeated four or five times. N even experiences the same accident without L in the car. However, at the time of the accident, the sound track brings L back, and her scream is heard again. This use of the sound track to denote subjective point of view (N's) and to foreshadow both the images and the spoken text is an elaboration of that used in Hiroshima, when the bells of Saint-Etienne at Nevers were heard in the opening images of Hiroshima.

In L'Immortelle the camera eye is also the narrator's eye. The N we see in the film is a visual projection of the unseen N who narrates. Thus, the images and the spoken text are often distorted by the subjective visions or hallucinations of the camera-narrator. Robbe-Grillet has indicated the narrator's function in the film in the following way:

> Pourquoi un N? Sans doute est-ce pour indiquer sa position très particulière dans le récit, qui est un peu comparable à celle du

> NARRATEUR dans un roman moderne: narrateur qui ne "raconte" rien, mais par les yeux de qui tout est vu, par les oreilles de qui tout est entendu, ou par l'esprit de qui tout est imaginé. Et c'est là ce qui lui donne, lorsqu'il est présent sur l'écran, cet aspect à la fois vide et gauche, qui n'est évidemment pas celui d'un "héros" de cinéma. De même se trouve-t-il le plus souvent, quant au cadrage, au montage, etc. en état d'erreur technique ou de "maladresse".[80]

Thus, subjectivity may be indicated by what N sees within a single image or a cluster of images. But it is usually in what he hears, that is to say, in a continuous musical sound track that disregards the images and the spoken text, that an extended sequence of subjective vision is portrayed. Perhaps the most striking example in _L'Immortelle_ of such an extended _hallucination vraie_ is the sequence of the Turkish belly dance.

The sequence begins in the market. N and L are walking away. The camera follows them. As they leave the arcade, the camera backtracks and comes to rest on a pillar, upon which is pasted an advertisement for a nightclub with a photo of a half-naked belly dancer.

> Mais elle (la caméra) découvre aussi, en premier plan, un panneau où sont placardées des affiches de spectacles érotiques, avec en particulier des photos de danseuses a moitié nues...

In terms of the image track, this photo is the trigger for all the subjective tableaux shots which follow. Those shots are discontinuously edited. As soon as the photo is clearly visible, the Turkish belly dance music begins on the sound track and the camera cuts. While the camera will continue to cut, the music will remain on the track. In other words, where the images are discontinuous, the musical track is sustained throughout the sequence.

Thus, the next image is that of a "live" belly dancer in the exact posture of the photo on the pillar. We have either jumped time and space frames or we have entered more deeply into N's subjective-camera visions. As the sequence develops, we realize that both are true. Robbe-Grillet's technique of bringing a painting or a photograph to life or, conversely, making a "still life" from already moving characters in Dans le labyrinthe is extended in L'Immortelle. From the belly dancer in the same posture she held in the photo on the pillar, the camera cuts to a reaction shot of all the men in the darkly-lit club. These men are stone-faced and totally immobilized. On an objective plane, it is certainly plausible that these men should be petrified or mesmerized by the erotic scene before them. On a more subjective plane, their immobility is a measure of contrast between them and the dancer or, more importantly, between them and N and L. N, the subjective narrator, foregrounds what he wants emphasized in his visions. Thus, what most attracts his attention in a scene may move. The rest of the scene, which is drawn to scale in an approximation of real-life proportions, is kept immobile.

As the camera shifts back to the dancer, the music figures more prominently. The increase in music volume is an effective device for further foregrounding, for it shuts out the image of the immobilized men. The focus is on the dancer and her music. As she turns her back to the audience(that is, to the camera-eye) she becomes transfixed. The camera shifts to reveal N and L, who have just arrived. N stands transfixed before the sight of the dancer while L looks anxiously at him, an indication of N's erotic obsessions.

The music mirrors his obsessions when it continues to dominate the sound track as N seats L at a table. Here, a different kind of foregrounding takes place. In the background of the frame, the dancer's bare back is still very visible. In the foreground of the frame, N continues to stand after having seated L. L is wearing a bare-backed dress, so that her figure becomes a kind of silhouette of the dancer's figure. N puts his hand on L's neck and gently squeezes it, an indication of his desire to do the same thing to the dancer. It is also an indication of the way in which he would like to perceive L, as if the dancer were a projection of N's vision of L. The frame is complicated by the fact that, while N, L and the dancer are all seen from the back, there is a man between their table and the stage who turns to stare directly at L. This man has appeared before in connection with the fat man who owns the two dogs. As if he were sent by the fat man to spy on L, this man disregards the stage and stares at L, a further indication that the "stage" may be illusory.

At this point, Robbe-Grillet injects an ingenious variation upon his theme. As long as the dance music corresponded to a photo of a dancer or a decor in which the dancer could be expected to be found, the music seemed to accompany the visuals. Now the music clearly accompanies the narrator's vision, for the camera shifts from the club to the street. Street sounds are added to the belly dance music, and that dance music is softened. N and L are in the same posture they were in the club: L is seated on a bench, N stands behind with his hand on L's neck. However, their costumes have changed. N, for example, wears the polo shirt and dress pants he wore in the scene on the beach. The street is a re-take of a previous view of the street. N and L now face the camera. Their exchange of dialogue reinforces the subjective quality of the image.

L. C'est aussi pour les touristes, vous voyez bien.
N. Mais il n'y a pas de touristes.
L. Il y a vous et moi.
N. Ni moi, ni vous. Je me demande bien ce que vous faites à Istanboul...
L. Je me promène avec vous...
N. Et le reste du temps?
L. Je vous attends, mon seigneur. Qu'est-ce que vous voulez que l'on fasse ici? Vous voyez bien que ce n'est pas une vraie ville...C'est un décor d'opérette, pour une histoire d'amour.

L's last response refers both to the legendary Byzantium of harems and kept women ("Je vous attends, mon seigneur") and to the Istanbul of post cards for tourists ("C'est aussi pour les touristes"), both of which are subjective falsifications of an elusive objective reality. The tension between the objective(natural sounds of the streets) and the subjective (continuation of the belly dance music) is effectively reproduced on the sound track.

N goes to kiss L and she refuses, saying there are people watching. Indeed, the camera reveals a woman in the window of one of the houses who watches, then disappears. It is an excellent transition device for Robbe-Grillet, for N's erotic obsessions are equalled by his paranoia about being seen. In addition, the visual of the woman in the window permits Robbe-Grillet to move his camera up to that window, that is, to change point of view. The camera now looks down on L and N in the street, even while its particular angle of vision duplicates that of N looking out his window in the opening shots of the film. That switch in camera angle is a psychological statement about N. He is a voyeur, and the fear of every voyeur is the fear of being watched. Having taken the place of the woman at the window, N turns from the window in his own apartment to L who is already in the room with him. The street sounds are gone and the belly dance music resumes its normal volume. L genuflects and assumes the same posture she had in the mosque. She begins to let her hair down and to take off her dress. The camera shifts to the face of N; his facial expression is identical to that in the club. Significantly, Robbe-Grillet indicates a shift in the music at this point. It becomes less sensual and less provocative. It becomes more irritating, both to indicate N's heightened arousal and the climax of the sequence. The camera shifts back to L, resuming the position of N's eyes. L is still on her knees and in her undergarments. She begins to undulate and reproduce the dance of the belly dancer. The identification of L with the dancer, suggested in the club with the mirrored image of the two bare backs, is now complete. N's desire is actualized.

What holds these disparate images together (the market, the club, the street, N's apartment) is the continuation of the belly dance music throughout the sequence. Without that music, the spectator would have much more difficulty in determining the relative objectivity or subjectivity of the images. The example just described is the most elaborate of the film, but it is only one of many. The film's aspirations toward opera are clearly indicated by the characters ("C'est un décor d'opérette"). Maurice LeRoux has also indicated the importance of the musical structure in L'Immortelle:

> Depuis <u>Hiroshima</u> et surtout avec <u>L'Immortelle</u>, il semble que l'art lyrique contemporain ouvre sur quelque chose qui n'est plus fragmentaire; grace à ce film, nous sommes en train de découvrir des ensembles cohérents qui désormais différent fondamentalement d'un cinéma - art de divertissement, conception tout à fait valable du reste. Appellons-les: spectacles musicaux, nouveaux opéras, films-opéras...en tout cas il s'agit d'un art audio-visuel de méditation dont la structure est musicale.[81]

The use of the musical sound track to reproduce the protagonist's interior visions is even more elaborate and more audacious in Robbe-Grillet's <u>L'Homme qui ment</u> (1968). Here, electronic music (sounds produced through an oscillating chamber) reproduce the thought waves of Boris Varissa/Jean Robin. Natural sounds, once they have been established as such, gradually merge with the abstract electronic sounds. For example, the film opens with shots of Boris running through the woods, being chased and shot at by Nazi soldiers. Thereafter, these gunshots reappear in the film, even though there are no guns visible in the images. Boris breaks a glass in the inn. Once the sound of the glass shattering is synchronized with the image of the glass shattering, those sounds become liberated in terms of their use or fixed in terms of their effect upon the protagonist. Thus, Boris seems to hear/contemplate the glass shattering in his room in the inn when he raises an imaginary glass (his hand is empty), drinks from it and then throws it to the floor. We again hear glass shattering at the chateau, even when there is no glass. Boris confronts Maria, the maid, in the bell-tower at the chateau. Those bells, once their sound has been established with their visual presence, become another mental leitmotiv. Thus, Boris repeatedly hears bells ringing when there are no bells to be seen.

Just as _Hiroshima_ could be broken down into a classification of themes ("oubli, " "corps," "Nevers," etc.), so too _L'Homme qui ment_ can be read on the basis of its leitmotivs: the gunshots, the glass shattering, the bells. The basic difference is that in the latter film these sounds are given realistic referents and then used anti-realistically; that is, as gauges of the protagonist's mechanism of thought, invention and memory, all of which are highly unreliable, as the title of the film would indicate. In addition, such aural leitmotivs create a complex network of associations and foreshadowings of future time or events, as when the glass shattering leads to an image of the balustrade breaking, which breaking Boris then "arranges" for the death of Jean Robin's father as a necessary step in the seduction of Robin's wife. Such associations and foreshadowings have, in addition, a boomerang effect, in the sense that all of Boris Varissa's invented visions are ultimately actualized. Thus, he invents the name of a doctor to convince the three women of his story at the film's beginning. That doctor surprises Varissa by appearing in the flesh at the time of the father's death. A snapshot of Jean Robin that Varissa sees in the pharmacy reappears as the "real" Jean Robin entering the study to shoot Boris.

With _L'Homme qui ment_, Robbe-Grillet successfully raises the sound track to the importance of the images. It is a film that must be read aurally as well as visually. The subjective hallucinations of the protagonist on the image track are both reinforced by and explained by the musical leitmotivs on the sound track. The _cinéma des auteurs_ has progressed a long way towards achieving the total art work and total art form with a film like L'Homme qui ment.

In her own way, Marguerite Duras has also advanced that progression. Significantly, for Duras the image track and the musical score are both assimilated in the spoken text. Thus, there are no rapid changes of scene, as one might expect in a film based on one of her novels or plays. The transitions between scenes are arbitrarily created through editing, but the justification for such changes is in the characters' lines, which often precede a scene or overlap onto a following scene. In the same way, there are few purely musical additions to the sound track, since the music is already contained in the recitatives of the characters. Yet, the structure is clearly musical and not simply poetic or linguistic. As Judith Gollub has noted of Peter Brook's adaptation of Moderato Cantabile:

> Moderato Cantabile, quoique mis en scène par un professionnel, transforme le roman qui était pur chant et fugue lyrique, en portrait de femme hystérique.[82]

Duras's apprenticeship was with Resnais on Hiroshima. In that film, the musical themes with variations paralleled the four long poem-fugues of the spoken text. The equal status of image, text and music in that film was due to Resnais who wanted a highly "literary" work at the same time that he wanted to go beyond both film and literature in heightening realism in all three domains:

> Dans son effort pour saisir à la fois tous les aspects de la réalité, le langage de Resnais ouvre la voie d'un opéra narratif, qui correspondrait à de très anciens appels de la littérature, cherchant en vain une expression de la simultanéité.[83]

Resnais thus parallels Robbe-Grillet's wish to play upon all the spectator's senses simultaneously. Duras has the same desire, with the difference that she condenses the various texts into one text: the spoken text. Thus, a film like _La Musica_ (1967) or _Jaune le soleil_ (1970) places an inordinate amount of importance upon the dialogues between characters. These films are operas without notes. The lines of the characters are chanted rather than spoken, and the full amplification or orchestration of these chants must come solely from the voice delivery of the actors. Thus, Duras spends a great deal of time rehearsing with her actors, not the _what_ of their lines but the _how_.

There is no music per se in _Détruire dit-elle_ (1969); yet, the film must be read musically. The film is a chant in four "voices" and the four characters embody those voices more than they embody any distinct personalities or any psychological motivations. At the film's conclusion, however, Duras resorts to sound to convey the terror and the power of the future. The three "wandering Jews" sit at the table and listen as the sounds emanating from the mysterious forest are those of drums, beating louder and louder. They eventually drown the dialogue exchanges of the characters. All the measured stasis of the film's previous images and spoken text are broken in the explosion of the drums. Those drums effectively elevate Duras to the level of experimentation of a Resnais or a Robbe-Grillet. With them, Duras clearly indicates the coming of the revolution.

> Et la musique - pour que ça prenne tout son sens. C'est la révolution, la musique. J'ai dù la massacrer jusqu'au bout.[84]

D. The Theme of Time

> "Pourquoi nier l'évidente nécessité de la mémoire?"
>
> -Riva in *Hiroshima mon amour*

In both literature and film, the problems in expanding time exploration are related to problems of narration and to the particular limitations on narration inherent in each medium. As George Bluestone has asserted,[85] space in the novel must be conveyed by moving from one point in time to another point in time, while time in film must be conveyed by moving from one point in space to another point in space. Christian Metz, in a similar vein, has noted the peculiarities of narration as it applies to both description and to images:

> L'une des fonctions du récit est de monnayer un temps dans un autre temps, et que c'est par là que le récit se distingue de la description (qui monnaye un espace dans un temps), ainsi que de l'image (qui monnaye un espace dans un autre espace).[86]

Literature must go to great lengths to convey spatial movement. Language may describe movement, but it cannot capture it. By contrast, there is seemingly nothing easier for a film camera: a simple pan or tilt captures movement, whether anything within the frame moves or not. Yet, by a simple switch in verb tense, literature can convey different time periods. Consider, for example, the following sentence: "If I had not come, you would not have remained here, but since I did come, you are going to stay." If I say that sentence, I express four different time frames. Film is seemingly incapable of such flexibility: thus, the artificiality of most film flashbacks, which are often awkwardly achieved (since they call attention to themselves) and which are ultimately unsuccessful (since, once they are achieved, they function as if in the present tense). The act of narration always involves some degree of artifice in both media. Thus, Jean-Paul Sartre has pointed out:

> Le réel ne raconte jamais d'histoires; le souvenir, parce qu'il est un récit, est pleinement imaginaire; un événement doit être en quelque façon terminé pour que--et avant que--sa narration puisse commencer.[87]

Sartre, thus, effectively demonstrates the inherent weakness in narration in both literature and film. The tyranny in the novel is the tyranny of the past tense. The present may be simulated (by verbs in the present tense, indicative mood, active voice), but it is an illusory present. The reader always assumes that the narrator knows the conclusion of his narration, and, thus, even though that narrator may pretend that events unfold in the present, the reader instinctively senses that those events are really in the past. By contrast, the artifice of narration in film is the tyranny of the present tense. A film may simulate the past tense only by rendering it in the present tense, because of the emphasis on motion in film and the ever-present orientation toward spatial relationships. This tyranny need not be seen as completely disadvantageous, however, for, even though film cannot effectively reproduce an objective past tense, its capabilities for rendering mental time and the subjective past tense (dreams, imaginations, memories, lies) seem infinite. As Marcel Martin has pointed out:

> Toute image filmique est donc au présent. C'est là un fait particulièrement important si l'on songe que tout le contenu de notre conscience est toujours au présent, aussi bien nos

> souvenirs que nos rêves: on sait en effet que le principal travail de la mémoire réside dans la localisation précise, dans le temps et dans l'espace, des schèmes dynamiques que sont les souvenirs; d'autre part les rêves sont étroitement déterminés (dans leur surgissement mais non dans leur contenu) par l'actualité de notre être physique et psychique et le cas des cauchemars montre bien que le contenu de nos rêves est d'abord perçu comme "présent." Cela permet de comprendre la facilité avec laquelle le cinéma peut exprimer le rêve.[88]

It seems paradoxical, then, that film, which must resort to illusion to convey the past in terms of content, should be so cursed by the past in terms of technology. It is fairly obvious that, if one records his voice on a tape recorder in the present, it immediately becomes past. He can play it back in the present, but his recording is one of a past moment. Similarly, a film may record an event in progress, which is to say that it may record the present. But the moment that film is projected, it becomes a projection of the past. Indeed, the fascination of many documentaries is that of seeing the past "come to life" again. We know that the events filmed have already taken place, but we willingly suspend disbelief and perceive them in the present for the duration of the film. Thus, we might add that a classic film necessarily ages more than a classical novel. As Susan Sontag has noted:

> This youngest of the arts is also the most heavily burdened with memory. Cinema is a time machine. Movies preserve the past, while theatres--no matter how devoted to the classics, to old plays--can only "modernize" . . . The historical particularity of the reality registered on celluloid is so vivid that practically all films older than four or five years are saturated with pathos.[89]

Alain Resnais's and Jean Cayrol's <u>Nuit et brouillard</u> was made in 1955. It could have been made in 1974 or 1990, because there is little in the film to date it: there are no actors and thus no hair styles, no dress codes, no dialogue to pinpoint the film as belonging to 1955. Cayrol's text is similarly timeless, because it is poetic: it does not attempt to reproduce everyday speech. And, because those exterior clues are absent in the film, the film effectively conveys the past, even though rendering it present, all the while not dating itself in a predetermined and dated present. In addition, because of the peculiar spatial properties of the medium, it explores time spatially. In other words, it transforms time into space without sacrificing the emphasis on temporality. As the German filmmaker, Jean-Marie Straub, recently pointed out: "Tout l'art du cinématographe n'est autre chose que l'application de l'espace au temps."[90]

There has perhaps been no coherent group of filmmakers who have made time as essential a theme in their films as has the _cinéma des auteurs_. The discussion which follows is an attempt to trace the various ways in which Alain Resnais, Jean Cayrol, Agnes Varda, Chris Marker, Marguerite Duras and Alain Robbe-Grillet have developed the theme of time in their films: how they have incorporated literature in their filmic treatment of time, how they have exploited to the fullest the subjective possibilities of film's "present tense," and how they have avoided "aging" through anti-realistic devices and through a spatialization of time. To that end, I will discuss the following films: Resnais's _Hiroshima mon amour_ (1959), _L'Année dernière à Marienbad_ (1961), and _Je t'aime je t'aime_ (1968); Agnes Varda's _Cléo de 5 à 7_ (1962); Chris Marker's _La Jetée_ (1963), Alain Robbe-Grillet's _L'Immortelle_ (1962) and _L'Homme qui ment_ (1968); and Marguerite Duras's _Détruire dit-elle_

(1969).

The theme of time has always been the most important theme in the films of Alain Resnais. An assiduous reader of Proust, Resnais "adapted" Proust's Les Yeux d'Albertine in 16 millimeter in 1945. Like Proust's fictional narrator in A la recherche du temps perdu, Resnais's characters in his feature films are neither free to remember nor to forget. They are "victims" in a sense of Proust's mémoire involuntaire or "involuntary memory." It goes without saying then that there are two kinds of time at work in the films of Resnais: objective, usually historical time (World War Two in Nuit et brouillard and Hiroshima, the Algerian war in Muriel), and mental time, which reflects the historical time upon an individual consciousness. This second and more subjective time always overrides the first, distorting time from clock chronology to personal meditation. As André Téchiné has pointed out:

> Le ton que prend Resnais en narrant ses récits ressemble fort à celui de quelque personne remuant dans sa mémoire ou dans son imagination, transformant toutes choses, insistant à chaque instant sur le fait que tout ne fût que provisoire et sans conséquences.[91]

This mental time assumes a restructuring of logic, of narrative flow, of emphasis upon thought over action. As Resnais has stated:

> For me, the film is an attempt, still very crude and primitive, to approach the complexity of thought, its mechanism . . . I believe that, in life, we do not think chronologically, that our decisions never correspond to an ordered logic.[92]

The first time evoked in Hiroshima is the historical time filtered through the biased eyes of a false eye-witness. What the

French woman has seen of Hiroshima is not the event of the bombing but the results: the newsreels, the museum, the reports of the victims. When the Japanese says to her, "Tu n'as rien vu à Hiroshima," he is referring to the fact that she, herself, did not live through Hiroshima. The film, then, evolves into another time, specifically the time that she did live through at Nevers. When Riva sees Okada's hand and associates it with the dead German's hand, we are in the presence of mémoire involuntaire, quite similar to Proust's network of associations triggered by the madeleine.

The Japanese senses the importance of Nevers to the understanding of Riva in the present. Consequently, he assumes the role if interrogator. Riva answers his questions unwillingly at first, but gradually both accept a false premise: the Japanese will ask questions and answer questions as if he were the German lover at Nevers. With this tacit agreement, never stated in the film, Riva submerges herself in the past. Film time in Hiroshima, thus, becomes mental time, the time of Riva's memories which gradually infect the present, so that when we see shots of the Hiroshima streets, they cannot be interpreted objectively, since Riva's voix intérieure dominates the sound track and constantly interprets the present in terms of the past.

The easy temptation for Resnais and Marguerite Duras would have been to construct a chronological past at Nevers, beginning with Riva's meeting the German soldier and ending with Riva riding off on her bicycle for Paris on the eve of the declaration of peace. Instead, the authors insisted on a past which would reproduce the disordered logic and reordering of chronology characteristically found in memories and dreams. Riva remembers by instinct, not by date.

Rene Predal has pointed out that Riva's memories of Nevers correspond to three distinct periods in the present: the bedroom, the cafe and again at another cafe. Those memories, for the most part, have very little do do with the German soldier alive. Rather, they "assume" his death and instead concentrate upon the punishment of Riva in the cellar with her head shaven. Thus, the first memory in each series emphasizes either the shaving of the head or the exile in the cellar: Riva with her head shaven in the cellar is the first memory in terms of the film, but it would be sixth, were one to reconstruct all memories chronologically. The first memory of the cafe remembrances, the shaving of her hair, is significant in that it is fourth in terms of the order of the film and also fourth in terms of real chronology, just as the last memory (her departure from Nevers) in the film is also the last memory in terms of real chronology. The equivalency in both is an emphasis of their psychic impact on Riva, the shaving of her hair at Nevers being repeated in her observations of the fallen hair of the women at the time of the bombing of Hiroshima, and her leaving Nevers being repeated in her anxieties about leaving Hiroshima. Resnais and Duras succeed in evoking both the present (which is already past) at Hiroshima and the past at Nevers which conditions that present by concentrating on "dead" time. Time is the tension between two events. An etenity seems to pass for Riva in the cellar, although, in reality, it was less than a year. An eternity seems to go by from that point in the film at which both Riva and Okada acknowledge that they have "sixteen hours to kill." "Dead" time refers to the time between events, the time perceived mentally and subjectively. As Jean Cayrol has pointed out:

> Or, le cinéma n'est véritablement un art que s'il se rend capable de témoigner, non seulement pour notre temps, mais pour les temps morts entre les événements; s'il restitue au temps son travail, son attente quand les hommes ne sont pas arrivés ou sont partis précipitamment; s'il raconte aussi des histoires qui ne sont pas historiques; s'il sait prendre l'Histoire aux moments ou émeutiers et historiens s'en détournent.[93]

Riva and Okada fill up those sixteen hours with the past. But, in reliving that past, they cease to act; rather, they react: they meditate. Time, the domain of memory, becomes the equal of space, the domain of movement and action. Resnais and Duras overcome the tyranny of the present tense in film by making an avowed past the entire present. If there is distance between Nevers and Hiroshima at the beginning of the film, there is none by the middle of the film. Riva comes to inhabit Nevers again, and, in so doing, she makes the past live again:

> Il faut faire entrer l'actualité dans le temps, c'est-à-dire en chercher les suites, les remords, les prolongements, l'existence persistante en marge d'une actualité renouvelée.[94]

Realizing that the image, nevertheless, corresponds to the present tense, unless that image is fixed (freeze-frames, photo-stills), Resnais and Duras counterbalance that image with a highly literary text: "L'image ne peut être que l'état présent d'un passé: seule la parole peut conjuguer."[95] To allow for more fluidity between Nevers and Hiroshima, Resnais composed his images so that Riva and Okada very seldom look directly at each other. The equivalent of that technique in the text of Duras is the use of voice-over narration. Characters are not present in the image when this narration takes place. When they are present, they are walking or simply looking; they are not speaking. This emphasis on dialogue (the text) over description (the camera) is a victory over the artifice of narration in film, since time thus explored appears more authentic, more "alive":

> Le cinéma essaie de s'éloigner de la fiction en substituant le temps du dialogue à celui de la description: le son direct à la voix, par exemple, d'un récitant invisible. Parole et image étant synchrones, et leur montage n'apparaissant pas clairement au spectateur, celui-ci est en mesure de croire que le temps véridique lui est présenté dans son exactitude mécanique . . .[96]

The poetic text of Duras triumphs over the present tense in that it renders both past and present subjectively from the point of view of Riva's mental time; thus, the boundaries between past and present are at least partially dissolved. The images remain present, because they involve movement. But the text renders them psychologically past. The text of Duras exploits literature's flexibility with verb tenses, and the film's images are an approximation of those verbs. Okada hears only the "description" of the past through the spoken (synchronous) words of Riva. The spectator hears her interior voice in addition, and the words of that interior voice are given body (the images).

The calculated ploy of the authors in the second half of the film is the slow merger of the two times. In a sense, time becomes diluted. More and more, the spoken text gives way to the interior voice of the woman. We hear more from her, while the Japanese hears less. The images give way in similar fashion. The longer takes of Hiroshima, involving walks during which Riva's interior voice communicates to us about Nevers but not to the Japanese, are balanced with the longer takes of Nevers, involving voiced commentary by Riva which is shared by both the Japanese and the spectator.

The "message" of Hiroshima, is there is one, seems to be the following: the only way around the past is through it. We continue to be haunted by the past until we relive it wholly and physically in the present. Indeed, the theme of time is succinctly developed at the very beginning of the film in a characteristically poetic and unrealistic exchange of dialogue:

> Elle: Ecoute-moi. Comme toi, je connais l'oubli.
> Lui: Non. Tu ne connais pas l'oubli.
> Elle: Comme toi, je suis douée de mémoire. Je connais l'oubli.
> Lui: Non. Tu n'es pas douée de mémoire.
> Elle: Comme toi, moi aussi, j'ai essayé de lutter de toutes mes forces contre l'oubli. Comme toi, j'ai oublié. Comme toi, j'ai désiré avoir une inconsolable mémoire. . . , une mémoire d'ombres et de pierres. J'ai lutté pour mon compte, de toutes mes forces, chaque jour, contre l'horreur de ne plus comprendre du tout le pourquoi du souvenir. Comme toi, j'ai oublié. Pourquoi nier l'évidente nécessité de la mémoire? . . . Ecoute-moi!

Memory is the link between the German lover and the Japanese lover

("Je te rencontre. Je me souviens de toi.") Memory precedes existence in a sense. Riva must "remember" the Japanese before she can love him. And loving him in turn insures her "forgetting" him. Memory is not a special talent for characters in the cinéma des auteurs; rather, it is a curse which must be overcome in order to live. Not overcoming that curse explains the inaction of so many characters in the cinéma des auteurs. This ode to amnesia in Hiroshima is echoed throughout the films of Resnais and the other directors of the cinéma des auteurs. As Anais Nin stated in her The Novel of the Future: "A child's forgetfulness helps him to live in the present." The child in Cayrol's La Frontière (1961) remembers similar advice from his mother: "Mon enfant, pour vivre il suffit de perdre la mémoire."[97] And Marguerite Duras said of Détruire dit-elle: "Si vous voulez, je parle d'un passage par le vide de l'homme. C'est qu'il oublie tout. Pour pouvoir recommencer."[98] When Riva says at the end of Hiroshima, "Je t'oublierai, je t'oublie déjà," she is speaking more to her dead German lover than to her present Japanese lover.

The final victory of Hiroshima over the present tense of the camera is the spatialization of time. Moments in time are juxtaposed in space: the hand on the bed in Hiroshima becomes the hand on the ground at Nevers. The past evoked by Riva's interior voice is visualized by a camera tracking the shots of Hiroshima by evening. The text "hollows out" the images by making them mental accessories, by transforming them from eventual to reflective:

> Les temps pleins creusés d'incertitude . . . n'évoquent plus l'action, mais les traces qu'elle laisse dans le personnage; or, cette rupture dramaturgique, qui met l'accent non plus sur le temps de l'événement mais sur la durée de l'homme, cette progressive implantation d'une structure proprement narrative n'est devenu perceptible que par la mise en relief de toutes les formes de mouvement qui permettent, au cinéma, de détacher le regard de l'image pour n'en suggérer que l'attente ou l'écho.[99]

Once hollowed out, these images can accurately reflect the temporality of the film. There can be no mistaking the spatialization of time in the film's closing lines, in which Riva identifies Okada as "Hiroshima" and Okada calls Riva "Nevers-en-France." The use of geography to name characters is a metaphor for the unspoken names of remembering and forgetfulness. Time is the tension between two events. It is also the distance ("dead" time) between two places. As André Téchiné has pointed out:

> La géographie resnaisienne stimule les grands voyages et fonde l'oeuvre entière. Au début il existe deux points isolés, tels Hiroshima et Nevers, Marienbad et le Reste, Boulogne et l'Algérie, Paris et l'Espagne. Chaque film raconte la distance qui unit et sépare ces lieux. Les derniers plans sont seuls décisifs: on quitte Hiroshima à l'aube, Marienbad à minuit, Boulogne au crépuscule et Paris en pleine lumière.[100]

The distance between two places is, thus, conveyed in terms of time: Hiroshima at dawn, Marienbad at midnight, Boulogne at twilight and Paris at noon.

L'Année dernière à Marienbad is even more audacious than *Hiroshima*, for both time and space are hypothetical: "last year" is probably an invention of the narrator, and Marienbad cannot be found on any maps. Robbe-Grillet insists that the time of the film is one hour and thirty-two minutes: the time of the film's running. There is no time and no space outside of those presented in the film. Thus, all time in Marienbad is mental time, and all time is visualized by being spatialized. Richard Blumenberg has pointed out three ways in which Resnais and Robbe-Grillet transform traditional film time:

> (1) the use of probability to suggest occurrence (rather than the use of possibility to convey actuality; (2) the use of paradox to imply the condition of relativity (rather than the use of linear time to determine "when" an event happened); (3) the use of tense juxtaposition to spatialize a temporal event (rather than the use of just the past tense to determine at what time an event in space occurred).[101]

There is the same interweaving of voice-over narration and dialogue in Marienbad that we traced in Hiroshima. In Hiroshima, however, the mental time of Nevers was given credibility by the historical event of Hiroshima. In Marienbad, there is no such credibility, for both past and present are fused in the mind of the narrator, who probably invents everything. That fusion suggests that time is cyclical. Resnais repeats the same images several times, and each time represents a cyclical return at the same time that it represents a new beginning. Blumenberg has commented on these shot repetitions:

> Resnais repeats the same shot (A on the bed with her arms up in defense) six times. Removed from the limitations and time-point sequence of narrative structure, the sequence projects the thematic idea of the emotion of fear from the rhythm of the shots. The rhythm carries the object as event (A's face and gesture as impending tragedy) to the emotion (fear) which both the rhythm and the image project, but which neither one projects individually through extended time. (The repeated shot is another way to use, and has a similar extra-chronological effect as, slow motion). It is not so much that "thought is externalized" as that the external (spatial) is internalized and temporalized.[102]

Repetition is a way to overcome the tyranny of the present tense in film. Even though the image presents movement, its repetition denies that movement: does A raise up her arms once or six times? Does A see only one picture in her drawer, as we might expect, or some fifty pictures of the same thing, as the image shows us?

Immobility is another way to combat the present tense. It is both a result of repetition and a contrast to it. There is often no sound when the spectator would expect to hear sound in Marienbad. Similarly, there is often no movement when the spectator could expect movement: the arrangement of the guests after the theatre performance, the same arrangement of the guests in fixed postures in the garden, with shadows when there should be no shadows.

> It is, however, exactly this fixity, this stability of positioning which, as the card game, is unbeatable, and which, as in the garden, existence loses meaning. To move into Memory is also to move into a world which needs Euclidean verification. This verification, which is form, however, can destroy.[103]

Where time is a dialectic (the tension between two events) in Hiroshima, time in Marienbad is spatial stasis (the two events become synonymous or identical). Everything is memory which transfixes in order to become real.

> Hence, all is Memory. For instance, in the famous shot in the Garden, the people are situated as chips or cards in a half-completed game of Nim. In one way or another, as chips or dominoes, as broken glass or as a pile of snapshots, or, finally, as torn bits of a letter, the disorder and the mathematical ordering of arranged pieces works in Memory . . . associatively.[104]

The tension in Marienbad is that between an X who creates a past and an A who struggles to disbelieve him. Tension is resolved when A's version of the past coincides with X's. At that point, "last year," which never existed, becomes this year: that is, last year is one hour and thirty-two minutes. The structural breaks in A's wall of memory are not linear but associative. The broken glass and the broken balustrade come to symbolize broken resistance. They negate the mathematical perfection of the Nim game. the garden poses, the torn bits of letter arranged in the Nim configuration. imilarly, when A stoops to tie her shoe in the garden, she "ties" her memory to that of X.

As long as X insists on a spatial memory (that is, insisting upon Marienbad), he cannot win. But the moment he begins to insist on time (that it was last year), A begins to succumb. She stammers: "Next year, here, the same day at the same hour . . . and I'll come with you, wherever you want." Without admitting to the past built up by X, A's projection into the future is a probability of the past (cyclical). Significantly, her stipulations are not spatial, but temporal. Neither X nor A believes in clock time, however, and any time indication is thus approximate and mythical. As X suggests: "But time, time doesn't count. I've come to take you away."

That this year at Marienbad is in reality last year unfolding is made evident by Robbe-Grillet's exploitation of literature's flexibility with verb tenses: "It would be a year ago that this story began . . . You wouldn't have been able to go on living among this _trompe l'oeil_ architecture, among these mirrors and these columns, among these doors always ajar, these stair-cases that are too long. . . In this bedroom always open."

Where Hiroshima moves into memory from the objective horrors of the war, Marienbad assumes memory as its primal vision and moves outward from it, infecting all dialogues, all gestures, all objects: all exteriors. As Blumenberg has pointed out: "Instead of a movement into the mind, then, the "story" of Marienbad is a movement from the mind's interior to the "outside world.'"[105] Proceed from the dream outward," Anais Nin would add.

Marienbad represents a triumph of memory over cognition, of dream over reality, of the subjective over the objective.

> Memory believes before knowing remembers. Believes longer than recollects, longer than knowing even wonders. Knows remembers believes a corridor in a big long garbled cold echoing building.

The quote seems to apply perfectly to Marienbad, although it does not come from either Resnais or Robbe-Grillet. It comes from William Faulkner in The Sound and the Fury. Time is made mythical in Marienbad by its circularity and made subjective by its very negation. The images can only be interpreted in terms of the equivocal verb tenses of the text, not in terms of the camera's mobility or fixity:

> The circularity of the film (emphasized by the "once more" of the beginning and the past tense of the end) suggests that the author intended the same kind of re-entry of the end into the beginning that one finds, for example, in Joyce's Finnegan's Wake. In this sense, nothing "exists" outside the film itself; last year is this year; the only reality is the here and now of the film's ninety minutes. All perspectives into another time or place are illusory.[106]

Resnais's Je t'aime je t'aime reverts to the fluidity of Hiroshima.

The time machine in the film is a device through which Resnais can explore the differences between a "real" event and Claude Ridder's subjective re-living of that event in time travel. More precisely, Resnais is interested in tracing the falsifications of the event through distortions in memory or through dreams or through deliberate lying to avoid confrontation with the truth of an event. In a sense then, time is the tension between two events, both of which are really one event, but since Ridder's consciousness has lived through the event, he can never re-live it exactly. There is something akin here to Borge's Pierre Menard who rewrites the Quixote word for word and creates a different work.

The experiment in time fails, because Claude Ridder cannot remain longer than a minute in any one period of his past. And, since he is nowhere long enough for the scientists at Crespel to get coordinates to bring him back, his time travel is dependent upon the caprices of his own mental time and not upon the technological expertise of the scientists. As with Hiroshima, Resnais reconstructs Claude Ridder's past achronologically. Ridder jumps in years as easily as he jumps in time, and the editing, often so quick that a scene is shown for less than a minute, is geared to convey a sense of falling, a sense of vertigo in the spectator:

> Il me semble que tout le film, dans sa continuité, devrait donner la sensation d'une chute dans le temps. Le contraire en somme d'un interminable fondu enchainé. Il faudrait que le spectateur ait vraiment la sensation de "tomber" dans les morceaux épars de la vie de Claude Ridder. C'est dire qu'il faudrait songer à un nouveau moyen de raccorder les séquences entre elles.[107]

That "new way of linking sequences" is in the poetic associations that Ridder makes between completely disparate time and space frames. The link between the hand of the Japanese lover and that of the German lover in Hiroshima is a relatively obvious link for the spectator. The links in Je t'aime je t'aime are not quite so obvious, partly because Ridder jumps so much in time and Resnais edits his scenes so swiftly. Whereas Riva in Hiroshima gradually accepts the fullness of her memory of Nevers and integrates herself with that memory, Claude Ridder cannot stay long enough in any one minute of his past to "get his bearings"; ultimately, his vertigo causes him to commit suicide, just as his boredom and sense of guilt had caused him to attempt suicide for the first time prior to the film's opening scenes.

The scenario of Jacques Sternberg indicates the precision with which he and Resnais constructed Ridder's past. Approximately the first dozen scenes, minus two brief returns to the time machine at Crespel, give the following dates and times:

(1) Tuesday, 5 September 1967 (the day of the experiment at Crespel)
(2) Monday, 5 September 1966 (Ridder and Catrine at the beach)
(3) Monday, 5 September 1964 (Ridder waiting for a tram in Brussels)
(4) Wednesday, 10 June 1959 (Ridder breaking off with a woman in France after meeting Catrine)
(5) Wednesday, 7 December 1951 (Ridder working as a packer in a book-packing shop in France)
(6) Tuesday, 15 September 1964 (Ridder and Catrine in Provence)
(7) Tuesday, 9 June 1959 (Ridder meets Catrine for the first time in a book-publishing house)
(8) Sunday, 12 February 1961 (Ridder and Bernard in a car, talking about Catrine)
(9) Monday, 29 March 1954 (Ridder working in a newspaper office)

(10) Tuesday, 18 September 1962 (Ridder and Catrine in a train in France)
(11) Wednesday, 8 February 1967 (Ridder is invited to dinner by the director of the publishing house)
(12) Monday, 4 January 1960 (Ridder discusses writing with Catrine)

Upon close examination, it is obvious that Sternberg and Resnais did not link such scenes haphazardly. The day of the experiment (1) gives way to the exact same date a year earlier, but the day is also one day earlier (2). If Ridder had been projected back to Tuesday, September 6, 1966, then perhaps the experiment might have been successful. That Monday gives way to the same Monday two years earlier, with the assumption that in 1965, September 5 would have fallen on a Tuesday. A Wednesday in 1959 (4) gives way to a Wednesday in 1951 (5), just as a Tuesday in 1964 (6) gives way to a Tuesday in 1959 (7). At this point, the achronology in terms of years becomes chronological in terms of days: Sunday (8), Monday (9), Tuesday (10) and Wednesday (11). One explanation for this change might be that all of the film's major themes have already been introduced: the time-travel, Catrine, vehicles which are metaphors for the time machine, the war experience, and working at various places which have to do with writing instead of writing creatively for oneself. Time travel, of course, relates to all these shots, although it is not the time machine at Crespel but the hyperactive mind of Ridder which makes such travel possible. The tram in Brussels (3), Bernard's car (8) and the train in France (10) all vehicles of time travel, just as the time machine at Crespel is. Thus, the train goes under a tunnel (sense of falling), and Ridder immediately reverts back for a moment to the time machine at Crespel. In addition, they all combine to make statements about Ridder and Catrine. They travel a great deal, but, whereas Ridder enjoys traveling (spatialization of time), Catrine does not. The woman in (4) and all the other women that Ridder sees in the film can be explained, in part, by Catrine's dislike for travel. Ridder's weakness, by contrast, is that of remaining still. When he is not traveling, he is not writing. Instead, he is working at minor jobs which involve other peoples' writing: the book-packing shop (5), the publishing house (7 and 12), and the newspaper office (9).

It seems that everything in the film can be neatly explained when one has the scenario in hand. The dates, however, are not given in the film. They are juxtaposed without indication of time or space. The viewer must fend for himself: that is, he must enter the mental time of Ridder. In so doing, he must in a sense "catch up" with Ridder. The scene of Ridder breaking off with a woman the day after he meets Catrine is explainable in the scenario (for we know it's the day after) but is rather puzzling in the film. The scene is very brief: Ridder says he's leaving and the woman turns to the camera and toots a horn. The woman never reappears in the film. The tooting of the horn is perhaps a deliberate calculation on the part of Resnais, so that the spectator will remember the scene, even though he might not understand its significance. Since the times and locales are not given to the spectator, there must be another way that "reading" of the film is made possible. That "way" is surely the association between images, regardless of time or place. For example, the scene immediately preceding Ridder's first and second suicides (Saturday, 5 August 1967) is that of Ridder counting packets in the book-packing shop. He seems to be counting "comme un automate." With the tone of an automaton, he, nevertheless, counts absurdly, mindlessly, almost nihilistically:

> Ridder: 46, 47, 48, 49, 50, 51, 52, 53, 54, 55, 56, 57, 56, 59 (musique) 60, 61, 62, 63, 64, 65, 66, 67, 68 . . .

The progression "56, 57, 56, 59" clearly approximates the kind of time travel that Ridder has been experiencing. The numbers can be "read" as years. 1958 is a year of oblivion for Ridder. He does not go to it. Thus, it is skipped in favor of a return to 1956. "58" is a "trou" or hole in Ridder's memory, just as the scene on the beach with Catrine represents an incomplete memory and, thus, must be returned to time and again. The series ends tentatively with "68" because that number represents the future. Ridder remembers that life ended for him in "67"! That sudden stop triggers the memory of the first suicide attempt, and Ridder returns to that suicide attempt: to relive it.

Within Ridder's time travels, there are explicit references to playing with time. When Ridder is most exasperated with the inanity of his work or the frustrations of not writing, he "plays" with time. At one point, he arranges several watches on his desk and pits bureau time against the time outside. At another point in the film, he calls "time" on the telephone and dialogues with the recording. His dialogue is a negation of time as an element which structures one's life. The banality of the minute is contrasted with the mythology of centuries:

> Il est trois heures de l'après-midi. Encore trois heures à franchir. Il y a trois minutes, il était déjà trois heures. Dans trois semaines, il sera encore trois heures. Dans un siècle aussi. Le temps passe pour les autres, mais pour moi seul, enfermé dans cette pièce, il ne passe plus. Je suis hors jeu, hors temps. Il est trois heures à tout jamais . . . Allo . . . ! L'horloge parlante? . . . Je vous signale qu'au troisième coup, il sera exactement quinze heures zéro minute zéro seconde. Comment? . . . D'accord! Demain, à la même heure, comme convenu. Mes amitiés chez vous.

When Ridder takes time seriously, however, he becomes its victim. His first re-entry into the past from the time machine is upon the beach with Catrine. The bubbles of Ridder breathing underwater effectively convey the sense of falling in time from the time machine. Ridder walks backwards out of the water toward Catrine. He does so because he is wearing fins, but he also does so because he is going backwards in time. That moment, his first in the past, is also the most important. Resnais repeats the sequence six times in rapid succession. Throughout the rest of the film, Ridder attempts to return to that moment and to stay there long enough to (1) understand what went wrong with Catrine and (2) to allow the scientists at Crespel to pull him out of the past. But each scene triggers another and Ridder cannot seem to get back to that beach long enough to solve both his and the scientists' problems. When he later returns to the scene, he is just going into the water or else he and Catrine are about to leave the beach. The most important moments in the film (those between the time Ridder leaves the water and the time he and Catrine leave the beach) are never shown in the film. Ridder must continually repeat scenes in his mind, whenever possible, in order to surround that moment which is a "hole" in his memory. In the repetition of his backing out of the water, Resnais triumphs over the present tense, just as the repetition of A raising her arms up in Marienbad or the repetition of François lifting his drowned wife's head in Agnes Varda's Le Bonheur (1965) accomplish the same triumph. The spectator does not know if the scene occurs once (all the repetitions adding up to one) or six times (each repetition being a new beginning).

In the very middle of the film, Ridder finds himself momentarily back in the time machine. He knows that something has gone wrong with the experiment. Further, he knows that he has not solved the guilt feelings he has over Catrine's death. He exerts all his forces to return conclusively to that moment on the beach:

> Il faut que je retrouve cette minute. Que je ne pense qu'à cette minute. Je suis dans l'eau. Il fait beau. Pas trop chaud.

The rhymed words (l'eau-beau-chaud) seem to me to be a deliberate attempt to create repetition, to poeticize the scene, to point out the impossibility of really returning to that scene in reality. Time is constantly spatialized in Je t'aime je t'aime, and Ridder's failure to integrate his past with his mental time is his failure to concentrate hard enough or long enough to reconstruct enough spatial details so that time would slow down and Ridder could re-live the moment. Ridder's past is an abrupt around-the-world tour when it should have been an in-depth re-experiencing of that one moment on the beach with Catrine.

Je t'aime je t'aime carries the spatialization of time to perhaps irrevocable extremes. As Marie-Claire Ropars-Willeumier has pointed out:

> Mais si _Je t'aime je t'aime_ achève ainsi le sens d'un itinéraire, il semble bien aussi, pour la première fois, le fermer: la spacialisation du temps mène à la destruction, puisque le suicide raté du personnage, antérieur à l'expérience, recommence au sein de cette expérience et la déborde, tout en ramenant le récit à son point initial: si le passé, une seconde fois vécu, éclate dans le futur, c'est parce que le futur répète ce passé; et le film se clot alors sur lui-même, à la différence de la spirale infinie dessinée dans _Marienbad_.[108]

The re-entry of _Marienbad_ is one of form, while the re-exit of _Je t'aime je t'aime_ is one of content. The constant shifts in time (that is, in editing) are too intriguing for the spectator to conclude so neatly. Thus, ironically, _Je t'aime je t'aime_ is at one and the same time Resnais's most artificial film (relying, as it does, on a gimmic or trick ending) and his most difficult film. Then again, perhaps the failure of Ridder's time travel infects the whole film. In other words, perhaps the failure in _Je t'aime je t'aime_ is a positive one, which reveals, as Jean Cayrol has suggested, the inevitable contradiction involved in time repeated:

> Revivre un drame, c'est vivre sa vie après le drame. Ce n'est pas se souvenir: la notion de temps n'entre plus dans cette survivance, dans cette mort déjà ancienne d'un être qu'on a laissé en vie quand il avait déjà toute sa vie derrière lui.[109]

Agnes Varda is both more successful and less successful than Resnais in her _Cléo de 5 à 7_. The film is an attempt to convey the time of the film with the time of the film's narrative. Thus, fictional time and real time coincide. In reality, _Cléo_ ends at six-thirty, not seven. One reason for this apparent contradiction is that the running time of the film is ninety minutes, not two hours. Were that the only reason, Varda could also be accused of gimmicry. There is in addition another reason, which is that Cléo fills up that objective, clock time with mental time. Within the hard chronology of the film's exterior, the perceptive spectator finds a more elastic time. As Cayrol has suggested:

> Un autre but, à la recherche d'une toujours plus grande exactitude (sa "vérité") demeure, depuis le début, de faire coincider le temps fictif et le temps réel d'une action: faire se dérouler en cent minutes ce qui est effectivement passé dans ce délai (Dans le film Cléo de 5 a 7, d'Agnes Varda, cet aspect est bien moins important que la durée RESSENTIE donnée effectivement au temps: non plus son écoulement regulier, mais une accélération ou un ralentissement, une élasticité du temps correspondant à l'impression de bonheur fugitif ou d'anxiété que nous a laissée tel ou tel moment.[110]

At the same time that Varda insists upon realistic clock time and the duration of objective time, she injects her film with subjective time which is elasticity or flux, not strict chronology. She explains this dialectic in the following way:

> Ce film se déroule "au temps présent." La caméra ne quitte pas Cléo de cinq heures à six heures trente. Si le temps est réel, les trajets le sont aussi; les "durées" sont vraies.
>
> Le film, dans son déroulement minute, observe une durée objective.
>
> A l'intérieur de ce temps mécanique, Cléo éprouve la durée subjective: "Le temps lui dure," ou "le temps s'arrête," ou "le temps glisse et l'entraine." Elle-même dit: "Il nous reste si peu de temps" et une minute après: "On a tout le temps."[111]

Cléo opposes the "time of the bureau" and the "time outside" every bit as much as Claude Ridder did in the Resnais film. The difference between the two is point of view. Claude Ridder's visions of the past often sacrifice objective reality for subjective hallucinations or dreams. Cléo, by contrast, lives a chronological present (5 to 7) with achronological eyes. Varda's film never sacrifices the documentary quality of the images. The real Paris is revealed in every shot. That real Paris takes on added meaning, however, if the spectator realizes Cléo's particular point of view, which is that of a woman who thinks she is about to die. Thus, shots of a shop exhibiting funeral wreaths, which exists in Paris, also refer to Cléo's double vision, the shots having been "selected" by Cléo's fearful eyes. Varda is more successful than Resnais in that she does not sacrifice the documentary quality of the images. She is less successful, however, since the spectator may see _Cléo_ without ever realizing that added subjective point of view.

Chris Marker's _La Jetée_ was the prototype of the subjective time-travel films, including Resnais's _Je t'aime je t'aime_ and Robert Benayoun's _Paris n'existe pas_ (1969). In a sense, Marker's film actualizes the hypothesis with which we began this discussion: that all times exist simultaneously rather than successively. Marker's success in _La Jetée_ derives in part from the fact that he does not attempt to resolve apparent contradictions in logic. Just as Luis Bunuel used editing in _Un Chien Andalou_ (1929) to make one character younger by sixteen years while allowing another character to retain his age, so too Marker plays with time through contradictions. _La Jetée_ opens with the affirmation that what is to follow is the story of a man traumatized by a memory from his childhood. The narrator states that a child once had a premonition on the jetty at

Orly Airport, that of seeing a man die. The man he saw dying was, of course, himself as an adult. When the man of the camps travels back to the jetty at Orly, he is conscious of the fact that the child he once was must also be there somewhere:

> Une fois sur la grande jetée d'Orly, dans ce chaud dimanche d'avant guerre où il allait demeurer, il pense avec un peu de vertige que l'enfant qu'il avait été devait se trouver là aussi, à regarder les avions.

Just as the man does not grow younger when he travels back into the past, so too he does not age when he travels to the future. The subjective explanation of such an apparent contradiction in logic is, of course, that all transpires in the mind of the man: thus, the body would not change.

> Mais l'esprit humain achoppait. Se réveiller dans un autre temps, c'était naître une seconde fois, adulte. Le choc était trop fort. Apres avoir ainsi projeté dans différentes zones du Temps des corps sans vie ou sans conscience, les inventeurs se concentraient maintenant sur des sujets doués d'images mentales très fortes. Capables d'imaginer ou de rêver un autre temps, ils seraient peut-être capables de s'y intégrer.

There are even contradictions within the various time zones, as, for example, when the woman asks the man about the medal he wears around his neck:

> Elle l'interroge sur son collier, le collier du combattant qu'il portait au début de cette guerre qui éclatera un jour. Il invente une explication.

A similar contradiction in logic exists in the future where the man uses a sophism to convince the people of the future of their obligation to help him:

> Il récita sa leçon. Puisque l'humanité avait survécu, elle ne pouvait pas refuser à son propre passé les moyens de sa survie. Ce sophisme fut accepté comme un déguisement du Destin. On lui donna une centrale d'énergie suffisante pour remettre en

> marche toute l'industrie humaine, et les portes de l'avenir furent refermées.

That projection into the future assumes *a priori* that humanity has survived.

Every image in the film is given multiple significance by the hypothetical tone of the spoken text. The man and woman visit two museums, but one of them is a museum of "eternal beasts," an indication of its subjective nature. The text adds that it is "un musée qui est peut-être celui de sa mémoire." Therein lies the reason for the profusion of images of "frozen time" as in a museum: statues, the rings of a tree, stuffed birds (all through *still* photography). The possibility of a dream is also reinforced by the text:

> Elle prononce un nom étranger qu'il ne comprend pas. Comme en rêve, il lui montre un point hors de l'arbre.[112]

> Lui ne sait jamais s'il se dirige vers elle, s'il est dirigé, s'il invente ou s'il rêve.

The text alone cannot create this multiplicity of meanings. It is in Marker's radically innovative handling of the images that the film's pluridimensionality is achieved. *La Jetée* is composed almost entirely with photo-stills. The use of photographs negates the present tense of film by immobilizing character movement. Photographs, thus, belong more to the past tense than to the present. Looking at photographs that are ten years old gives one more a sense of the past than looking at most films which are thirty or forty years old. The photograph captures a present moment and freezes it, immediately making that present moment a past moment. But Marker is not only concerned with establishing the sense of the past in La Jetée; in addition, there is a deliberate attempt to make the past, among all three times zones, "come to life." What prevents the spectator from summarily deciding that the woman is a figment of the man's imagination is that one moment of actual film, in which the woman's eyes blink from sleep and the sound of crickets appears on the sound track.

It is a strange kind of spatialization of time at work in La Jetée. Totally different time zones and spatial areas are related through camera movement or through editing. Marker zooms in on a photograph when he enters a different time zone and zooms out from a photograph to build up a scene. Like the Surrealists did before him, Marker often presents a close-up first and then an establishing shot. The effect is that of putting the spectator momentarily off-guard, for he does not immediately see the character in his surroundings. It is perhaps an oversimplification to see La Jetée in this way, but one might even postulate that the close-ups reinforce the protagonist's mind and subjective vision, whereas the establishing shots reinforce the authenticity or objective construction of those visions. Marker also uses editing to link different times and spaces. The text says: "Un jour, elle se penche sur lui." On the image track, there is a lap dissolve, from the woman's head leaning in the past to the man's face in the underground camps. Through the dissolve, the woman does indeed seem to be leaning on the man, although they are occupying two different time zones. When the man "runs" on the jetty at the end of the film, spaces are "skipped" to convey movement. At the same time that the photos immobilize the man's movement, the editing restores the sense of movement. Several quick cuts with photos that show the man increasingly in close-up give the spectator an eerie sense of the man's flight.

Visual clues also reinforce the sense of time as a fluid spectrum. The man usually wears white blinders in the camp but reappears in the past with nothing over his eyes. When he travels to the future, however, he wears dark glasses. Similarly, when the people of the future project him back into the past, he is wearing the dark glasses. He is shot by the doctor from the camp, wearing the gas-mask goggles of the camp. Only the woman seems locked in a particular time and space.

This very fluid time sense enables the spectator to interpret _La Jetée_ in several ways. There is, of course, a sound basis for assuming that all times and all decors in the film emanate from the mind of the protagonist. There is also the hypothesis that all times exist simultaneously rather than successively. The film seems to indicate that the jetty is the past, the camps are the present, and the men and women with black spots on their foreheads are the future. But, since the past comes to life with the filming of the woman's eyes blinking, the jetty may also be seen as the present, in which case both the camps and the black-spotted people would represent progressions into the future. The film also posits that the people of the future travel freely into the past. At that point, the future becomes the present, and the camps and the jetty become different degrees of past-ness, which would explain why the director of the camps suddenly appears on the jetty with the man. But, since time is treated so fluidly, perhaps the real answer is that "past" and "present" and "future" are only arbitrary terms imposed by man's need for clock time. If this is the case, then time in La Jetée may be seen as a spiralling series of random moments, more random even than those developed by Kurt Vonnegut in Slaughterhouse Five.

Whichever interpretation the spectator opts for, he must deal with the final contradiction in logic at the film's conclusion, which reaffirms that the man and himself as child cohabit the same time zone, although time travel is ultimately not possible:

> Et lorsqu'il reconnut l'homme qui l'avait suivi depuis le camp souterrain, il comprit qu'on ne s'évadait pas du Temps et que cet instant qu'il lui avait été donné de voir enfant, et qui n'avait pas cessé de l'obséder, c'était celui de sa propre mort.

Perhaps the real protagonist of the film is this unseen child, from whose mind the whole film, including the projection of himself as an adult, springs forth.

The use of photo-stills was an ingenious device for immobilizing the present tense of the film image. Those photos become film through the camera mobility and the associative editing. As Christian Metz has affirmed, the passage from one to two photos is the passage from the image to language:

> Le roman-photos est très souvent employé à raconter l'intrigue d'un film préexistant: conséquence d'une rassemblance plus profonde, qui découle elle-même d'une fondamentale dissemblance:

> la photo est si inapte à raconter que quand elle veut le faire, elle devient cinéma. Le roman-photos n'est pas un dérive de la photo mais du cinéma. Une photo isolée ne peut rien raconter; bien sûr! Mais pourquoi faut-il que par un étrange corollaire deux photos juxtaposées soient forcées de raconter quelque chose? Passer d'une image à deux images, c'est passer de l'image au langage.[113]

And that resultant language is deliberately poetic, that is, pluridimensional. Even the title of the film is multiple. _La Jetée_ refers objectively to the jetty or air-strip at Orly Airport. It also refers to a ballet term, a _jetee_ being a kick or leap. Just as Maya Deren played with different times and spaces in her films (_Meshes of the Afternoon_--1944, _Ritual in Transfigured Time_--1946, or _A Study in Choreography for Camera_--1950, for example) through having a character "dance" with the camera and with the editing, so too the protagonist of Marker's film enacts a ballet leap through otherwise illogically related times and spaces. Finally, the title of the Marker film also refers to the woman, and, in this context, means "the abandoned one." True exploration of time in film can only come, it seems, from such a pluridimensionality of meaning.

Alain Robbe-Grillet's _L'Immortelle_ also plays with time through subjective point of view and through the superimposition of one time frame upon another. The geography of _L'Immortelle_ is modern day Istanbul, but it is an Istanbul falsified by post-card cliches. At the same time, it is Byzantium, the Turkey of legends and dreams, another falsification made possible by the subjective point of view of the camera-narrator.

N, the narrator of the film, is a voyeur. As such, everything in the film comes filtered through his eyes. Ingeniously, Robbe-Grillet also portrays this voyeur who tries to immobilize everything and everyone as a camera which cannot stand to be looked at. As soon as a character begins to turn toward the camera (that is, toward the narrator's eyes), there is a cut in the film. Several random examples should suffice to prove my point.

> M, avec ses lunettes noires et toujours dans le même costume, assis seul à une table où il est en train de lire un journal turc, largement déplié devant lui, qu'il quitte bientôt des yeux pour lever le regard face à la caméra. Le plan est coupé lorsque son regard s'est fixé sur celle-ci. (p. 46 of the published text)

> Le même pecheur, dans la même position exactement et au même endroit, mais vu de plus près, bien que sous le même angle, comme par un homme debout. . . Dès le début du plan il commence à tourner la tête lentement vers la gauche, tout en relevant les yeux. Lorsque son regard est face à la caméra, le plan change. (p. 23)

> Mais M se retourne aussitôt pour regarder vers la droite. . . Puis il lève lentement la tête, en tournant le corps, jusqu'à ce que son regard soit dirigé vers la caméra. Le plan change à cet instant. (p. 27)

> Lorsqu'elle a disparu, M ramène son regard vers la caméra et le plan est coupé. (p. 32)

> N se penche davantage vers elle, pour la saisir de nouveau, par la nuque; comme pour surveiller les alentours, elle se tourne alors vers la caméra. Le plan est coupé lorsque son regard est sur l'objectif. (p. 54)

> Au bout de quelques secondes de contemplation, la jeune femme a un sourire, et jette un regard à son compagnon, qui ne détourne pas les yeux du spectacle. Le plan est coupé lorsqu'elle reporte les siens sur la caméra. (p. 72)

Significantly, shots are also cut off when N, the physical projection of the unseen narrator, turns toward the camera, as if this uniquely subjective point of view were dependent upon the two N's never looking directly at each other:

> Pour dire le dernier mot il s'est retourné vers la caméra et a designé, du bras tendu, les fenêtres du premier étage. Le plan est coupé sur ce geste. (p. 33)

> N se retourne avec lenteur vers la caméra, tandis que claque une portière d'automobile. Et le plan est coupé, lorsque le visage de N se présente de face (sur la fin de ce claquement). (p. 55)

In a sense, then, time and space change every time the camera-narrator blinks or "edits" his visions.

Camera mobility is used, as in Maya Deren's films, to juxtapose unrelated or irrational times and spaces. The camera, for example, slowly pulls back from a shot of N and L paddling a canoe to reveal N and L in close-up, seen from the back, upon a larger boat. Both the boat and the canoe, that is, both sets of N and L, are visible in the same frame. The objective shot of the two of them in the canoe becomes a subjective shot of N in the big boat imagining the canoe. That shot of them in the big boat becomes a subjective shot in turn, and the film progresses, thus, in terms of spatial perspectives or subjective mental time. At another point in the film, a continuous camera movement from left to right reveals N and L facing the camera on a bridge, then N and L "displaced" farther on along the bridge, this time their backs to the camera, then "displaced" again still farther. This is strikingly similar to Deren's "displacements" of a dancer in _A Study in Choreography for Camera_, in which Talley Beatty begins a pirouette and finishes it in three different spaces in a woods, while the camera continuously pans laterally.

Image fixity is another device Robbe-Grillet uses to insist upon the subjective nature of his narrator and to counteract the present tense in film. When N meets Catherine Saroyan in a cafe to discuss L, all of the other men in the cafe are fixed and rigid in their seats. They are as if dead or else intently listening and spying on the conversation between N and Catherine. Form rejoins content, for, as Robbe-Grillet has explained, the immobility is due to the sadism in N's character, to the subjectivity of his visions and to the link between voyeurism and immobilization.

> Les personnages appelés sadiques dans mes romans ont toujours ceci de particulier qu'ils essaient d'immobiliser quelque chose qui bouge. Lui est là, il regarde ça, et j'ai l'impression qu'on sent naître chez lui le désir d'arrêter ça. . . Cet homme qu'on voit dans mes romans et dans mes films, c'est quelqu'un qui effectivement a besoin de voir et d'immobiliser, les deux choses étant constamment liées.[114]

Another means of negating the present tense is to negate the very content of the images. L's function as a character seems precisely to negate the authenticity of everything that N sees. She says that everything is false appearances, due either to deceptions on the part of the land itself or to N's imaginations or dreams. Thus, a cemetary is a false cemetary, a mosque is a reconstruction for tourists, and all the boats are false boats. Again, several examples from L's various dialogue exchanges should prove my point.

> Tout ça, ce sont vos imaginations . . . Vous voyez . . . Vous êtes sur la Bosphore. Vous longez la rive d'Asie. . .

> L: Tout ca est faux, naturellement.
> N: Tout quoi?

L: Ce qu'il disait. Ca n'est pas ancien du tout, on l'a reconstruite après la guerre.

L: Vous voyez bien que ce n'est pas une vraie ville. . . c'est un décor d'opérette, pour une histoire d'amour.

L: Vous voyez bien que tout est faux. . . Byzance! . . . Ils sont même en train de le construire.

L: Regardez. . . Une mosquée comme dans vos rêves. . . Elle est en train de s'écrouler. . . Et voilà un navire comme dans vos rêves. . . Un navire qui ne tenait pas la mer. . . Il faut maintenant tout recommencer. . .

L: Ce ne sont pas de vraies tombes. . . On n'enterre jamais personne. . .

L: Vous arrivez dans une Turkie de rêve. . . Fausses prisons, faux remparts, fausses histoires. . . Vous ne pouvez plus revenir en arrière. . . Et pour vous échapper. . . Ce sont de faux bateaux, aussi, vous voyez bien.

L. insists continually upon the "vous voyez bien," even when the subjective visions of N obviously don't take into account all these false appearances. Thus, a counterpoint is established. The camera reveals the visions of N, which, once revealed, take on an aspect of authenticity. By contrast, the spoken text, and especially the lines of L, negate the content of those images. Jacques Doniol-Valcroze, who played the part of N, has said of this innovative treatment of mental time in L'Immortelle:

> Ce qui me parait le plus important et le plus nouveau dans ce film c'est que le labyrinthe de sa structure tente de nous donner le premier équivalent cinématographique d'un "temps mental." Un temps qui est perpétuellement au "présent." Il ne s'agit ni de retours en arrière ni d'incursions en avant, il s'agit de ce qui se passe dans la tête d'un monsieur debout devant une fenêtre et qui pense à une femme qu'il a aimée, pensée qui, dans le temps et dans l'espace, ne peut être ni continue, ni logique, ni chronologique, ni certaine et qui chemine avec ses trous, ses blancs, ses défaillances, ses erreurs d'interprétation, ses phantasmes, ses mensonges même, conscients ou non.[115]

I would argue with Doniol-Valcroze's contention that L'Immortelle is the first film to succeed in portraying mental time or that everything in the film is "au présent." If that present is given, it is a present without linear movement and without chronological logic.

L'Homme qui ment expands the treatment of time and space developed in L'Immortelle. Here again, the role of everyone in the film who surrounds Boris Varissa is to negate the veracity of what he says. Boris is an inveterate liar, but he is the only narrator we have in the film. Thus, we are led to believe again and again what he says, until the images or the characters' dialogues prove us wrong--again and again. The same camera mobility from objective reality to subjective vision is at work in L'Homme qui ment as in L'Immortelle, with the added complication that many scenes are prefigurations or flash-forwards created by Boris before he enacts them. A Nazi soldier shoots a machine-gun into an opening in a wall. Only later in the film do we discover, when that image is restored to its rightful place, that the first image was a flash-forward. Boris walks up the stairs of the inn and, through a continuous camera movement, he is walking up the stairs with Jean Robin in the "past": that is, inside one of his fabrications. Likewise, immobility is also used to project into the future. Boris sees snapshots of his own "death" in the pharmacy before the actual scenes in which the post cards will "come to life." Robbe-Grillet has defined this new treatment of time through subjective point of view and this new concept of verisimilitude in the following way:

> On mesure à quel point le "vraisemblable" et le "conforme au type" sont loin de pouvoir encore servir de critères. Tout se passe même comme si le FAUX--c'est-à-dire à la fois le possible, l'impossible, l'hypothèse, le mensonge, etc.--était devenu l'un des thèmes privilégiés de la fiction moderne; une nouvelle sorte de narrateur y est né: ce n'est plus seulement un homme qui décrit les choses qu'il voit, mais en même temps celui qui invente les choses autour de lui et qui voit les choses qu'il invente. Dès que ces héros-narrateurs commencent un tant soit peu à rassembler à des "personnages," ce sont aussitôt des menteurs, des schizophrènes ou des hallucinés (ou même des ecrivains, qui créent leur propre histoire).[116]

Time is again completely spatialized in Marguerite Duras's _Détruire dit-elle_. The retreat chateau of the film is as illusory as the chateau in Resnais's and Robbe-Grillet's _L'Année dernière à Marienbad_, and the mythology of time that Resnais created in _Je t'aime je t'aime_ between "bureau time" and the "time of centuries" or that created between Istanbul and Byzantium in Robbe-Grillet's _L'Immortelle_ is here reproduced in a recreation of the "wandering Jew" and "Flying Dutchman" myths. Alissa, Max Thor and Stein seemed doomed to forever wander through illusory spaces and achronological times, unless, as with the Flying Dutchman, they can convince someone, in this case Elizabeth Alione, to return the love they bear and to be willing to "die" ("détruire") for that love. Contradictions in logic abound, as in Marker's _La Jetée_. When Elizabeth's husband asks Max Thor how long he's known Alissa, he responds that he's just met her. The statement is perhaps true, if we understand by it that Max Thor continually re-invents Alissa (he's a writer) or that he sees her in a new way each day.

Alissa, Max Thor and Stein are mutants, in the words of Duras. They have no past, because their task is the restructuring of the present in terms of the future. They are amnesiacs in the same way that the missing "husband" in Henri Colpi's Une Aussi Longue Absence (1960) or the protagonist of Marker's La Jetée have no past. They must "build" their past as they go along in the present. Robbe-Grillet's words are perhaps apropos here: "Je ne transcris pas, je construis."[117] And Elizabeth Alione's "sin" in Détruire dit-elle is her inability to accept the present because she cannot let go of her past. She continues to re-invent that past, to suffer from sins of omission and to linger on her few sins of commission. She cannot play the "game" of the other three, which is to invent the truth of each moment. She constantly resists the advances of the other three, because those advances are in contrast with the past she struggles with. Memory is the original sin in Détruire.

Duras provokes the spectator by images which insist upon a present tense: long takes, little camera movement, little actor movement. But the immobility of the camera and the actors is paralleled by the spoken text, which negates the present which surrounds the characters and projects "real" time beyond the mysterious forest and the invading drums of the film's conclusion. Tension springs from the fact that what appears to be a soap-opera refuge in the images is, in reality, an apocalyptic battle-royal in the text. Détruire ends in the same way that Mike Nichols' Who's Afraid of Virginia Woolf? (1967) ends: with a sense of the past wiped clean, a sense of false peace in the present and an awesome terror waiting in the future. The terror in both films is the terror from the power of love, which does not observe strict chronology or restricted space.

The spatialization of time that we have discussed is not, then, a temporality conveyed through objective space. Indeed, new temporality in film can only come, it seems, from a radical restructuring of spatial relationships from the objective to the subjective, that is, from an impersonal camera to a subjective point-of-view camera. As Marie-Claire Ropars-Willeumier has pointed out:

> Si donc le langage cinématographique parvient à devenir totalement narratif, ce ne peut être qu'en acquérant cette temporalité propre au roman, et par là même en modifiant le rapport spatio-temporel qui le définit à l'origine: car l'espace immédiatement perçu enferme l'image cinématographique dans l'éternel présent qui caractérise une présentation dramatique; aussi faut-il, pour que le temps devienne perceptible dans sa réalité sensible, estomper la présence de cet espace; à quoi s'est efforcé tout le cinéma moderne, jusqu'à atteindre un pouvoir d'abstraction.[118]

The use of photo-stills, of subjective camera mobility, of image fixity and of a text which negates the content of the image in films like _Hiroshima_, _Marienbad_, _Je t'aime je t'aime_, _Cléo_, _La Jetée_, _L'Immortelle_, _L'Homme qui ment_ and _Détruire dit-elle_ are attempts to radically restructure filmic space to meet the needs of a more subjective and more fluid temporality that transcends the tyranny of the present tense.

Notes

[1] Van Gogh, Le Mystère de l'Atelier Quinze and Le Chant du Styrène are available in L'Avant-scène du cinéma (no. 1, February 1961) along with the complete text for Hiroshima mon amour, Les Statues meurent aussi (text by Chris Marker) is available in Chris Marker's Commentaires (Paris: Editions du Seuil, 1961). Nuit et brouillard is available in L'Avant-scène du cinéma (no. 1, February 1961) and Toute la Mémoire du monde is available in L'Avant-scène du cinéma (no. 52, October 1956).

[2] Alain Resnais, Ciné-Club (no. 3, December 1948). Reprinted in the two volumes devoted to Resnais in Etudes Cinématographiques (nos. 64-68, 1968), p. 21.

[3] Lewis Jacobs, "The Mobility of Color" in The Movies as Medium (New York: Farrar, Straus and Giroux (Noonday), 1970), p. 193.

[4] Jacobs, p. 193.

[5] René Prédal, Etudes Cinématographiques (nos. 64-68, 1968), p. 20.

[6] Prédal, p. 21.

[7] Prédal, p. 23.

[8] Prédal, p. 24.

[9] Prédal, p. 25.

[10] Prédal, p. 26.

[11] Jean Cayrol and Claude Durand, Le Droit de regard (Paris: Editions du Seuil, 1963), p. 20.

[12] Cayrol and Durand, p. 22.

[13] The complete texts for On vous parle, La Frontière, Madame se meurt, and De Tout Pour Faire un Monde can be found in Le Droit de regard.

[14] Agnes Varda, Cahiers du Cinéma (1965).

15 Les Statues meurent aussi, Dimanche à Pékin, Lettre de Sibérie, L'Amérique rêve, Description d'un combat and Cuba si are available (complete texts) in Chris Marker's Commentaires I (Paris: Editions du Seuil, 1961). Le Mystère Koumiko, Yo Soy Mexico and Si j'avais quatre dromadaires are available in Commentaires II (Paris: Seuil, 1967).

16 This quote appears on the jacket of Commentaires I.

17 Marie-Claire Ropars-Willeumier, L'Ecran de la mémoire (Paris: Editions du Seuil, 1970), pp. 164-165.

18 Hiroshii Teshigahara, Cahiers du Cinéma (1969).

19 Ropars-Willeumier, p. 166.

20 Ropars-Willeumier, p. 166.

21 Jacobs, p. 196.

22 Agnes Varda, La Côte d'Azur (Paris: Gallimard, 1958), p. 4.

23 Ropars-Willeumier, p. 164.

24 Ropars-Willeumier, p. 163.

25 Ropars-Willeumier, p. 162.

26 Jacobs, p. 212.

27 Ropars-Willeumier, p. 163.

28 Ropars-Willeumier, p. 164.

29 Ropars-Willeumier, p. 172.

30 Ropars-Willeumier, p. 170.

31 Ropars-Willeumier, p. 170.

32 Prédal, p. 164.

33 Ropars-Willeumier, p. 170.

34 Ropars-Willeumier, p. 165.

35 Ropars-Willeumier, p. 160.

36 Ropars-Willeumier, p. 168.

[37] Ropars-Willeumier, p. 169.

[38] Ropars-Willeumier, p. 168.

[39] Jacobs, p. 208.

[40] Cayrol and Durand, p. 98.

[41] Cayrol and Durand, pp. 99-100.

[42] The one exception here is the Paul Eluard poem for _Guernica_. Although Resnais did not ask for an original script, he did ask that Eluard expand the original work.

[43] Alain Resnais, _Esprit_ (6 June 1960). Reprinted in Prédal, p. 28.

[44] Alain Resnais, _Ciné-Club_ (3 December 1948). Reprinted in Prédal, pp. 34-35.

[45] Marcel Martin, _Le Langage cinématographique_ (Paris: Eds. du Cerf, 1955), p. 63.

[46] See further Eisler's compositional process in Chapter VI of his _Composing for the Films_ (New York, 1951).

[47] Henri Colpi, _Défense et illustration de la musique dans le film_ (Lyons: Serdoc, 1963), p. 129.

[48] Prédal, p. 29.

[49] Colpi, p. 134.

[50] Colpi, p. 134.

[51] Colpi, pp. 134-135.

[52] Colpi, p. 135.

[53] Colpi, p. 135.

[54] André Hodeir, "An Analysis of Alain Resnais' Film _Hiroshima mon amour_" (New York: Grove Press, 1960). Reprinted in _Evergreen Review Reader_, ed. Barney Rosset (New York: Castle Books, 1967), pp. 283-289.

[55] Colpi, p. 136.

[56] Colpi, p. 136.

[57] Hodeir, p. 285.

[58] Hodeir, p. 285.

[59] Ropars-Willeumier, p. 20.

[60] Ropars-Willeumier, p. 20.

[61] Alain Resnais, Image et Son (February 1960). Reprinted in Prédal, p. 28.

[62] Colpi, p. 128.

[63] Alain Resnais, Esprit (June 1960). Reprinted in Prédal, p. 28.

[64] Colpi, p. 129.

[65] Colpi, p. 128. Colpi goes on to elaborate upon the Rivette quote: "Par exemple, la définition que Stravinsky donne de la musique--'une succession d'élans et de repos'--me semble parfaitement convenir au film d'Alain Resnais. Qu'est-ce à dire? La recherche d'un équilibre supérieur à tous les éléments de création. Stravinsky utilise systématiquement les contrastes et, en même temps, à l'instant même où il les utilise, met en évidence ce qui les unit" (Colpi, p. 138).

[66] Colpi, p. 128.

[67] Ropars-Willeumier, p. 116.

[68] Prédal, p. 30.

[69] Alain Resnais, France-Observateur (18 May 1961). Reprinted in Prédal, p. 30.

[70] Prédal, p. 30.

[71] Ropars-Willeumier, p. 72.

[72] Alain Resnais, "Cinq à la zéro," Cahiers du Cinéma, 146 (August 1963), p. 30.

[73] Armes, p. 99.

[74] Prédal, p. 28.

[75] Alain Resnais, Clarté, 33 (February 1961).

[76] Agnes Varda, Cahiers du Cinéma, p. 44.

77 Agnes Varda, Cléo de 5 à 7 (Paris: Gallimard, 1962), pp. 9-10.

78 Varda, Cléo de 5 à 7, pp. 9-10.

79 The quote comes from the introduction on the jacket of Chris Marker's Le Coeur net (Paris: Editions du Seuil, 1950).

80 Alain Robbe-Grillet, L'Immortelle (Paris: Editions de Minuit, 1963), p. 9.

81 Maurice LeRoux, quoted by Jacques Doniol-Valcroze, Cahiers du Cinéma, 143 (May 1963), p. 57.

82 Gollub, p. 130.

83 Ropars-Willeumier, p. 236.

84 Jean Narboni and Jacques Rivette, "Entretien avec Marguerite Duras," Cahiers du Cinéma, 217 (November 1969), p. 48.

85 George Bluestone, Novels into Film (Berkeley and Los Angeles: The University of California Press, 1966).

86 Christian Metz, Essais sur la signification au cinéma (Paris: Eds. Klincksieck, 1971), p. 27.

87 Metz, p. 31.

88 Martin, p. 26.

89 Susan Sonntag, Styles of Radical Will (New York: Dell (Delta), 1966), p. 113.

90 Jean-Marie Straub, Cahiers du Cinéma, 180 (July 1966), p. 51.

91 André Téchiné, Cahiers du Cinéma, 181 (August 1966), p. 25.

92 Armes, pp. 96-97.

93 Cayrol and Durand, p. 17.

94 Cayrol and Durand, p. 19.

95 Cayrol and Durand, p. 20.

96 Cayrol and Durand, p. 32.

97 Cayrol and Durand, p. 161.

98 Narboni and Rivette, p. 51.

99 Ropars-Willeumier, p. 229.

100 Téchiné, p. 24.

101 Richard Mitchell Blumenberg, _The Manipulation of Time and Space in the Novels of Alain Robbe-Grillet and in the Narrative Films of Alain Resnais, With Particular Reference to Last Year at Marienbad_ (Ph.D. Ohio University, 1969), p. 17.

102 Blumenberg, p. 133.

103 Blumenberg, p. 83.

104 Blumenberg, p. 124.

105 Blumenberg, p. 127.

106 Bruce Morrissette, _Alain Robbe-Grillet_ (New York: Columbia University Press, 1965), p. 35.

107 Alain Resnais and Jacques Sternberg, _Je t'aime je t'aime_ (complete scenario) in _L'Avant-scène du cinéma_, 91 (April 1969), p. 29.

108 Ropars-Willeumier, p. 123.

109 Cayrol and Durand, p. 20.

110 Cayrol and Durand, p. 32.

111 Agnes Varda, _Cléo de 5 à 7_, pp. 8-9.

112 The word she pronounces is apparently "Hitchcock."

113 Metz, p. 53.

114 Andre Gardies, _Alain Robbe-Grillet_ (Paris: Seghers (Cinéma d'aujourd'hui), 1972), p. 74.

115 Jacques Doniol-Valcroze, "Istanbul nous appartient," _Cahiers du Cinéma_, 143 (May 1963), pp. 55-56.

116 Alain Robbe-Grillet, _Pour un nouveau roman_ (Paris: Gallimard, 1963), p. 177.

117 Robbe-Grillet, p. 177.

118 Ropars-Willeumier, p. 228.

VI

From *La Politique des Auteurs* to *Les Auteurs de la Politique*

The "French New Wave" is a term that provides for aesthetic classifications or categories by implying that there was something like "an old wave" against which the New Wave films reacted. The term does not explain, however, how the New Wave films came to be made in any cultural context: specifically, in any economic or political context. It would be naive to assume that aesthetic factors alone permitted the young Cahiers du Cinéma critics like Truffaut and Godard to one day stop writing articles and successfully begin making films or that those same aesthetic factors alone explain how the literary New Wave filmmakers like Resnais and Varda began making feature films that were admittedly not for mass audiences. Both groups can be delineated historically: 1955 marks a shift in one direction, while 1968 marks a shift in another. Those shifts can only be understood in light of the prevailing economic conditions, especially as they influenced modes of production and distribution, and in light of the prevailing political climate, and especially as it changed the French government's attitude toward the film industry and the filmmakers' attitudes toward both the government and the film industry.

Economic Considerations

"Un film c'est aussi un auteur."
-Claude Degand

There are very few studies of the economic situation of the French cinema before World War Two,[1] but Claude Degand estimates that approximately 250 million spectators brought in a total of 1.5 million francs, and since the census figures for 1938 showed that the French population had grown to 42 million inhabitants, Degand estimates that each person went to the cinema six times a year.[2] What followed in terms of the war years' statistics seems a paradox: the French film industry flourished, at least in terms of total gate receipts. The number of spectators grew from 250 million in 1938 to 300 million in 1943, from there to 400 million in 1945 during the Liberation and finally to 424 million in 1947, the top figure for any year in French film history. Correspondingly, the gate receipts increased seven-fold from 1938 to 1947. What is misleading about this last figure is that it doesn't take into account the increase in film prices per spectator, which were one and one-half times that of the 1938 price of six francs in 1943 and almost six times that 1938 price in 1947. And all of these statistics, which represent a measure of reception in terms of audience, must also be counterbalanced by statistics pertaining to film production costs and film productivity. In 1938 film production ran between 130 and 140 films (feature films) per year at an average cost of 2.8 million francs. That average cost had doubled by 1942, and by 1947 it had reached 30 million francs. This enormous increase in film costs might help explain the decrease in the number of features produced per year: from 140 or so in 1938 to 72 in 1947.[3] Translating all these statistics, one comes up with another paradox: where the gate receipts reveal a film industry unparalleled in its own prosperity, the number of features produced (and a corresponding decrease in movie theaters) reveals an industry plagued with financial troubles. Rising costs explain both factors: the rising costs of the average ticket explains the inflation in gate receipts, while it also explains in part the gradual decrease in spectator attendance after 1947; the rising costs of producing the average feature film explain the decrease in the number of films made per year, while they also explain in part the gradual decrease in the number of movie theaters after 1947.

By 1947 the government had already intervened in several ways, ironically taking its precedent from the deposed Vichy government. This latter government had realized the importance of film both as an information or news service and as a means of propaganda. Accordingly, in 1942 it created the Comité d'Organisation de l'Industrie Cinématographique (C.O.I.C.) under the control of the Ministry of Information. The C.O.I.C. established government-controlled price regulations on ticket purchases and gate receipts at the same time that it assumed ideological control (censorship) over the kind of films being made and financial control (in the form of subsidies) over the kind of films it wanted made.

The C.O.I.C. was eventually replaced by the C.N.C. (Centre National de la Cinématographie), which is still in existence. The establishment of the C.N.C. was an attempt, as one Minister put it, to put an end to "the reign of anarchy in the industry." In fact, the C.N.C. was established as a filter between the government and the film industry. It looked on the surface like efficient organization and common sense. In reality the C.N.C. with the government behind it would come to operate very much in the manner of the C.O.I.C.

Degand refers to the period 1947-1957 as "les belles années" ("the good years"), but he does so with some tongue-in-cheek, for governmental policy in that decade created more problems for the film industry than it solved.

The government made its presence felt in the French film industry in three distinct ways from the Liberation to 1957. First, it assumed a policy of protectionism toward the domestic film industry, which, among other things, entailed a more aggressive attitude toward foreign films. Second, it began a complicated system of subsidies for the production of French films. Finally, it officially sanctioned and actively encouraged the co-production of films. These policies of protectionism, subsidies and co-production sponsorship are still prevalent today; indeed, they apply to most of the other Western European countries as well.

The first signs of protectionism were in evidence as early as May of 1946 when the Blum-Byrnes accord was signed. This accord established a quota system, whereby domestic film theaters had to show French films for four out of every thirteen weeks. In 1948 the number was extended to five out of every thirteen weeks. In reality this latter legislation was more permissive than the former. Whereas the accord of 1946 related to feature films, the accord of 1948 encompassed short films as well, so that a recent French short would serve the purpose of a feature in terms of one of the weeks.[4] The accord was the first sign of a policy of nationalism, aimed especially at the long arm of Hollywood. The long-term effects of these accords were minimal for many reasons, not the least of which was the French people's enormous appetite for American films. Prior to 1940 there were approximately 180 foreign films shown in France commercially each year of which 140 were American films.

In 1948 after the second of the quota accords had been legislated, there were 186 import visas given to foreign films: of these 186, American films comprised 121, which meant there were 65 for all other countries combined.[5]

Whereas the policies of protectionism were aimed at weakening the stronghold of Hollywood, the policies of financial aid were intended to strengthen the domestic film industry. Those policies only strengthened the government's control over the French film industry. One of the first ways in which the government tried to make the home industry self-sufficient was to establish a system of links between the C.N.C. and the Crédit National, the latter providing loans of up to one-half a film's total production costs in the years 1948-1952. That percentage gradually decreased until 1960 when the Crédit National advances were eliminated, to be replaced by a system of surtaxes on tickets purchased by spectators. In retrospect, the affiliation between the C.N.C. and the Crédit National amounted to acknowledged intervention on the part of the government, which was tantamount to saying to the rest of the world that France had a state-run film industry which (1) could not prevent Hollywood from dominating the country's film sector, which (2) could not improve the economic conditions surrounding the domestic film industry unless that industry voluntarily reformed itself, and which (3) did, however, discourage foreign investment (specifically American) for a time in French film production costs. Obviously the surtaxes were no solution, since they taxed the spectator in order to help the industry. Predictably, the

French spectator responded by watching television more and going to films less.

The third official policy, that of encouraging co-productions, was even more complicated. Technically speaking, a co-production involved a financial partnership between production firms from at least two different countries. This policy, like the other two, was aimed at competing with American films in Europe. Thus, the policy applied primarily to feature films and particularly to fiction films. Degand states that the arrangement was usually one of a major-minor partnership on a reciprocal basis.[6] Accordingly, a hypothetical French production firm would finance 30% of an Italian film, thus assuming the role of minor partner in that film. The Italian production firm would supply the remaining 70%; in addition, it would agree to provide for 30% of the financing for the next French film produced by our hypothetical French production firm. The system of co-production was a radically innovative step in European film history, and, for a time, it served its purpose very well: it competed with American films. Many of the New Wave films were produced under this system. Ironically, the idea of a European film community prefigured that of the European economic community (the Common Market). Ultimately, it proved much more feasible than the Common Market. But its very reason for being was also its greatest drawback: nationalism. For the co-production countries, competing with America also came to mean competing with each other.

In 1949 France and Italy put their official stamp of approval on the co-production system. It was natural that Italy should be France's first partner. Italy had the strongest post-war film industry in Europe and with France was in the best position to compete with Hollywood. The preamble to this accord was two-fold: the two countries would join in co-producing films de qualité; they would also compete with America abroad as well as at home. Their emphasis on "quality" should be understood in economic terms, not artistic ones. As Degand points out, Hollywood was exporting its most expensively produced films to Europe; the European countries felt somehow compelled to respond in kind. Thus, co-production came to mean "more expensive" which was not necessarily "better". Their desire to spread the reputations of French and Italian films throughout the world became a desire to compete with each other at times in the name of cultural nationalism. In a way, the co-produced films were treated like citizens; that is, they were given double nationality. Economically, this meant that the films could cross borders without tariffs or quotas to worry about. But culturally, this double nationality meant that each country could claim a film as its own. In effect the film community functioned not unlike the later Common Market community: that is, each country was happy to work communally with the others as long as it was deriving benefits from the partnership. On every issue, nationalism undermined the strength of the community as a whole. Ultimately, the co-production system was subverted by the invader; rather than fight the system, America joined it, either by co-financing

French films directly or by giving money to Italian producers like Carlo Ponti and Dino de Laurentiis, thus co-financing the French films indirectly. The French government could do little about it: the co-production system was irreversible. By 1970, the most recent year documented by Degand with accurate statistics, there was ample evidence of the failure to compete with Hollywood in terms of "quality" films. There were 138 films produced in France in 1970; of that number, 66 were entirely French-produced, while 72 were co-produced. Significantly, the latter were produced at an average cost of three times that of the former. Only one of the films was in black-and-white. Only one was made in 16 millimeter. These statistics are perhaps not surprising in terms of international trends. What is surprising, for a country that had aspired to compete with America in terms of "spectacle", is that only one of those films was done in cinemascope, and only two were done in techniscope.[7] The most successful of the three governmental policies had also failed.

Degand cites 1957 as the year of crisis. This in itself is yet another in a long line of paradoxes. First, the film industry had flourished during the war years, contrary to what one might expect. Next, the "good years" began in 1947, the last good year French film has had in terms of spectator attendance. The year 1952 was a good one for the government: the Pinay stabilization plan stopped the rampant post-war inflation. It was a bad year for the film industry. The year 1957 was a good one for the government: the Common Market agreements were signed. It was a crisis year for the film industry.

It would seem, then, that there is an inverse relationship between the fortunes of the French government and those of the film industry. I would posit that this same inverse relationship operates between French film economics and French film art during this period. In terms of artistic achievement, 1959 was a very important year for French film; but it should be clear from this discussion that the achievement of French films at the Cannes film festival in 1959 must be understood in light of economic conditions within the industry that had never been worse. A final paradox pertaining to this discussion involves the apparent blindness of the industry to economic trends. If 1957 was the beginning of a financial crisis which still exists, it is because film production was in inverse proportion to spectator attendance: 1957 marked at the same time the most remarkable drop in attendance since the Liberation and the most remarkable jump in film production. What explains this paradox is the fluctuation in ticket prices. For the previous five years (since 1952), the industry had seen its profits steadily rise, and so they continued to produce more and more films. But the profit increase was due to an increase in ticket prices, not a corresponding increase in attendance figures. In fact, as Degand notes, there was a decrease in attendance each time there was an increase in ticket price.

Degand also notes that the statistics concerning profits must be understood in terms of geography. For example, Nice is statistically the best French city for films. Based on the population of Nice, the frequency of attendance at films for the average person is eleven times per year. By contrast, Paris is second; by contrast, because the frequency of attendance is less (eight times per year), but the average ticket price is more expensive than that of Nice.[8] Degand summarizes the problem of understanding geography in terms of the film economic market this way:

> Que de variantes, par exemple, si on analyse le marché par zones urbaines-rurales ou par grandes agglomérations. Les communes de moins de 5000 habitants - qui comptent 40% des salles - n'apportent que 8,5% de la recette, tandis que les communes de plus de 15000 habitants - qui groupent elles aussi près de 40% des salles - drainent 80% de la recette... Les résultats par agglomération - les 40 de plus de 100.000 habitants et qui, avec 12% des salles apportent 29% des spectateurs et 38% de la recette - permettent de délivrer des brevets de "bonne fréquentation" ou de "forte dépense" à quelques villes dont l'énumeration peut apporter quelque surprise. 9

Degand cautions that film should not be isolated from the other arts (if film is understood as an art form) or other entertainment possibilities (if film is understood as an industry). Film attendance statistics are in direct proportion to those for the theater as well as to those for sports events. But because of film's enormous production costs, it suffers more. Degand even proposes the idea that film is moving away from the "popular" art it once was toward the status of a luxury art like the theater now is.

> Faudrait-il y voir le signe d'une évolution - dénoncée en Angleterre par l'économiste J. Spraos - qui conduirait le cinéma du stade du spectacle "populaire" - sortie non préparée et quasi occasionnelle, encouragée par un bas prix de vente - vers le spectacle "de choix", celui qu'on prémédite, mais que, du même coup, on répète moins souvent par suite d'une moindre disponibilité de temps et de l'argent? En d'autres termes est-ce que le style de la "consommation" cinématographique se rapprocherait petit à petit de celui de la consommation du théâtre? Nouvelle question, qui attend sa réponse... 10

More important than the comparison Degand makes between the cinema and the theater is the very real comparison to be made between film and television. Jean-Patrick Lebel notes the same trend in the cinema, but he relates it both to the familiarization with television and to the projected growth of video in a three-step process of audio-visual literacy:

> -La télévision (l'émission), comme familiarisation massive avec la lecture des images et des sons. Peu à peu la magie première de "l'image", du "pris sur le vif", du "direct" se dissipe et se développe en retour la capacité à déchiffrer les images et les sons.
>
> -La cinéphilie et la tendance qui se répand de plus en plus à CHOISIR les films que l'on va voir, comme indices des progrès de la lecture du langage cinématographique; et déjà la téléphilie qui apparait à son tour.
>
> -Et, bien entendu, phénomène plus récent mais considérable, les magnétoscopes, vidéo-cassettes, vidéo-disques, etc., et tous les progrès de la vidéo et de l'image magnétique qui vont permettre de développer d'une manière extraordinaire les deux faces du langage audio-visuel (lecture et écriture). 11

The literacy envisioned by Lebel is at the level of pure technology and not in terms of human personalities or government intervention. The French film industry has looked upon the rapid growth of television in France, since the inception of the latter in 1950, as an usurpation of a privileged domain. Again, an inverse proportion exists. Degand notes that in those European countries where the film industry was strongest (France and Italy) the development of television was weakest. England would be an exception here, due to a very different system of production-distribution relationships. Degand's point is that the retardation of the growth in television expansion in France makes that country more receptive to the latest television technology and especially to the latest advances in video. Despite the retardation of television in France in relation to its neighbors, the fact remains that television attracted an ever increasing share of France's former film-going spectators. The reasons are both economic and political. Degand notes that the relative economic prosperity which France enjoyed from 1952 to 1957 permitted more and more people to purchase television sets. And, whereas the government's protectionist and interventionist policies toward the film industry were weakened by the already established position of French film in the world, its policies toward the television industry met much less opposition. Indeed, television from its very beginnings in France was tied to the government; in this respect, the film industry was perhaps justified in feeling that the rise of television was an usurpation, especially since it involved a governmental sponsorship that the film industry did not enjoy. For the latter, subsidies were mostly in the form of advances against earnings, which meant that the film in question had to do well at the box office in order to receive any appreciable government aid. To do well at the box office, the French film had to compete financially (in terms of production costs) with lavish Hollywood films. Thus, the film industry had to compete with Hollywood from the outside and the government-encouraged infant television industry from within.

Following the example of Britain, where the BBC monopoly was ended in 1955 with the establishment of a second channel (to be run as a private enterprise), French television also expanded. The addition of a second channel (there is now a third) meant an increasing use of film on the part of television. To satisfy television's increasing appetite for film consumption, the O.R.T.F. (the official radio and television firm) was expanded to become a power in film production. M.P. Louyet sees this expansion into the film industry proper on the part of television as being similar to that in America, where in 1955 the newest of the television networks (ABC) took control of an established film-producing firm (RKO Pictures). ABC's acquisition meant an immediate warehouse of films to be used for television. Indeed, Louyet sees the complex relationship between television and film in Europe as a political problem, one which involves an inability to cope with American invasion in either film or television, one which involves enormous new expenditures for technology, and one which involves the non-cooperation of the two media:

> Aux Etats-Unis la production et la distribution sont en effet fortement concentrées et impriment le mouvement à l'exploitation, aux salles de cinéma. En Angleterre, la situation est à peu près la même. C'est de ces deux pays-là qu'est venu ce mouvement de politique de force du cinéma vis-à-vis de la télévision. Cette politique, nous pouvons la suivre sur deux plans. Il y a d'abord un plan offensif, à savoir le changement de la politique cinématographique, quant au fond, en essayant de faire d'autres films. Vous avez tous remarqué qu'à la naissance de la télévision, on a vu se multiplier les formes diverses de cinéma. Il y a eu du cinémascope, la couleur s'est généralisée, on a commencé à faire des films qui étaient plus coûteux, qui étaient beaucoup plus spectaculaires, et on a réduit considérablement le nombre des films. 12

Louyet notes that the changes in technology (cinemascope, color films) were paralleled with changes in content. Film's subject matter became openly more audacious, more controversial. The "adult" film was in part a response to television: in effect, this meant fighting a new form with a new content.

> En Europe surtout dès que la télévision a percé la politique a changé plus encore et s'est attachée davantage au fond qu'à la forme. Il est significatif que se multiplient à l'heure actuelle les films plus "osés", qui ont une certaine clientèle que la T.V. ne peut satisfaire parce que tenue à certaines règles de morale conventionnelle. 13

Louyet concludes by noting that this relationship of rivalry for spectators could only intensify in terms of non-cooperation between the media.

> Les grandes firmes qui possèdent l'immense majorité des films ne veulent pas collaborer avec la télévision au point de vue information et diffusion cinématographique et refusent de donner à la television des films qui ne sont plus dans le commerce, qui n'ont donc pour eux pratiquement plus aucune valeur commerciale, pour enlever ainsi à la television l'attrait que peut avoir pour la masse la diffusion des films à grandes vedettes etc. Il est évident que cette politique a couté énormément et au cinéma et à la télévision. 14

The result of this non-cooperation was the expansion of firms like O.R.T.F. from television into film production (often for television use) on the one hand and the relatively competition-free diffusion of American television programs and films in French television. Thus, the "threat" that French television represented for the French film industry was as much due to a failure to capitalize upon a new market on the part of the film industry itself as it was due to disappearing spectators or to protective government policies.

To summarize our discussion thus far, we need to point out that the economic difficulties of the French film industry in 1957 were due to ill-fated government policies as well as to a near-sighted film industry. Protectionism, the first of three government policies, largely failed because there was no way to enforce the quota system, and, when the quota system was adhered to, it was economically detrimental to the movie theaters. Finally, the quota system was subverted by the co-production system, the first and third government policies thus working at cross-purposes. Financial aid in the form of Crédit National loans, advances against earnings and subsidies, the second government policy, largely failed because the aid was not enough and not in the right sectors. The financial aid system was in effect a kind of merit system: if French films could prove themselves at the box office, the government would reward them. That aid was earmarked for feature films. What aid there was for short films was also based on a merit system. There were "prizes" for films of "quality" ("prix à la qualité"). In effect, then, short films were only compensated in the form of festivals like the famous court-métrage festivals at Tours. Not until April of 1967 did the government provide subsidies for short films. In addition, the government legislated aid in two other sectors which concern us here: (1) to the so-called Cinéma d'Art et d'Essai for wider distribution of "difficult" films; and (2) to the Cinéma National Populaire, providing subsidies for exhibitors screening films from countries whose production is little known in France. The aid to both of these sectors, however, was largely hypothetical, since distribution outlets in both these sectors were too limited to take advantage of the legislation.

Co-production, the third government policy, was unique in that the government sanctioned the practice but did not enforce it. In terms of film production output, the co-production system was effective. It was so effective that America joined the system, largely replacing the Italian firms in the late 1960's. Co-production also delayed a phenomenon that took place in American film production during the decade 1960-1970: the rise of the "independents", small film production units for films made outside of the major studio system.

Finally, the failure of the French film industry to interpret correctly shifts in spectator attendance created a crisis in 1957: the industry had overproduced in terms of a diminishing audience. The result was the massive closing of many movie theaters, most of them located in the provinces. Cooperation with the rising television industry could have alleviated the crisis to some degree, but the film industry remained adamantly opposed to the new medium, again failing to understand that the French population would watch television, whether it offered them movies or not.

Only against this economic picture can the artistic achievements of 1959 be understood fully. The New Wave filmmakers did not revolutionize the film industry as some critics alleged at the time. They merely took advantage of the economic conditions. They proved that France could compete with Hollywood more cheaply than had been supposed by both the government and the film industry. Using unknown or "no-name" actors, using 16 millimeter effectively, reducing overhead expenses by minimizing on camera crews, on camera equipment and on sets, all of these New Wave techniques had as many economic repercussions as aesthetic repercussions. At the time, Truffaut and the other *Cahiers* directors represented at Cannes painted the picture of a moribund film industry resisting the winds of change. Actually the financially plagued industry welcomed the new filmmakers. They assimilated the "young Turks" with little difficulty. They foresaw the potential of a new audience sector (students and young adults) and also the potential for new distribution outlets (film societies and ciné-clubs). From 1959 to 1962 young filmmakers were encouraged in different ways. It allowed the young filmmakers to get studio backing without a long apprenticeship as an assistant director, and it was financially feasible for the studios to back the unknown directors, since their aesthetics were based on cheaply-made films. By 1962 the *Cahiers* directors were a little older and no longer a novelty, the fad for youth had dwindled in terms of audience response, and the Cannes film festival (government-conceived and government-sponsored) could not continue to proclaim the "new". For a time Cannes functioned to alleviate the industry's production problems by serving as free publicity for French film in the world. But the semblance of fairness had to be maintained for the festival to remain effective outside of France; in other words, other countries had to win awards too.

A close examination of the enclosed production table will reveal some interesting patterns in the genesis of New Wave films, especially in terms of the relationship between *courts métrages* and feature films at the level of production and in terms of the co-production system.[15]

Production Table

The following table indicates the major producers of French New Wave films during the period 1955-1971. However, special emphasis is placed on the years from 1955 to 1968. Production and distribution patterns changed drastically in France in the mid-sixties, so I have not included many of the most recent films. The most influential of the individual producers are listed next to their respective production companies. Since most of these films were co-productions (involving more than one production company), several films are cross-listed. Furthermore, only those companies which repeatedly financed these directors' films are listed; for example, _Muriel_ (Alain Resnais, 1963), a co-production of several companies (Argos, Alpha, Eclair, Films de la Pléiade and Dear Films) is listed only under Argos and Films de la Pléiade, because the other companies did not finance any other Resnais films.

Argos

Nuit et brouillard (Resnais, 1955)
Dimanche à Pékin (Marker, 1955)
Lettre de Sibérie (Marker, 1957)
Du Côté de la Côte (Varda, 1958)
Les Astronautes (Marker, 1959)
Hiroshima mon amour (Resnais, 1959)
On vous parle (Cayrol and Durand, 1960)
Madame se meurt (Cayrol and Durand, 1961)
Chronique d'un été (Rouch, 1961)
L'Année dernière à Marienbad (Resnais, 1961)
De Tout Pour Faire un Monde (Cayrol and Durand, 1963)
A Valparaiso (Ivens, 1963)
Muriel (Resnais, 1963)
La Jetée (Marker, 1963)
La Guerre est finie (Resnais, 1966)
Masculin-Féminin (Godard, 1966)

Les Films Tamaris

La Pointe courte (Varda, 1954-55)
L'Opéra mouffe (Varda, 1958)

Films de la Pléiade (Pierre Braunberger)

Toute la Mémoire du monde (Resnais, 1956)
Le Coup du berger (Rivette, 1956)
O Saisons ô chateaux (Varda, 1957)
Tous les Garçons s'appellent Patrick (Godard, 1957)
Charlotte et son Jules (Godard, 1958)
Une Histoire d'eau (Godard, 1958)
Le Chant du styrène (Resnais, 1958)
Tirez sur le pianiste (Truffaut, 1960)
La Frontière (Cayrol and Durand, 1961)
Cuba si! (Marker, 1961)
La Pyramide humaine (Rouch, 1961)
Vivre sa vie (Godard, 1962)
Muriel (Resnais, 1963)
La Punition (Rouch, 1964)
Le Coup de grace (Cayrol and Durand, 1965)

Como (Samy Halfon)

Nuit et brouillard (Resnais, 1955)
Hiroshima mon amour (Resnais, 1959)
L'Année dernière à Marienbad (Resnais, 1961)
Une Aussi Longue Absence (Colpi, 1961)
Codine (Colpi, 1962)
L'Immortelle (Robbe-Grillet, 1962)
Trans-Europ Express (Robbe-Grillet, 1966)
L'Homme qui ment (Robbe-Grillet, 1968)
L'Eden et après (Robbe-Grillet, 1970)
N. a pris les Dés (Robbe-Grillet, 1971)

Pathe

Hiroshima mon amour (Resnais, 1959)
Salut les Cubains (Varda, 1963)

Sofracima (André Heinrich)

Le Joli Mai (Marker, 1963)
Le Mystère Koumiko (Marker, 1965)
Le Coup de grace (Cayrol and Durand, 1965)
La Guerre est finie (Resnais, 1966)

O.R.T.F.

La Jetée (Marker, 1963)
Le Mystère Koumiko (Marker, 1965)
N. a pris les Dés (Robbe-Grillet, 1971)
La Femme du Gange (Duras, 1973)

Parc Films (Mag Bodard)

Les Parapluies de Cherbourg (Demy, 1964)
Les Demoiselles de Rochefort (Demy, 1965-66)
Le Bonheur (Varda, 1965)
Les Créatures (Varda, 1966)
Je t'aime je t'aime (Resnais, 1968)

AJYM Films (Claude Chabrol)

Le Beau Serge (Chabrol, 1958)
Les Cousins (Chabrol, 1959)
Paris nous appartient (Rivette, 1957-60)

Pierre Roustang

L'Amour à vingt ans (1962) (Including Truffaut's Antoine et Colette)
Les Plus Belles Escroqueries du monde (1964) (Including Godard's Le Grand Escroq and Chabrol's L'Homme qui vendit la tour Eiffel)

Les Films du Losange (Barbet Schroeder)

Paris vu par... (1964) (Including sketches of Godard, Chabrol and Rouch)

Les Films Marceau (Leopold Schloberg)

Les Mauvaises Rencontres (Astruc, 1955)
Les Liaisons dangéreuses (Vadim, 1959)
La Proie pour l'ombre (Astruc, 1960)
Les Carabiniers (Godard, 1963)
La Curée (Vadim, 1966)

Les Films du Carrosse (François Truffaut and Marcel Berbert)

Les Mistons (Truffaut, 1957)
Les Quatre Cent Coups (Truffaut, 1959)
Paris nous appartient (Rivette, 1957-1960)
Jules et Jim (Truffaut, 1961)
La Peau douce (Truffaut, 1964)

Cocinor

Et Dieu créa la femme (Vadim, 1956)
Les Godelureaux (Chabrol, 1961)
L'Immortelle (Robbe-Grillet, 1962)
La Curée (Vadim, 1966)

Robert and Raymond Hakim

A Double Tour (Chabrol, 1959)
Les Bonnes Femmes (Chabrol, 1959)
La Ronde (Vadim, 1964)

S.N.C. (Georges de Beauregard)

A Bout de Souffle (Godard, 1959)
Le Petit Soldat (Godard, 1960)

Anouchka/Orsay

Bande à part (Godard, 1964)
Une Femme mariée (Godard, 1964)
Masculin-Féminin (Godard, 1966)

Rome-Paris Films (Georges de Beauregard, Carlo Ponti, Dino de Laurentiis)

Lola (Demy, 1960)
Une Femme est une femme (Godard, 1961)
L'Oeil du malin (Chabrol, 1962)
Cléo de 5 à 7 (Varda, 1962)
Les Carabiniers (Godard, 1963)
Le Mépris (Godard, 1963)
Landru (Chabrol, 1963)
Marie-Chantal contre le Docteur Kah (Chabrol, 1965)
Pierrot le fou (Godard, 1965)
Suzanne Simonin, La Religieuse de Diderot (Rivette, 1966)

The first striking feature revealed by the table is the amount of film production in terms of courts métrages that took place prior to 1959. In this respect, 1955 was a very productive year, marking a shift in production practices. Nuit et brouillard, Dimanche à Pékin, La Pointe courte and Les Mauvaises Rencontres all came out in 1955. The table shows that most of the shorts produced prior to 1959 were by Argos and Films de la Pléiade. Specifically, they were produced by Pierre Braunberger, who deserves credit for recognizing the talents of both the Cahiers directors and the literary New Wave filmmakers. Indeed, Braunberger has been a force in film production throughout the twentieth century. He produced Luis Bunuel's first two films (Un Chien Andalou (1929) and L'Age d'or (1930)) and three of Jean Renoir's films (Nana (1926), La Chienne (1931) and Une Partie de campagne (1936, released in 1946)). And it was Braunberger who produced Resnais's first three documentary films: one for Films de la Pléiade (Gauguin (1950)) and two for Les Films du Panthéon (Van Gogh (1948) and Guernica (1950)). Braunberger was equally helpful to the career of Jean-Luc Godard, producing three shorts and one feature.

Argos and Films de la Pléiade were primarily helpful to the filmmakers of the literary New Wave (Resnais, Marker, Varda, Cayrol). But these firms concentrated on courts métrages and could provide only limited support in terms of feature films. Godard and Truffaut moved on to other production firms, probably for this very reason. This concentration on the non-commercial short might also explain the plight of someone like Chris Marker, who was fortunate to find someone like Braunberger to back his films (Marker once referred to Braunberger as "un producteur supersonique"), but Marker's financial support and his market possibilities are both limited by the kind of films he makes. Argos and Films de la Pléiade would both be rewarded for their faith in people like Marker and Jean Rouch when, in 1962 the original enthusiasm for the *Cahiers* directors' New Wave had waned, critics and audiences became aware of a current called *cinéma vérité* whose chief proponents were thought to be Marker and Rouch in France. Indeed, Ian Cameron notes a critical shift from attention paid to the New Wave from 1959 to 1962 to attention paid to *cinéma vérité* from 1962 to 1964.[16]

The second feature revealed by the table which concerns these formative years (1955-1959) is the initiative taken by the *Cahiers* directors in the sector of production: specifically, self-production. These directors economized from within (writing each other's scripts, serving as camera operator or technical advisor, acting in each other's films) and from without (linking directing to producing). This link between directing and producing was an outgrowth of their critical aesthetic of *la politique des auteurs*. In other words, it was necessary to insure production in order to give the director total aesthetic control. François Truffaut formed a production company called Les Films du Carrosse which totally financed many of Truffaut's early features. Significantly, it was Truffaut's *Fahrenheit 451* (1966) which initiated the French-British co-productions. It is also interesting to trace the production development of Truffaut's films, from full production responsibilities by Carrosse in his earlier features (Jules et Jim, La Peau douce) to co-productions with American studios, which began with La Mariée était en noir in 1967 (co-production of Carrosse and United Artists). Baisers volés (1968) and La Sirène du Mississippi (1969) were also co-productions between Carrosse and United Artists. From co-productions Truffaut in effect became an American director, for with Domicile conjugal (1970) he shifts from United Artists to Columbia. Columbia in turn became the distributor of the film. Une Belle Fille comme moi (1972) is both produced and distributed by Columbia. With La Nuit américaine (1973) there is another shift involving an agreement between two major American studios. Columbia and Warner Brothers both put money into production, and both assumed distribution rights for their investment; the film is distributed by both Columbia and Warner Brothers in Great Britain and by Warner Brothers in America. It is ironic that someone like Truffaut, who was concerned enough with production to help form a production company, should turn almost exclusively to American studios for production and distribution in his later films.

The case of Claude Chabrol is equally enlightening. Chabrol too was concerned about production. He formed his own production company AJYM. From 1956 to 1961 that production company was very prolific. In addition to two of Chabrol's films (Le Beau Serge (1958) and Les Cousins (1959)), AJYM produced seven other films: Jacques Rivette's Le Coup du berger (1956) and Paris nous appartient (1957-1960) (both in collaboration with other production firms); Eric Rohmer's Le Signe du lion (1959); Philippe de Broca's Les Jeux de l'amour (1959) and

Le Farceur (1960); Jacques Doniol-Valcroze's L'Eau à la bouche (1959); and the first film of Chabrol's editor: Jacques Gaillard's La Ligne droite (1961). If Chabrol's production company had demonstrated both efficiency and productivity with an output of nine films in five years, it was not able to sustain this generosity for friends. Chabrol's financial dilemmas are evident as early as 1959 with his dependency upon the Hakim brothers for the production of two other films (A Double Tour and Les Bonnes Femmes). The price that directors as prolific as Chabrol and Godard have to pay is in terms of production: specifically, using up available producers. Godard has run the gamut of French production firms (Argos, Films de la Pléiade, Pierre Roustang, Les Films du Losange, Les Films Marceau, S.N.C., Anouchka/Orsay and Rome-Paris Films) and has had to find money from American, British, German and Italian firms to continue his pace. Chabrol has been more fortunate. After Le Scandale (The Champagne Murders), which was produced by Raymond Eger for Universal and distributed by Universal in 1966, Chabrol found a producer (André Génovès) and a production firm (Les Films la Boétie) for all of his subsequent films: La Route de Corinthe (1967), Les Biches (1968), La Femme infidèle (1968), Que la Bête meure (1969), Le Boucher (1969) and La Rupture (1970).[18]

The table is also helpful in seeing which producers and which firms backed which part of the New Wave. With respect to the firms, Pléiade, Carrosse, Cocinor, S.N.C., AJYM and Rome-Paris Films were the major backers of the Cahiers directors. Individual producers important to this part of the New Wave were Chabrol and Truffaut, the Hakim brothers, Pierre Roustang, Barbet Schroeder, Georges de Beauregard,

Carlo Ponti and Dino de Laurentiis. The latter three are especially important in terms of co-productions and will be discussed later.

For the literary New Wave, the major firms were Argos, Pléiade, Les Films Tamaris, Pathé, Como, Sofracima, O.R.T.F. and Parc Films, the latter four backing the feature films in the same way that the former four had backed the shorts. The most important individual producers for the literary New Wave were Braunberger, Samy Halfon, André Heinrich and Mag Bodard. What Braunberger's input meant to both New Waves in terms of shorts was paralleled by the input of Beauregard and Ponti for the Cahiers directors, Halfon and Bodard for the literary New Wave directors.

What differentiates the two New Waves is often a degree of backing. For example, it is not generally known that many of the shorts of the literary New Wave directors were commissioned films. Agnes Varda's O Saisons ô chateaux (1957) and Du Côté de la Côte (1958) were commissioned for television. Resnais's Nuit et brouillard (1955) was commissioned by the Committee for the History of World War II Deportation. His Toute la Mémoire du monde (1956) was commissioned by the French Ministry of Foreign Affairs, and his Le Chant du styrène (1958) was commissioned by the Pechiney plastics firm.[19]

The passage from short film to feature film is an interesting genesis to trace with these directors. Resnais's first feature, Hiroshima mon amour (1959) is a case in point. Based upon the success of his earlier Nuit et brouillard in dealing with the themes of war and memory, Argos, Les Films de la Pléiade and Braunberger decided to back another Resnais documentary, this time about the effects of the atomic bomb on Hiroshima and Nagasaki. When he arrived in Japan, Resnais saw that he could not make a documentary and that the film would have to be a fiction film. Françoise Sagan (unavailable) and Simone de Beauvoir ("too political") were suggested as possible screenwriters. Resnais jokingly suggested Marguerite Duras, since he had enjoyed her novel _Moderato Cantabile_. Both the producers and Duras complied. The only remaining problem was money; Argos and Pléiade and Pathé could not finance the feature that Resnais envisioned. Money was obtained from the chief producer at Daiei studios in Japan on the basis that Okada, who plays the Japanese lover in the film, would be a "drawing card". The money was in the form of a loan, a kind of advance-against-earnings agreement, whereby the French firms would repay the loan within eighteen months of the film's first commercial run. They were able to do this, because they were able to "sell" the film to French audiences in two ways. The first was to sell the film as an "adult" film, a mature love story involving nudity and much discussion of sexuality. Then, the film was billed as an "intellectual" film in order to appeal to educated film-goers and students from the film societies and cine-clubs.[20] _Hiroshima_ is typical of a pattern. The financial backers of the literary New Wave filmmakers were less affluent than the producers of the _Cahiers_ directors on the one hand, and, on the other hand, they were less able to justify their expenditures in terms of commercial success. The films of the literary New Wave directors were too short, too experimental, too involved with mixing documentary and fiction and too "intelligent" to justify continued investments. Consequently, the literary New Wave directors were eventually forced into co-productions.

These co-productions were slightly different in terms of method and scope from the co-productions of the *Cahiers* directors. Whereas the latter directors remained in France and co-produced with Italian firms (see the table for Rome-Paris Films) and American studios, the literary New Wave directors often worked out elaborate arrangements in which a foreign firm would agree to co-produce if the filmmaker would do part of his film in that producer's country. Thus, Alain Robbe-Grillet obtained financial backing from Bratislava Films in Czechoslovakia for both *L'Homme qui ment* (1968) and *L'Eden et après* (1970) by filming segments in both films in Czechoslovakia and using Czech crews for those segments.[21]

The alternative to this kind of co-production is the multi-production involving small investments from many firms. Alain Resnais's *L'Année dernière à Marienbad* (1961) is a good example of this trend; it was produced by the following firms: Terra Films, Films Tamara, Films Cormoron, Précitel, Como, Argos, Cinétel, Silver Films and Cinériz. Such multi-production arrangements are difficult to work out; they help to explain such gaps as the six years between *Je t'aime je t'aime* (1968) and *Stavisky* (1974) in Resnais's career.

On the other hand, the table provides solid evidence of the kind of franco-italian co-productions discussed by Degand. Rome-Paris Films is significant here. The French producer was usually Beauregard, while the Italian producer was usually Ponti. A close look at the filmographies for Fellini, Antonioni and other Italian directors of this period would show how Ponti's co-production of French films was reciprocated by French firms in terms of Ponti's Italian films. The irony here is that by legal standards the films of Godard and those of Fellini are equivalent, since both share this French-Italian double nationality. In terms of our table, one can easily see that Godard (four films) and Chabrol (three films) were the major beneficiaries of these co-productions. Agnes Varda's _Cléo de 5 à 7_ (1962) is the lone example from the literary New Wave directors here. The Beaurégard-Ponti co-productions in effect meant comfortable budgets, dependable backing and little or no say in the distribution of the films for these directors. In addition, the table only shows evidence of French and Italian co-productions; it does not show the amount of American money behind the names of Ponti and Dino de Laurentiis. This American influence can only be surmised from a close examination, not of production statistics, but rather of distribution statistics. Without any accurate data, I can only state that studios like Paramount, United Artists and Columbia put enough money into the projects to gain ultimate distribution of the films in many cases.

Sometimes there was more involved than just money in these productions. For example, one of the "selling" points for Godard's _Le Mépris_ (1963), one of the Rome-Paris co-productions, was that Godard was basing his film (very loosely, it turns out) on the Italian novelist Alberto Moravia's novel _Ghost at Noon_.

Again in terms of co-productions, an interesting feature of the table are the productions of Barbet Schroeder and Pierre Roustang. These films are generally referred to as sketch films or compilation films; they are films in which several directors are given a theme or topic (very general) like "love in the city" or "love and the French woman" or "the seven deadliest sins" and those directors are then financially backed for a very short film or sketch. Interestingly, I think that the precedent for these compilation films comes from Italy with films like L'Amore in citta (Love in the City, 1953), involving sketches from Fellini, Antonioni, Dino Risi, Alberto Lattuada and Cesare Zavattini and the later Boccaccio 70 (1962), involving segments by Fellini, Visconti, de Sica and Monicelli. Whatever the precedent was, there were a rash of compilation films in the sixties. I have made a list which may very well be incomplete, since many of these films are not available for distribution. But the list here presented should suffice for our discussion. Often they involved films made over a period of years, so I have noted the variation in years first.

1961-1962: L'Amour et la française (Love and the French Woman). With segments by Henri Décoin, Jean Delannoy, Michel Boisrond, René Clair, Henri Verneuil, Christian-Jacque and Jean-Paul Le Chanois.

1962: Les Parisiennes (Tales of Paris). With segments by Jacques Pointrenaud, Michel Boisrond, Claude Barma and Marc Allegret.

1962: Trois Contes d'amour (Three Fables of Love). With Alessandro Blasetti, Hervé Bromberger and René Clair.

1962: L'Amour à vingt ans (Love at Twenty). With segments by Francois Truffaut, Andrzej Wajda, Renzo Rossellini, Marcel Ophuls and Shintero Ishikaro.

1962: RoGoPaG. With segments by Jean-Luc Godard, Roberto Rossellini, Pier Paolo Pasolini and Ugo Gregoretti.

1962: Les Sept Péchés capitaux (The Seven Capital Sins). With segments by Claude Chabrol, Jean-Luc Godard, Edouard Molinaro, Jacques Demy, Roger Vadim, Philippe de Broca and Sylvain Dhomme.

1962-1964: Les Plus Belles Escroqueries du monde. With segments by Claude Chabrol, Jean-Luc Godard, Iromichi Horikawa, Ugo Gregoretti and Roman Polanski.

1964: Les Adolescents (The Adolescents). With segments by Gian Vittorio Baldi, Michel Brault, Jean Rouch and Hiroshii Teshigahara.

1964-1966: Paris vu par.... With segments by Claude Chabrol, Jean-Luc Godard, Eric Rohmer, Jean Rouch, Jean Douchet and Jean-Daniel Pollet.

1967: Le Plus Vieux Métier du monde (The Oldest Profession). With segments by Jean-Luc Godard, Franco Indovino, Mauro Bolognini, Philippe de Broca, Michel Pflughar and Claude Autant-Lara.

1967: L'Aller et retour des enfants prodigues. Segment by Godard entitled Vangelo '70. Other segments by Italian directors.

1967: La Contestation. With segments by Jean-Luc Godard, Bernardo Bertolucci, Pier Paolo Pasolini, Carlo Lizzani and Marco Bellochio.

1967: Loin du Vietnam (Far From Vietnam). With segments by Jean-Luc Godard, Alain Resnais, Agnes Varda, Joris Ivens, Claude LeLouch, William Klein. Edited by Chris Marker.

In aesthetic terms most of these films are not very good. They mixed known directors with unknowns, often resulting in mediocre work from the known directors and poor work from the unknowns. But these compilation films are still interesting to study for several reasons.

First, the general topics or themes were geared to coax spectators, often centering on the "new woman", sexual mores of the young or exploring prostitution: Love and the French Woman, Love at Twenty, Three Fables of Love, The Adolescents, The Oldest Profession. At their most daring, the images in such films were soft pornography, while the thematic undertones remained very moral.

Perhaps more interesting than the themes in terms of our discussion is the mode of production involved in the compilation films. Using directors from several different countries (predominantly French and Italian directors with the required Japanese or Pole thrown in) insured financial backing from all of those countries. In effect, the compilation films were often multinational co-productions. Such films enjoyed all of the advantages the co-production laws provided, advantages which extended to several countries instead of just two. At the same time, they represented relatively small financial risks for the producers of each director, since the input was often proportionate to the segment.

While most of these films merely provide an extension of the kind of co-productions Beauregard and Ponti did, Paris vu par... offers an alternative at the level of filming as well as at that of production-distribution. All of the segments for that film were shot in 16 millimeter and then enlarged to 35 millimeter for distribution. It was an interesting concept that, unfortunately, was not followed by the other films.

Loin du Vietnam is the exception to all that has been said about compilation films. It is significantly the only film on the list involving the literary New Wave directors. The idea for the film and the production money behind it both came from the filmmakers themselves. The film was not widely distributed for commercial use, and it, thus, did not return its original investment. The film is important, however, because it is one of those rare films in which economic considerations were set aside in favor of political considerations. We will return to Loin du Vietnam in the next section.

The table, then, shows two distinct patterns which reflect the differences in the two New Waves. The Cahiers directors revealed an immediate concern for self-production in their early films (Carrosse, AJYM). They were prolific directors, and so they were constantly changing producers (see the table on Godard, for example). They gradually attached themselves to the richer companies and entered into co-productions involving Italian and American firms. They made several compilation films involving individual producers (Pierre Roustang and Barbet Schroeder) and multinational co-productions.

On the other hand, the literary New Wave directors maintained their roots in the court-métrage (Argos, Films de la Pléiade); thus, they maintained ties with the less affluent production firms. Their attachment seems to have been more to individual producers (Braunberger, Samy Halfon, André Heinrich, Mag Bodard) than to the companies these producers represented. Their production is correspondingly less prolific. When they became involved in co-productions, it was usually with countries not known for affluent production money (Czechoslovakia for Robbe-Grillet, Sweden for Resnais in La Guerre est finie and for

Agnes Varda in Les Créatures, Cuba for Marker and Varda, Japan for Marker and Resnais). Whereas the Cahiers directors received Italian money without going to film in Italy, the literary New Wave directors often filmed in the countries that co-financed their films. Their alternative, in terms of domestic production, was the cumbersome multi-production (L'Année dernière à Marienbad, for example). And, because of their fidelity to the short film and the documentary/experimental formats established with Argos and Pléiade, they have not been able to find financing for their later films. Henri Colpi has not made a feature film since 1967; Jean Cayrol has not made a feature film since 1965. Agnes Varda has made her last two features in America. In one of them, Lion's Love (1969), she provides a very succinct portrait of the filmmaker vis-a-vis the producer.

The film is about Shirley Clarke (noted director of cinéma vérité documentaries on the East Coast and its inner cities) playing herself. Clarke goes to Hollywood to make a fiction film. Clarke is obviously Agnes Varda of the shorts (L'Opéra mouffe, Salut les cubains) being asked to make a Hollywood film (Lion's Love). At one point in the film Clarke says she's used to directing but not to acting, and she doesn't know how to play a particular scene in which she is supposed to be suicidal. Varda switches places with her, takes off her blouse and plays the scene. Max Raab plays himself as the producer of Clarke's hypothetical film. In fact, he was the producer of Lion's Love. Varda shows Raab talking finances with two "independents"; their talk centers on the reputation of Clarke and her lack of familiarity with the Hollywood system. Will she sell? They project a minimum-budget film with a limited audience. The talks break down, however, on a political issue rather than an economic one. Raab feels he is taking enough risks in co-financing the project. For his investment, he wants final cut privileges, which means that the final print of the film can be re-edited or cut down in length at the discretion of the producer. The independents argue that Clarke is a serious filmmaker with an established reputation within the film community for the kind of films she makes and that she should have final cut privileges, which would mean that nothing could be changed from the final film without her approval. Raab refuses. Totally confused by the tinsel and glitter of Hollywood, Clarke attempts suicide. She never does make her film.

Such a scene, which shares the decision-making process beyond the films with the audience, is a new phenomenon in the films of the former New Wave directors. These directors are opening up the process, so that the final film is not a closed product for the viewer. One thinks of the cancelled checks during the credits of Godard's *Tout va bien* (1972) as another example of this kind of sharing. In essence, such scenes indicate a shift from *auteur* theory with its emphasis upon the director's spiritual and artistic control to marxist criticism with its emphasis on the modes of production/distribution in a cultural/ideological context. Marxist criticism posits that the critic should see the film as a product, reminding us that the cinema is an industry as well as an art. Thus, the critic should study film's production and distribution, and he should interpret those economics in terms of politics. In other words, French critics in the last ten years have moved away from the director as the focal point of film scholarship to a study of the studio system and analyses of modes of production/distribution. This shift from the director to the studio to the studio's culture and from the individual film as an artistic entity to the film as a cultural byproduct prompted former *auteur* critic Jean-Louis Bory to note the following:

> Dans l'optique américaine, le DIRECTOR n'est guère plus important que les WRITERS, ce n'est qu'un technicien supérieur. Le vrai maitre du film, son auteur, c'est le PRODUCER, ou plutôt la firme pour laquelle il travaille, la MGM, la Fox, la Paramount, la Columbia. D'où la prééminence, au générique, de l'image de marque, la dame en chemise de la Columbia, la neigeuse cime de Paramount, le ballet de projecteurs de la Fox ou le lion MGM qui fait grrr. C'est la vraie signature du film. 22

The awareness of the importance of production is in part responsible for (1) the *Cahiers* directors being so concerned about self-production (so that the director could have full aesthetic control and the *auteur* theory could have validity in their works) and (2) for the literary New Wave directors repeatedly denying the *auteur* theory and insisting upon the collective or communal nature of film. Equally aware of the modes of production/distribution and conscious of their dependence upon those modes of production/distribution, the younger filmmakers in France insist upon collectivity if they have any political sense of the cinema at all.

> Plus radicalement des cinéastes comme Marin Karmitz, Jacques Kebadjan, René Vautier recusent avec un haut-le-corps la notion même d'auteur. Insistent sur le caractère collectif de leur travail. 23

The examples of both Chris Marker and Jean-Luc Godard are illuminating in this respect. Since the events of May 1968, Marker has been working collectively with SLON, a group of workers from the CGT (Communist Party), making films without signature that are oriented to labor issues. Marker's role has been that of a producer and technical advisor. He has provided the workers with the equipment and the suggestions for operating the equipment. The production/distribution sector resists this collectivity. There has been little money put into these projects, and there is little chance of such films being seen on a wide scale. In other words, Marker involves the workers in the process of filmmaking, without regard to the end product. Critics like Peter Wollen who have seen these films generally agree that they are not very good aesthetically or technically. They fail to see that the process is more important than either the production or the ultimate audience. These are films made by the workers about the workers and essentially for the workers. On the other hand, Marker's name is enough to guarantee at least limited distribution of his own films made during this period. If SLON had made _Cuba: Battle of the 10,000,000_ (1970) or _The Train Rolls On_ (1972), New Yorker films would probably not be distributing them in this country. Marker's name in the film is enough; despite the filmmakers themselves, the _auteur_ theory lingers.

At about the same period that Marker became involved with SLON, Godard associated himself with Jean-Pierre Gorin and the Dziga-Vertov Group. Yet the group's films are still credited to Godard. Critics speak of Vent d'Est (Wind From the East, 1969) as Godard's film, not Gorin's film or the Dziga-Vertov Group's film. Paramount financed Tout va bien (1972), because it was Godard's film and because he would be using Jane Fonda and Yves Montand in the film. They were not financing a collective film of the Dziga-Vertov Group.

The irony in both Godard's and Marker's cases is that critics and producers alike resist their (the directors') anonymity. It is as though their names are needed to (1) justify the making of a film and (2) justify a critical analysis of that film. The more things change, the more they stay the same. The old ideas and systems return to subvert the new. As Godard jokingly put it: "Ceux de Lacan, Althusser et Barthes ont été rendus démodés par ceux de Montaigne."[24]

The question of authorship in film remains pertinent. As Degand has pointed out, French law interprets film (an entity) as an author, so that the individual components of that film must share in the rights of authorship. There are legal provisions for the director, the screenwriter, the musical composer, the camera-person. There is no provision for the producer, except a short statement to the effect that the producer must follow his own conscience in dealing with these other sectors, since ultimate financial responsibility rests with him.

This legislation concerning authorship in film (March 11, 1957)[25] is crucial to the theory and practice of the ciné-roman. Resnais as director shared legal authorship rights with his various screenwriters, but, because those writers had these limited rights, they were able to determine where the scenario of the film would be published in book form. That several of these writers were already associated with publishing houses (Cayrol and Marker with Les Editions du Seuil, for example) was also crucial to the proliferation of the _ciné-roman_. Each successive screenplay was published with the publisher with whom the writer had already worked. Marguerite Duras's novels are published by Gallimard by and large; consequently, the scenario for _Hiroshima mon amour_ was published by Gallimard. Alain Robbe-Grillet's novels are published by Les Editions de Minuit; consequently, the scenario for _L'Année dernière à Marienbad_ was published by Minuit. Jean Cayrol's novels are published by Les Editions du Seuil; in addition, Cayrol works as an editor for Seuil. Consequently, the scenario for _Muriel_ was published by Seuil. Jorge Semprun publishes with Gallimard; so, _La Guerre est finie_ and _Stavisky_ are published by Gallimard. This link between film and publisher is an important outgrowth of the legislation of 1957.

This publication of scenarios is related more to distribution than to production in terms of the film. Regardless of the cost of making a film, the published scenario is not going to sell unless the film is widely distributed. Unfortunately, statistics for the distribution of individual films are not as easily available as those for production, so it is difficult to assess accurately the invisible links between production and distribution. But Claude Degand does present statistics for the distribution outlets in France as of 1967, from which we could introduce several hypotheses.

Degand's table takes into account the number of distribution outlets, their specialization and their fiscal percentage of the total money outlay.[26]

French Distribution Outlets in 1967

Number			Specialization	Fiscal Percentage
35			national outlets	53.7 %
	25		specializing in "Salle Arts et Essais"	1.9 %
	10		Sociétés (big corporations)	
		3	French	13.7 %
		7	American	38.1 %
8			multi-regional outlets	13.8 %
78			restricted to one region	32.5 %
121 societes or outlets				100 %

Of the thirty-five national outlets (servicing all of France), twenty-five are art cinema outlets (Salle Arts et Essais) and ten are Societies. These thirty-five comprise over half of the total money outlay. But within the thirty-five the contrast could not be greater. Those twenty-five art cinema outlets make up only 1.9 % of the total fiscal outlay: a minimal percentage. On the other hand, the ten Sociétés make up 51.8 % of the total fiscal outlay. Significantly, American firms outnumber the French firms by seven to three, and the percentage in terms of fiscality of the American firms is almost three times that of the French firms. The seventy-eight outlets which are restricted to a single region can perhaps be explained by France's rural geography vis-à-vis the few big cities. This provincialism in terms of the location of distribution outlets proves more a disadvantage than an advantage.

> Enfin il y a une poussière de distributeurs "locaux", ne travaillant que sur un coin de France. L'explication doit en être cherchée dans le taux de ruralité qui est plus élévé en France que dans les pays voisins, les salles de cinema se trouvant ainsi éparpillées sur de grandes surfaces. Un tel éparpillement alourdit plutôt que favorise la productivité de la branche distribution: comment réduire, par film distribué, le cout de la circulation, de la vérification, de la facturation, etc.? 27

These geographically restricted outlets outnumber the American Sociétés by seventy-eight to seven, yet those seven Sociétés account for 5.6 % more of the total fiscality.

At the top of the list for any individual outlet was United Artists. MGM was third. Their positions explain in part why barely one-third of all the films distributed in France in 1967 (feature films, that is) were French films. Related to their preeminence in the French distribution system is the system of co-productions at the level of production.

The director deals with the producer and the producer arranges distribution. As the system is set up, the director has very little say in the matter of how his film is distributed. We have already noted the genesis of Truffaut, the way in which United Artists, then Columbia, then Warner Brothers became co-producers and then sole distributors. We have noted that Rome-Paris films, backed by American money, turned to American firms for distribution. We have noted that Godard became involved with Paramount and Chabrol with Universal.

What has not been noted yet is the extent to which American firms have distributed the films of the literary New Wave directors. Resnais's _Muriel_ was distributed by United Artists; his _Je t'aime je t'aime_ was distributed by Fox. Alain Robbe-Grillet's _Glissements progressifs du plaisir_ (1973) was also distributed by Fox. Here again it is worth repeating that those same factors which discourage producers from financing the films of the literary New Wave directors apply as well to the distributors. In other words, it would seem that the French filmmaker today has to be aware of American money in production as well as in distribution. For directors like Marker, Cayrol, Colpi, Duras, Varda, Robbe-Grillet and Resnais, that money is in short supply.

Political Considerations

> "Film is truth twenty-four times a second."
> -Jean-Luc Godard

In the enthusiasm following the French triumphs at Cannes in 1959, there was very little mention of the fact that Cannes was, after all, a government-sponsored festival. Everything about the festival, from the selection of films to the selection of critics for the Jury, bears the stamp of the French government. Such festivals as that of Cannes for feature films and that of Tours for short films fulfill both an economic and a political function for the government. Short films until 1967 could only gain government support by winning awards in competitive festivals. Producers and distributors, both domestic and foreign, kept a close eye on the winners at Cannes. The government made an exception to the Blum-Byrnes accord when it stated that foreign films winning awards at Cannes would be exempt from the quota system. Thus, economic remuneration serves as a political tool. The French government realized the effectiveness of Cannes at home and decided to intervene in the selection of films to be entered in foreign festivals as well in 1964.

> In France, for example, a special commission was appointed in 1964 charged with the responsibility of advising upon the films to be entered by France at international festivals. On the advice of the Commission the Minister for Cultural Affairs in conjunction with the Minister for Foreign Affairs decides which films shall represent France officially. Except for the nominees of the Minister of Cultural Affairs, the composition of the Commission is not defined. 28

For the French government the opposite of festival (awards) is censorship (punishment). Often that censorship took place at the festivals. Resnais' _Nuit et brouillard_, for example, was retired from the Cannes film festival for fear of offending Germany in 1955. Resnais' and Chris Marker's _Les Statues meurent aussi_ had already been banned by the censors from 1953 to 1963. It was finally released in mutilated form. Resnais' _Hiroshima mon amour_ was partially retired from the 1959 Cannes festival, because festival officials feared that the film might be offensive to the United States. Nevertheless, the film received two special jury prizes. Marker's _Cuba Si!_ was banned by the censors from 1961 to 1963. His 1967 film _A bientôt, j'espère_ was censored and then released in mutilated form. Even when these filmmakers won awards, it was for political as well as aesthetic reasons. Marker's _Dimanche à Pékin_ won the Gold Medal of Moscow two years after the film's release in 1955. Since the film (_Sunday in Peking_) was a satire on modern China, it is clearly understandable that the film should be awarded by Moscow. Significantly, the year was 1957, the same year that Marker's *Lettre de Sibérie*, a satirical documentary on modern Russia, appeared, for which Marker received no such recognition. With an increasingly unstable economy, with labor unrest and a stronger, more unified Communist Party opposition, with the rise of marxist-leninist and Maoist student groups at the country's universities, and with the increasing importance of television as a communications medium, the Gaullist government relied more and more heavily on the festivals and on censorship in the 1960's, culminating in the events of May 1968.[29]

Cahiers du Cinéma:1954-1968/ Cannes: 1959-1968

When François Truffaut launched *la politique des auteurs* in 1954 with an article entitled "Une Certaine Tendance du cinéma français" in *Cahiers du Cinéma*, the New Wave had a manifesto, one which was as enthusiastic, as dogmatic and as naive politically as Breton's two manifestoes for Surrealism had been.[30] The article was intended as an attack on films of "quality" (well-scripted films) and a declaration of independence from the well-made studio films. While not explicitly saying so, Truffaut's article was actually a declaration of independence from the tutelage of Andre Bazin. From 1952 to 1958 Truffaut, Godard, Chabrol and Rohmer developed their own personal tastes in directors. Yet, with the exception of Godard (from 1966 on), these directors neither found a new aesthetic nor advanced any new political ideology. _La politique des auteurs_ had more to do with _auteurs_ than with politics. Truffaut, Chabrol and Rohmer remained right-wing, Catholic, personalist, aesthetic critics and filmmakers. Social problems, but not the social conditions which spawned those problems, were treated in their films, as though France had never been touched by World War Two, by the Algerian War, by the Vietnam war. There was little mention of capitalism or marxism, of the De Gaulle regime, of unemployment in their films. The so-called working class was conspicuously absent from their films. And, as long as their films continued to win awards at international festivals, producers could be found to support more films.

Once established as directors, the _Cahiers_ critics began to recant. The enthusiasm that the _nouvelle vague_ had generated for film dissipated in the early 1960's. Without an established record of commercial successes, new filmmakers could not find producers to back them. The plight of politically committed filmmakers or of filmmakers who specialized in _courts métrages_, in documentary films or in the so-called "arts et essais" films was even worse. Ironically, the period was also one of growing political awareness on the part of film journals and intellectuals alike. _Cahiers du Cinéma_, for example, which had been the proving grounds for Truffaut, Chabrol, Rohmer and Godard, began to reject the _auteur_ theory as early as 1965. As Claire Clouzot has noted:

> C'est l'époque de la révision. En novembre 1965, les _Cahiers_ apportent un correctif à ce qu'ils appellent "la dogmatisation de la politique des auteurs et la valorisation systématique du cinéma américain." La théorie des auteurs, axiome d'abord, puis

> postulat et hypothèse de travail, disparait comme principe de base d'une esthétique que les rédacteurs jugent dépassée. 31

In its stead, Cahiers began to concentrate on structuralism, on semiology and on marxism. They began to combine Freud and Marx in analyses whose vocabulary came from structuralism. Thus, deliberately and abruptly, they shifted from director-oriented pieces, from hierarchies of film preferences (the ten best lists), from content analyses and from a certain apolitical playfulness to elaborately annotated and often abstract pieces that stressed theories over films. From structuralism they borrowed a methodology with which to analyze film form: shot-by-shot analyses rather than film-by-film pieces. From semiology they borrowed the means for studying film language in terms of linguistics and for studying bodies of films (as opposed to individual films) as coherent systems. Thus, they treated Soviet films of the 1920's (Eisenstein, Pudovkin, Dziga-Vertov, Kuleshov) as a "system" of films. From marxism they developed an interest in placing films in their socio-political or historical contexts, in accepting pieces that had as much, if not more, to do with those contexts than with the films, themselves; they also developed an interest in emphasizing national cinemas, especially those of the Third World, and in emphasizing new directors, especially non-French directors, whose aspirations were overtly political (Jean-Marie Straub, André Delvaux, Nagisa Oshima, Alain Tanner, Glauber Rocha, Costa-Gavras).

Three events further politicized Cahiers du Cinéma: (1) the Langlois affair, (2) the May 1968 strikes and (3) the fight with Daniel Filipacchi. In the early part of 1968 the government, represented by

André Malraux as Minister of Cultural Affairs in the De Gaulle regime, fired Henri Langlois, the long-time director of the Cinémathèque in Paris. Godard and Truffaut took the lead in protesting Langlois's firing. Truffaut wrote two articles bitterly attacking Malraux as a traitor to his (Malraux's) artist-intellectual past.[32] The _Cahiers_ critics backed Truffaut and Godard. In effect, their journalism turned the firing into a personal vendetta between Malraux and Langlois. Malraux partially retracted, allowing Langlois to remain as head of the Cinémathèque Archives but not permitting him to schedule film programs.

The May strikes in 1968, involving both workers and students, applied pressure on _Cahiers_ from the outside to deal with films more in terms of their cultural and ideological contexts. What was already latent in their political about-face was made manifest in 1969 when Daniel Filipacchi, one of the controlling shareholders in the magazine, objected to the increasingly leftist approach at _Cahiers_ and used his stock for leverage. The younger critics at _Cahiers_ - Jean Narboni, Jean-Louis Comolli, Francois Weyergans - bought up Filipacchi's shares and ceased publication for a short time. When publication resumed, there was an editorial manifesto attached, which stated three goals that _Cahiers_ would pursue:

(1) continuer le travail d'information et de réflexion critique

(2) susciter la circulation et la diffusion de films peu ou non connus

(3) continuer l'élaboration d'une théorie critique fondée sur

> la science marxiste du matérialisme historique et les principes du matérialisme dialectique. 33

Thus, by 1969 the three most influential film journals in France - *Cahiers du Cinéma*, *Positif* and *Cinéthique* (the latter two having been politically oriented from their beginnings) - were all politically committed: *Cahiers* to dialectical marxism, *Positif* to a combination of Marx, Breton and Trotsky, and *Cinéthique* to marxist-leninism. The articles at *Cahiers* became more "scholarly"; very strangely, they combined the erudition and heavy annotations of linguistics and structuralism with the often predictable polemics of politics. Understandably, their readership declined. *Positif*, which had always set itself up as the alternative to *Cahiers*, continued to do the opposite of whatever *Cahiers* did. Thus, while remaining politically committed, they moved in 1968 from theoretical pieces to special issues and studies of individual directors - the very things *Cahiers* had just moved away from. *Cinéthique*, founded in 1969 by Gerard Leblanc, had also advertized itself as the alternative to *Cahiers*, accusing the latter of opportunistic marxism and fair-weather politics. Since *Cinéthique* had been projected for a low budget and a limited readership, it could use the cheapest grains of paper and eliminate expenses like reproducing stills. Their space was then liberated for theoretical debate. Not only was their readership limited, but so was their list of "possible" directors. Godard seems to have been one of the fortunate few to receive *Cinéthique's* seal of approval. For a director that they considered politically aware (which meant a director whose politics were marxist-leninist), like Godard, Cinéthique would devote an entire issue and would return to that director in subsequent issues. When no such director was available, the issues would simply avoid directors and even avoid films altogether. In that case, their articles would speak to what they thought the cinema should be or would deal with the following: the theory of performance, the economics of distribution, the relationships between film and the working class or the psychology of audience reception and perception. Cinéthique's avowed stance was a daring one: they were not in existence to chronicle the existing cinema. Their existence was to prepare the way for a cinema to come. Leblanc and the other editors at Cinéthique saw their journal as an encouragement or challenge for a marxist-leninist cinema to come forth.

Film criticism in France had, thus, come full circle from the Cahiers manifestoes in the mid-fifties. The journal which had largely ignored the literary New Wave in the 1950's and early 1960's now became interested in Chris Marker, Agnes Varda and Marguerite Duras for their political perspectives. That same journal turned on some of its founding fathers, attacking the aestheticism of Truffaut, Chabrol and Rohmer.

Another full circle can be traced from the Cannes film festival of 1959 to that of 1968. Those same directors who most benefited from the festival of 1959 - Truffaut and Godard - would use the festival of 1968 as a showcase for their dissatisfaction with the Gaullist regime. The politicization of the Cannes festival was in large part foreshadowed by the making of Loin du Vietnam in 1967.

Chris Marker and Agnes Varda had grown increasingly political in their attitudes toward the cinema prior to the making of Loin du Vietnam. They had begun to place more emphasis upon cinéma vérité images and less emphasis upon lyrical, poetic or merely witty soundtracks and texts. Varda's case is especially enlightening. Her disappointment at the critical confusion and hostility surrounding Les Créatures (1966) caused her to return to the image-témoin (camera eye-witness) format of her earlier documentaries. As Carlos Clarens has noted:

> C'était à Vénise, l'année où Les Créatures y firent un four, qu'Agnes commença à interroger ses films au même titre que ceux des autres. Pour elle, cela voulait dire que le film de fiction avait été déplacé par le film-témoignage. 34

Loin du Vietnam was a significant film in its overtly political stance, its departure from traditional production and distribution systems, its collectivity and its non-hierarchical decision-making processes. In retrospect, it was to be a kind of swan song to the close collaboration which had characterized the literary New Wave's cinéma des auteurs. Deeply concerned about the Vietnam war, they felt compelled to make a film which would put the war in a global perspective, showing the differences between North and South Vietnam, the differences between France and the United States in their approaches to the war, showing demonstrations for and against the war in America, showing the wife of Norman Morrison two years after he had immolated himself in front of the Pentagon, showing the plight of one refugee wife and mother in France. Loin du Vietnam is an indictment of the continued American participation in the war; but it is also an acknowledgment of guilt for the French responsibility in the war. Further, it pays tribute to the heroism of the people of North Vietnam, while it reveals the impotence of the intellectual left in France.

Chris Marker oversaw the production of the film, and it was he who edited the final sequences together. The resulting film is an interesting mixture of cinéma vérité involvement and Brechtian withdrawal, of documentary and fiction, of hope and cynicism. The reportage segments were done by Joris Ivens in South Vietnam and by Agnes Varda in North Vietnam. Her images of a guerilla theater performance in North Vietnam are reminiscent of the children with masks edited with a wall proclaiming "Peace in Algeria" in L'Opéra mouffe. But the most poignant parts of the film are also the most detached, the most withdrawn: the segments of Godard and Resnais.

Godard's segment is entitled "Caméra-Oeil": it is an interview of Godard by Godard before the camera. In this minimalist piece Godard explains that the North Vietnamese did not trust him enough to permit his filming the segment in North Vietnam. Further, he explains that they were right to refuse him. There is nothing visually interesting in the segment; if the spectator continues to watch the segment, it is because of the spoken text. Godard forces this emphasis upon his language with the suggestion that this language is what would betray the North Vietnamese, if indeed he would betray their cause.

The lack of camera movement and the de-emphasis of the image track reinforces the thematic idea that Godard's speech is one of impotence. Godard talks to the camera because he feels inept to film anything which would change the war situation.

Resnais's segment, although a piece of fiction, says the same thing: the French intellectual is impotent vis-à-vis the Vietnam war. A writer named Claude Ridder (the name given to the protagonist in *Je t'aime je t'aime* - 1968) who is played by Bernard Fresson (who also plays the friend of Claude Ridder in *Je t'aime je t'aime*) stands before the camera and paces around his room in France. He explains why he as a writer is incapable of writing anything about the war or about the book on the escalation of the war by Herman Kahn that he was supposed to review. Assuming that Fresson's speech reflects to some degree the sentiments of Resnais, the message seems to be the following: the intellectual left in France is concerned about the war but is totally incapable of taking any constructive action, least of all any artistic action, to put an end to the war. Fresson's room is full of books and other artifacts of intellectual life: typewriter, paintings, etc. Resnais restrains his usually mobile camera in order to prevent the spectator from interpreting Fresson in any subjective way. The restrained camera reinforces distance between the character and the audience at the same time that it punctuates the anguished detachment of the writer.

The sequence of Resnais fits very well with the portrait of the revolutionary Diego in *La Guerre est finie* (1966), in which

Resnais abstained from showing any "glory" in political struggle or even the possibility of change by such struggle. Resnais laid bare the grim realities behind Diego's political struggle: the boredom and fatigue, the lack of family ties, of friends, of a strong self-identity, the necessity for lying or living incognito, the neuroses and paranoia involved in clandestine politics. Diego is portrayed as an anachronism: a man bound by 1936, not a man who can think beyond 1966. Diego accomplishes no more than the writer in Resnais's segment for Loin du Vietnam, who simultaneously admits concern and defeat.

Loin du Vietnam was the first real sign of a passage from la politique des auteurs (with its aesthetic concerns) to les auteurs de la politique (with an emphasis on socio-political concerns).

With some retrospect one can now appreciate with some degree of understanding the chaotic first six months of 1968 in France. The Langlois affair polarized the intellectuals against Malraux and the entire Gaullist regime. The filmmakers' revenge was in the form of organizing all communications workers into the Etats Généraux du Cinéma. The Langlois protests took place in February and March of 1968. In May, Godard, Truffaut and other concerned filmmakers convinced the actors attending the Cannes film festival to walk out. The filmmakers were also convinced to withdraw their films from the festival. It must have been a strange phenomenon, one in which cinema and life were contrasted. Mag Bodard, the producer of Je t'aime je t'aime (made that year) and Jacques Sternberg (who wrote the screenplay for the film) found themselves on opposite sides. Sternberg began a speech at the festival with the following words: "J'ai déjà fait la guerre mais je n'avais encore jamais fait une révolution."[35] He was hooted and booed. He never finished his speech. His few words do, however, point up a very important difference in the two New Waves. There is a distinct generation gap and political gap between the two. Resnais, Jean Cayrol, Chris Marker, Armand Gatti and Henri Colpi might have said the same things. Their generation had participated in the war and in the resistance. For someone like Cayrol who had seen the concentration camps first-hand, storming the Cannes film festival would hardly seem to be in the same class of political activity. Conversely, Truffaut and Godard had never seen the war. From their early student days at the Cinémathèque, their memories had always been cinematic memories. It is significant that the Cahiers directors-led protests focused first on the Langlois affair at the Cinémathèque and then on the Cannes film festival, cause and effect thus both being tied intimately to their own film experience. It is also ironic that their revenge should come at Cannes, the festival that launched their careers. Only Godard remained constant in his political opposition to the festival and the politics behind it. Truffaut seems to have a schizophrenic history with Cannes. In 1958 he created a scandal by showing up at the festival as the only uninvited critic to attack the festival and its critics. In 1959 he was one of the major winners at the festival. In 1968 he helped to shut the festival down; in 1969 he was back, this time to enter one of his films.

Godard and some of his followers began making ciné-tracts in 1968. These were short reportage films like those one would see on television news programs, except that the content of these cine-tracts was too radical for French television. Thus, these 16 millimeter shorts were made and shown clandestinely. With their marxist perspective, such films offered an alternative to the government's intervention in, and censorship of, the news media. More than the subversion of the Cannes festival, these cine-tracts are an important sign for the future. The distance between filmmaker and audience, always great because of the production/distribution system, can be reduced by video, which is the natural extension of the cine-tract. The kind of control over the medium that the Cahiers critics/directors had assumed in their auteur theory is possible with video, provided that new distribution systems for video do not imitate their film counterparts.

From the period of the cine-tracts comes a Godard pun which might serve as an answer to Sternberg's objections: "La Révolution = L'Art Evolution."[36] Radically altering the form of a medium (the cine-tracts, Marker's work with SLON, Godard's present excursions in video) is to alter the content: is to make a revolution.

The directors of the literary New Wave make political films, but they do not advocate any specific political programs. Consequently, they have been attacked by both the right and left in France. One remembers Resnais's cryptic statement about revolution as the only concrete pronouncement of the literary New Wave on political change: "Révolution et rêve commencent par le même mot."[37] Resnais seems to suggest that the only revolution possible is one which begins from within: from within the artist, from within the medium. If one accepts his definition, then Resnais and the other New Wave directors have done much to concretize the dream at the root of the revolution.

Notes

1 For the best study of the economic and political aspects of French film prior to World War Two, see Paul Leglise, *Histoire de la politique du cinéma français: Le Cinéma et la Troisième République* (Paris: Librairie Generale de Droit et de Jurisprudence, 1970).

2 Claude Degand, *Le Cinéma...cette industrie* (Paris: Editions Techniques et Economiques, 1972), p. 19.

3 Degand, p. 20.

4 James Quinn, *The Film and Television as an Aspect of European Culture* (Leyden: A.W. Sijthoff, 1968), p. 134.

5 Degand, pp. 26-27.

6 Degand, p. 32.

7 Degand, p. 38.

8 Degand, p. 52.

9 Degand, p. 52.

10 Degand, p. 54.

11 Jean-Patrick Lebel, *Cinéma et idéologie* (Paris: Editions Sociales, 1971), p. 223.

12 M.P. Louyet, "De Quelques Problèmes actuels et à venir de la télévision," in *Le Cinéma, fait social*, ed. M.A. Doucy (Brussels: Université Libre/L'Institut de Sociologie, 1959), p. 128.

13 Louyet, p. 128.

14
Louyet, pp. 128-129.

15
For the best source of information regarding the production of French New Wave films, see the filmography in Roy Armes, French Cinema Since 1946, 2 vol. (London and New York: A. Zwemmer and A.S. Barnes and Company, 1966).

16
Ian Cameron, "Introduction," in Second Wave, ed. Ian Cameron (London: Praeger, 1970), p. 5.

17
For a complete filmography of Francois Truffaut, see C.G. Crisp, François Truffaut (London and New York: Praeger, 1972) and Don Allen, François Truffaut (London: Secker and Warburg, 1974).

18
For a complete filmography of Claude Chabrol, see Robin Wood and Michael Walker, Claude Chabrol (London and New York: Praeger, 1970).

19
For a complete filmography of Alain Resnais, see Roy Armes, The Cinema of Alain Resnais (London and New York: A.Zwemmer and A.S. Barnes and Company, 1968).

20
Raymond Ravar, "Du Côté du distributeur et de l'exploitant," in "Tu n'as rien vu à Hiroshima", ed. Raymond Ravar (Brussels: Université Libre/L'Institut de Sociologie, 1962).

21
For a complete filmography of Alain Robbe-Grillet, see André Gardies, Alain Robbe-Grillet (Paris: Seghers, 1972).

22
Jean-Louis Bory, Questions au cinéma (Paris: Stock, 1973), p. 64.

23
Bory, p. 65.

24
Michel Vianey, En attendant Godard (Paris: Bernard Grasset, 1966), p. 111.

25
Degand, p. 92.

26 Degand, p. 66.

27 Degand, p. 66.

28 Quinn, p. 119.

29 For a discussion of censorship in France, see Patrick Séry, "French Cinema--Blunting the Censor's Scissors," Le Monde (March 8, 1971) and Michel Delain and Guillemette de Véricourt, "La Censure clandestine," L'Express (February 14-29, 1972).

30 See André Breton, Manifestes du surréalisme (1924-1929) (Paris: Gallimard, 1965).

31 Claire Clouzot, Le Cinéma français depuis la nouvelle vague (Paris: Fernand Nathan, 1972), p. 182.

32 François Truffaut, "L'Antimémoire courte," Combat, 7334 (February 12, 1968) and "Toujours la Cinémathèque," Combat, 7362 (March 15, 1968).

33 Clouzot, p. 183.

34 Cahiers du Cinéma, 214 (July-August 1969), p. 13.

35 Michel Delahaye, "Fin d'un festival: Cannes," Cahiers du Cinéma, 203 (August 1968), p. 26.

36 For a discussion of the cine-tracts of Godard, see Guy Monreal, "Qui n'a pas son petit Godard," L'Express (July 15-28, 1968), pp. 51-52. There is an excellent discussion of the ciné-tracts of Godard and of the political implications of the events of May 1968 from a marxist viewpoint in Julia Lesage's forthcoming dissertation on Godard and Brecht (Indiana University, 1975).

37 Alain Resnais, Le Monde (May 11, 1966).

Bibliography I

General Works: Selected Bibliography

A Selected Bibliography

Agel, Henri. Esthétique du cinéma. Paris: Presses Universitaires de France, 1962.

Alter, Jean. La Vision du monde d'Alain Robbe-Grillet: Structures et significations. Geneva: Droz, 1966.

Armes, Roy. The Cinema of Alain Resnais. London and New York: A. Zwemmer and A.S. Barnes and Company, 1968.

Armes, Roy. French Cinema Since 1946. 2 Vols. London and New York: A. Zwemmer and A.S. Barnes and Company, 1966.

Bachelard, Gaston. La Dialectique de la durée. Paris: Boivin, 1936.

Baechlin, Peter. Histoire économique du cinéma. Paris: La Nouvelle Edition, 1947.

Barthes, Roland. Le Degré zéro de l'écriture. Paris: Seuil, 1953.

Barthes, Roland. Essais critiques. Paris: Seuil, 1964.

Barthes, Roland. S/Z. Paris: Seuil, 1970.

Bazin, André. Cinéma: un oeil ouvert sur le monde. Lausanne: Clairefontaine, 1952.

Bazin, André. Qu'est-ce que le cinéma? 4 Vols. Paris: Cerf, 1958-1962.

Bernal, Olga. Alain Robbe-Grillet: Le Roman de l'absence. Paris: Gallimard, 1964.

Bloch-Michel, Jean. Le Présent de l'indicatif: Essai sur le nouveau roman. Paris: Gallimard, 1963.

Bluestone, George. Novels into Film. Berkeley and Los Angeles: University of California Press, 1966.

Blumenberg, Richard Mitchell. The Manipulation of Time and Space in the Novels of Alain Robbe-Grillet and in the Narrative Films of Alain Resnais, with particular reference to Last Year at Marienbad. Diss. Ohio University, 1969.

Borde, Raymond with Freddy Buache and Jean Curtelin. Nouvelle Vague. Lyon: Serdoc, 1962.

Bory, Jean-Louis. Des Yeux pour voir. Paris: 10/18, 1971.

Bory, Jean-Louis. Questions au cinéma. Paris: Stock, 1973.

Breton, André. Manifestes du surréalisme (1924-1929). Paris: Gallimard, 1965.

Burch, Noel. Praxis du cinéma. Paris: Gallimard, 1969.

Butler, Ivan. The Making of Feature Films--A Guide. Baltimore and London: Penguin Books, 1971.

Caillois, Roger. Les Jeux et les hommes. Paris: Gallimard, 1969.

Cayrol, Jean. De L'Espace humain. Paris: Seuil, 1968.

Cayrol, Jean and Claude Durand. Le Droit de regard. Paris: Seuil, 1963.

Cayrol, Jean. Lazare parmi nous. Paris: Seuil, 1950.

Clouzot, Claire. Le Cinéma français depuis la nouvelle vague. Paris: Fernand Nathan, 1972.

Cocteau, Jean. Entretiens autour du cinématographe. Ed. André Fraigneau. Paris: André Bonne, 1951.

Cohen-Seat, Gilbert. Essais sur les principes d'une philosophie du cinéma. Paris: Presses Universitaires de France, 1958.

Colpi, Henri. Le Cinéma et ses hommes. Montpellier: Causse, Graille and Castelnau, 1947.

Colpi, Henri. Défense et illustration de la musique dans le film. Lyon: Serdoc, 1963.

Degand, Claude. Le Cinéma... cette industrie. Paris: Editions Techniques et Economiques, 1972.

Deren, Maya. An Anagram of Ideas on Art, Form and Film. Yonkers: Alicat Bookshop Press, 1946.

Doucy, M.A. Le Cinéma, fait social. Brussels: Université Libre/ L'Institut de Sociologie, 1959.

Durgnat, Raymond. Nouvelle Vague: The First Decade. Loughton, Essex: Motion Monographs, 1963.

Eco, Umberto. L'Oeuvre ouverte. Paris: Seuil, 1965.

Eisenstein, Sergei. Film Form. Trans. and ed. Jay Leyda. New York: Harcourt, Brace and Company, 1949.

Gardies, André. Alain Robbe-Grillet. Paris: Seghers (Cinéma d'aujourd'hui), 1972.

Genette, Gerard. Figures. Paris: Seuil, 1966.

Genette, Gerard. Figures II. Paris: Seuil, 1969.

Genette, Gerard. Figures III. Paris: Seuil, 1972.

Goldmann, Lucien. Pour une sociologie du roman. Paris: Gallimard, 1964.

Gollub, Judith Podselver. "Nouveau Roman et Nouveau Cinéma." Diss. UCLA, 1966.

Graham, Peter. The New Wave. New York: Doubleday, 1968.

Guback, Thomas. The International Film Industry. Bloomington and London: Indiana University Press, 1969.

Hamelin, Henry. L'Industrie du cinéma. Paris: Société Nouvelle Mercure, 1954.

Hauser, Arnold. The Social History of Art (Vol. IV). New York: Knopf, 1951.

Huaco, George. The Sociology of Film Art. New York and London: Basic Books, 1965.

Humphrey, Robert. Stream of Consciousness in the Modern Novel. Berkeley and Los Angeles: University of California Press, 1965.

Jacob, Gilles. Le Cinéma moderne. Lyon: Serdoc, 1964.

Jacobs, Lewis. The Movies as Medium. New York: Farrar, Straus and Giroux, 1970.

Jaffé-Freem, Elly. Alain Robbe-Grillet et la peinture cubiste. Amsterdam: Meulenhoff, 1966.

Janvier, Ludovic. Une Parole exigeante: le nouveau roman. Paris: Minuit, 1964.

Kawin, Bruce. *Telling it Again and Again: Repetition in Literature and Film.* Ithaca and London: Cornell University Press, 1972.

Kristeva, Julia. *Sēmeiōtikē: Recherches pour une sémanalyse.* Paris: Seuil, 1969.

Kristeva, Julia. *Le Texte du roman.* The Hague: Mouton, 1970.

Lebel, Jean-Patrick. *Cinéma et ideologie.* Paris: Editions Sociales, 1971.

Leehnart, Jacques. *Nouveau Roman: hier et aujourd'hui.* Paris: 10/18, 1972.

Léglise, Paul. *Histoire de la politique du cinéma français: Le Cinéma et la Troisième République.* Paris: Librairie Générale de Droit et de Jurisprudence, 1970.

Le Sage, Laurent. *The French New Novel.* University Park, Pennsylvania: Penn State University Press, 1962.

L'Herbier, Marcel. *Intelligence du cinématographe.* Paris: Corréa, 1947.

Limbacher, James. *Four Aspects of the Film.* New York: Brussel and Brussel, 1968.

Lukacs, George. *La Théorie du roman.* Paris: Gonthier, 1963.

Magny, Claude-Edmonde. *L'Age du roman américain.* Paris: Seuil, 1948.

Malraux, André. *Esquisse d'une psychologie du cinéma.* Paris: Gallimard, 1941.

Marker, Chris. *Commentaires I.* Paris: Seuil, 1961.

Marker, Chris. *Commentaires II.* Paris: Seuil, 1967.

Martin, Marcel. *Le Langage cinématographique.* Paris: Cerf, 1955.

Mercillon, Henri. *Cinéma et monopoles.* Paris: Armand Colin, 1953.

Metz, Christian. *Essais sur la signification au cinéma.* Paris: Klincksieck, 1971.

Metz, Christian. *Langage et cinéma.* Paris: Larousse, 1971.

Miesch, Jean. Alain Robbe-Grillet. Paris: Editions Universitaires, 1965.

Mitry, Jean. Esthétique et psychologie du cinéma. Paris: Editions Universitaires, 1963.

Mitry, Jean. Les Structures. Paris: Editions Universitaires, 1963.

Morin, Edgar. Le Cinéma ou l'homme imaginaire: Essais d'anthropologie sociologique. Paris: Minuit, 1956.

Morrissette, Bruce. Les Romans d'Alain Robbe-Grillet. Paris: Minuit, 1963.

Mourlet, Michel. Sur un art ignoré. Paris: La Table Ronde, 1965.

Nin, Anais. The Novel of the Future. New York: Macmillan, 1968.

Pingaud, Bernard. Ecrivains d'aujourd'hui: 1940-1960. Paris: Bernard Grasset, 1960.

Pouillon, Jean. Temps et roman. Paris: Gallimard, 1946.

Prédal, René and Jacques Belmans, Jacques Sternberg, Christian Zimmer. Alain Resnais. Etudes Cinématographiques. 64-68 (1968).

Quinn, James. The Film and Television as an Aspect of European Culture. Leyden: A.W. Sijthoff, 1968.

Ravar, Raymond. "Tu n'as rien vu à Hiroshima". Brussels: Université Libre/L'Institut de Sociologie, 1962.

Raynal, Jean and André Rouanet de Vigne-Lavit. Le Droit du cinéma. Paris: Armand Colin, 1962.

Ricardou, Jean. Pour une théorie du nouveau roman. Paris: Seuil, 1971.

Ricardou, Jean. Problèmes du nouveau roman. Paris: Seuil, 1967.

Robbe-Grillet, Alain. Pour un nouveau roman. Paris: Gallimard, 1963.

Ropars-Willeumier, Marie-Claire. De la littérature au cinéma. Paris: Armand Colin, 1970.

Ropars-Willeumier, Marie-Claire. L'Ecran de la mémoire. Paris: Seuil, 1970.

Sadoul, Georges. Histoire d'un art: Le Cinéma des origines à nos jours. Paris: Flammarion, 1953.

Sarraute, Nathalie. L'Ere du soupçon. Paris: Gallimard, 1956.

Sarraute, Raymond and Michel Gorline. Droit de la cinématographie. Paris: Librairie du Journal des notaires et des avocats, 1955.

Sarris, Andrew. The Film. Indianapolis: Bobbs-Merill, 1968.

Sartre, Jean-Paul. Situations II. Paris: Gallimard, 1948.

Siclier, Jacques. Nouvelle vague?. Paris: Cerf, 1961.

Sitney, P. Adams. Film Culture Reader. New York: Praeger, 1970.

Sontag, Susan. Against Interpretation. New York: Dell, 1961-1966.

Stoltzfus, Ben F. Alain Robbe-Grillet and the New French Novel. Carbondale: Southern Illinois University Press, 1964.

Sypher, Wylie. Rococo to Cubism in Art and Literature. New York: Random House, 1960.

Tanner, Carlton. La Politique des Auteurs as a Critical Aesthetic. Diss. University of California, 1968.

Todorov, Tzvetan. Poétique de la prose. Paris: Seuil, 1971.

Truffaut, François with André Bazin, Jacques Becker, Charles Bitsch, Claude Chabrol, Michel Delahaye, Jean Domarchi, Jacques Doniol-Valcroze, Jean Douchet, Jean-Luc Godard, Fereydoun Hoveyda, Jacques Rivette, Eric Rohmer and Maurice Schérer. La Politique des auteurs. Paris: Champ Libre, 1972.

Varda, Agnes. La Côte d'Azur. Paris: Gallimard, 1958.

Vianey, Michel. En attendant Godard. Paris: Bernard Grasset, 1966.

Ward, John. Alain Resnais or the Theme of Time. New York: Doubleday, 1968.

Wollen, Peter. Signs and Meaning in the Cinema. Bloomington and London: Indiana University Press, 1972.

Zeltner, Gerda. La Grande Aventure du roman français au XXeme siècle: Le Nouveau Visage de la littérature. Paris: Gonthier, 1967.

Bibliography II

Literature and Criticism

Jean Cayrol

Poetry:

Les Phénomènes célèstes. Paris: Cahiers du Sud, 1939.

Miroir de la rédemption. Paris: Seuil, 1944.

Poèmes de la nuit et du brouillard. Paris: Seghers, 1946.

Passe-temps de l'homme et des oiseaux. Paris: Seuil, 1947.

Les Mots sont aussi des demeures. Paris: Seuil, 1952.

Pour tous les temps. Paris: Seuil, 1955.

Poésie-journal. Paris: Seuil, 1969.

Fiction:

Je vivrai l'amour des autres. Paris: Seuil, 1947-1952.

La Noire. Paris: Seuil, 1948.

Le Vent de la mémoire. Paris: Seuil, 1951.

L'Espace d'une nuit. Paris: Seuil, 1954.

Le Déménagement. Paris: Seuil, 1956.

La Gaffe. Paris: Seuil, 1957.

Les Corps étrangers. Paris: Seuil, 1959. Translated by Richard Howard as *Foreign Bodies* (New York: Putnam, 1960).

Les Pleins et les déliés. Paris: Seuil, 1960.

Le Froid du soleil. Paris: Seuil, 1963.

Histoire d'une prairie. Paris: Seuil, 1969.

N'oubliez pas que nous nous aimons. Paris: Seuil, 1971.

Histoire d'un désert. Paris: Seuil, 1972.

Kakémono hôtel. Paris: Seuil, 1974.

Jean Cayrol

Critical Works:

Lazare parmi nous. Paris: Seuil, 1950.

Le Droit de regard. Paris: Seuil, 1963.

De L'Espace humain. Paris: Seuil, 1968.

Henri Colpi

Critical Works:

Le Cinéma et ses hommes. Montpellier: Causse, Graille and Castelnau, 1947.

Défense et illustration de la musique dans le film. Lyons: Serdoc, 1963.

Marguerite Duras

Theater:

Les Viaducs de la Seine-et-Oise. Paris: Gallimard, 1960.

Théâtre I (*Les Eaux et forêts*, *Le Square* and *La Musica*). Paris: Gallimard, 1965.

Théâtre II (*Suzanna Adler*, *Des Journées entières dans les arbres*, *Yes, peut-être*, *Le Shaga* and *Un Homme est venu me voir*). Paris: Gallimard, 1968.

Détruire dit-elle. Paris: Gallimard, 1969.

Fiction:

Les Impudents. Paris: Plon, 1943.

La Vie tranquille. Paris: Gallimard, 1944.

Un Barrage contre le Pacifique. Paris: Gallimard, 1950. Translated by Herma Briffault as *The Sea Wall* (New York: Pellegrini and Cudahy, 1953) and (New York: Farrar, Straus and Giroux, 1967).

Le Marin de Gibraltar. Paris: Gallimard, 1952. Translated by Barbara Bray as *The Sailor From Gibraltar* (London: Calder and Boyars, 1966).

Les Petits Chevaux de Tarquinia. Paris: Gallimard, 1953.

Des Journées entières dans les arbres. Paris: Gallimard, 1954.

Le Square. Paris: Gallimard, 1955. Translated by Sonia Pitt-Rivers and Irma Murdoch as *The Square* (New York: Grove Press, 1960).

Moderato Cantabile. Paris: Minuit, 1958. Translated by Richard Seaver as *Moderato Cantabile* (New York: Grove Press, 1960).

Dix heures et demie du soir en été. Paris: Gallimard, 1960. Translated by Anne Borchardt as *Ten-thirty on a Summer Night* (New York: Grove Press, 1962).

L'Après-midi de Monsieur Andesmas. Paris: Gallimard, 1962.

Marguerite Duras

Le Ravissement de Lol V. Stein. Paris: Gallimard, 1964. Translated by Richard Seaver as *The Ravishing of Lol Stein* (New York: Grove Press, 1966) and by Eileen Ellenbogen as *The Rapture of Lol V. Stein* (London: H. Hamilton, 1967).

Le Vice-consul. Paris: Gallimard, 1966.

L'Amante anglaise. Paris: Gallimard, 1967.

Abahn Sabana David. Paris: Gallimard, 1970.

L'Amour. Paris: Gallimard, 1971.

Chris Marker

Fiction:

Le Coeur net. Paris: Seuil, 1950.

Critical Works:

Giraudoux par lui-meme. Paris: Seuil, 1959.

Alain Robbe-Grillet

Fiction:

Les Gommes. Paris: Minuit, 1953. Translated by Richard Howard as *The Erasers* (New York: Grove Press, 1962).

Le Voyeur. Paris: Minuit, 1955. Translated by Richard Howard as *The Voyeur* (New York: Grove Press, 1958).

La Jalousie. Paris: Minuit, 1957. Translated by Richard Howard as *Jealousy* (New York: Grove Press, 1959) and republished by Howard in *Two Novels by Robbe-Grillet* (New York: Grove Press, 1965).

Dans le labyrinthe. Paris: Minuit, 1959. Translated by Richard Howard as *In the Labyrinth* (New York: Grove Press, 1960) and republished by Howard in *Two Novels by Robbe-Grillet* (New York: Grove Press, 1965). Also translated by Christine Brooks-Rose as *In the Labyrinth* (London: Calder and Boyars, 1967).

Instantanes. Paris: Minuit, 1962. Translated by Bruce Morrissette as *Snapshots* (New York: Grove Press, 1968). Also translated by Barbara Wright in *Snapshots and Towards a New Novel* (London: Calder and Boyars, 1965).

La Maison de rendez-vous. Paris: Minuit, 1965. Translated by Richard Howard as *La Maison de Rendez-vous* (New York: Grove Press, 1966).

Projet pour une révolution à New York. Paris: Minuit, 1970. Translated by Richard Howard as *Project for a Revolution in New York* (New York: Grove Press, 1972).

Les Demoiselles. Paris: Minuit, 1973. Translated by Martha Egan as *Sisters* with photographs of David Hamilton (New York: Morrow, 1973).

Topologie d'une cité fantôme. Paris: Minuit, 1976.

La Belle Captive. Paris: La Bibliothèque des Arts, 1976.

Critical Works:

Pour un nouveau roman. Paris: Gallimard, 1963. Translated by Richard Howard as *For a New Novel: Essays on Fiction* (New York: Grove Press, 1965). Also translated by Barbara Wright in *Snapshots and Towards a New Novel* (London: Calder and Boyars, 1965).

Bibliography III

Published Screenplays

Jean Cayrol

Nuit et brouillard (1955) is published in _L'Avant-scène du cinéma_ 1 (February 1961). The English translation is to be published by Grove Press in _Film: Book 2: Films of Peace and War_, edited by Robert Hughes.

On vous parle (1960) is published in Cayrol's and Claude Durand's _Le Droit de regard_ (Paris: Seuil, 1963).

La Frontière (1961) is published in _Le Droit de regard_.

Madame se meurt (1961) is published in _Le Droit de regard_.

De Tout Pour Faire un Monde (1963) is published in _Le Droit de regard_.

Muriel (1963) is published in book form: _Muriel_ (Paris: Seuil, 1963).

Le Coup de grace (1965) is published in book form: _Le Coup de grace_ (Paris: Seuil, 1965).

Marguerite Duras

Hiroshima mon amour. Paris: Gallimard, 1960. Translated by Richard Seaver as Hiroshima mon amour (New York: Grove Press, 1961).

Une Aussi Longue Absence (with Gerard Jarlot). Paris: Gallimard, 1961.

La Musica. Paris: Gallimard, 1967.

Détruire dit-elle. Paris: Gallimard, 1969.

Nathalie Granger. Paris: Gallimard, 1973.

La Femme du Gange. Paris: Gallimard, 1973.

Chris Marker

Les Statues meurent aussi (1953) is published in *Commentaires I* (Paris: Seuil, 1961).

Dimanche à Pékin (1955) is published in *Commentaires I*.

Lettre de Sibérie (1957) is published in *Commentaires I*.

L'Amérique rêve (1959) is published in *Commentaires I*.

Description d'un combat (1960) is published in *Commentaires I*.

Cuba si! (1961) is published in *Commentaires I*. Also published in *L'Avant-scène du cinéma* 6 (July 1961).

La Jetée (1963) is published in *L'Avant-scène du cinéma* 38 (June 1964).

Le Mystère Koumiko (1965) is published in *Commentaires II* (Paris: Seuil, 1967).

Yo Soy Mexico (1965) is published in *Commentaires II*.

Si j'avais quatre dromadaires (1966) is published in *Commentaires II*.

Alain Resnais

Van Gogh (1948) is published in *L'Avant-scène du cinéma* 1 (February 1961).

Guernica (1950) is published in *L'Avant-scène du cinéma* 38 (June 1964).

Les Statues meurent aussi (1953) is published in Chris Marker's *Commentaires I* (Paris: Seuil, 1961).

Nuit et brouillard (1955) is published in *L'Avant-scène du cinéma* 1 (February 1961).

Toute la Mémoire du monde (1956) is published in *L'Avant-scène du cinéma* 52 (October 1956).

Le Mystère de l'atelier quinze (1957) is published in *L'Avant-Scène du cinéma* 1 (February 1961).

Le Chant du styrène (1958) is published in *L'Avant-scène du cinéma* 1 (February 1961).

Hiroshima mon amour (1959) is published in *L'Avant-scène du cinéma* 1 (February 1961). It is also in book form: *Hiroshima mon amour*. Paris: Gallimard, 1960. Translated by Richard Seaver as *Hiroshima mon amour* (New York: Grove Press, 1961).

L'Année dernière à Marienbad. Paris: Minuit, 1961. Translated by Richard Howard as *Last Year at Marienbad* (New York: Grove Press, 1962).

Muriel. Paris: Seuil, 1963.

La Guerre est finie. Paris: Gallimard, 1966. Translated by Richard Seaver (New York: Grove Press, 1967).

Je t'aime je t'aime. Paris: Gallimard, 1968.

Stavisky. Paris: Gallimard, 1974.

Alain Robbe-Grillet

L'Année dernière à Marienbad. Paris: Minuit, 1961. Translated by Richard Howard as _Last Year at Marienbad_ (New York: Grove Press, 1962).

L'Immortelle. Paris: Minuit, 1963. Translated by A.M. Sheridan Smith as _The Immortal One_ (London: Calder and Boyars, 1971).

Glissements progressifs du plaisir. Paris: Minuit, 1974.

Agnes Varda

Du Côté de la Côte (1958) is published in *La Côte d'Azur* (Paris: Gallimard, 1958).

Cléo de 5 à 7. Paris: Gallimard, 1962.

Salut les cubains. Paris: Gallimard, 1963.

Filmography

Jean Cayrol

Short Films:	Distributor U.S.A.
(with Claude Durand)	
On vous parle (1960)	not available
La Frontière (1961)	not available
Madame se meurt (1961)	not available
De Tout Pour Faire un Monde (1963)	not available
(by Cayrol alone)	
La Déesse (1969)	not available
Feature Films:	
Le Coup de grace (1965)	not available

Henri Colpi

Feature Films:	
Une Aussi Longue Absence (1961)	formerly Macmillan Audio/ Brandon, now out of circulation
Codine (1962)	Twyman
Mona l'étoile sans nom (1966)	not available
Heureux qui comme Ulysse (1967)	not available

Marguerite Duras

Feature Films:	Distributor U.S.A.
La Musica (1967)	not available
Détruire dit-elle (1969)	Grove Press, Impact Films
Jaune le soleil	not available
Nathalie Granger (1972)	not available
La Femme du Gange (1973)	Monument Films
India Song (1974)	not available

Adaptations:	
Moderato Cantabile (Peter Brook, 1960)	Columbia Cinematheque
10:30 P.M. Summer (Jules Dassin, 1966)	United Artists
The Sailor From Gibraltar (Tony Richardson, 1967)	United Artists

Armand Gatti

Feature Films:	
L'Enclos (1963)	not available

Chris Marker

Short and Feature Films:	Distributor U.S.A.
Les Statues meurent aussi (1953)	not available
Dimanche à Pékin (1955)	Contemporary/McGraw-Hill
Lettre de Sibérie (1957)	New Yorker
Les Astronautes (1959)	not available
L'Amérique rêve (1959)	not available
Description d'un combat (1960)	not available
Cuba si! (1961)	not available
La Jetée (1963)	Janus Pyramid Films
Le Joli Mai (1963)	Contemporary/McGraw-Hill
Le Mystère Koumiko (1965)	Contemporary/McGraw-Hill
Yo Soy Mexico (1965)	not available
Si j'avais quatre dromadaires (1966)	not available
Loin du Vietnam (1967)	New Yorker
A bientôt, j'espère (1967)	not available
Cuba: Battle of the 10,000,000 (1970)	New Yorker
The Train Rolls On (1972)	New Yorker

Alain Resnais

Short Films:	*Distributor U.S.A.*
Van Gogh (1948)	not available
Gauguin (1950)	not available
Guernica (1950)	Grove Press
Les Statues meurent aussi (1953)	not available
Nuit et brouillard (1955)	Contemporary/McGraw-Hill, Pyramid Films
Toute la Mémoire du monde (1956)	not available
Le Mystère de l'atelier quinze (1957)	not available
Le Chant du styrène (1958)	not available

Feature Films:	
Hiroshima mon amour (1959)	Contemporary/McGraw-Hill, Macmillan Audio/Brandon
L'Année dernière à Marienbad (1961)	Macmillan Audio/Brandon
Muriel (1963)	United Artists
La Guerre est finie (1966)	Macmillan Audio/Brandon
Je t'aime je t'aime (1968)	New Yorker
Stavisky (1974)	Cinema 5

Alain Robbe-Grillet

Feature Films:	Distributor U.S.A.
L'Immortelle (1962)	Films Incorporated (Grove Press Collection)
Trans-Europ-Express (1966)	Macmillan Audio/Brandon Modern Sound Pictures United Films Westcoast Films
L'Homme qui ment (1968)	Films Incorporated (Grove Press Collection)
L'Eden et après	Mundial Films (Los Angeles)
N. a pris les Dés (1971)	not available
Glissements progressifs du plaisir (1973)	Mundial Films
Le Jeu avec le feu (1975)	Mundial Films
Piège à fourrure (1977-1978)	not available

Agnes Varda

Short Films:	Distributor U.S.A.
O Saisons ô chateaux (1957)	FACSEA (French-American Cultural Exchange-New York)
L'Opéra mouffe (1958)	Films Incorporated (Grove Press Collection)
Du Côté de la Côte (1958)	FACSEA
Les Fiancés du Pont Macdonald (1961)	not available
Salut les Cubains (1963)	not available
Oncle Janco (1967)	not available

Feature Films:	
La Pointe courte (1955)	not available
Cléo de 5 à 7 (1962)	Contemporary/McGraw-Hill
Le Bonheur (1965)	Janus
Les Créatures (1966)	New Yorker
Elsa (1966)	not available
Black Panthers: A Report (1969)	Films Incorporated (Grove Press Collection)
Lion's Love (1969)	EYR Films
Daguerréotypes (1974)	not available

DISSERTATIONS ON FILM

An Arno Press Collection

Anderson, Patrick Donald. **In Its Own Image:** The Cinematic Vision of Hollywood. First publication, 1978

Bacher, Lutz. **The Mobile Mise En Scene:** A Critical Analysis of the Theory and Practice of Long-Take Camera Movement in the Narrative Film. First publication, 1978

Beaver, Frank Eugene. **Bosley Crowther:** Social Critic of the Film, 1940-1967. First publication, 1974

Benderson, Albert Edward. **Critical Approaches to Federico Fellini's "8½".** First publication, 1974

Berg, Charles Merrell. **An Investigation of the Motives for and Realization of Music to Accompany the American Silent Film, 1896-1927. First publication, 1976**

Blades, Joseph Dalton, Jr. **A Comparative Study of Selected American Film Critics, 1958-1974.** First publication, 1976

Blake, Richard Aloysius. **The Lutheran Milieu of the Films of Ingmar Bergman.** First publication, 1978

Bohn, Thomas William. **An Historical and Descriptive Analysis of the "Why We Fight" Series.** First publication, 1977

Cohen, Louis Harris. **The Cultural-Political Traditions and Developments of the Soviet Cinema: 1917-1972.** First publication, 1974

Dart, Peter. **Pudovkin's Films and Film Theory.** First publication, 1974

Davis, Robert Edward. **Response to Innovation:** A Study of Popular Argument about New Mass Media. First publication, 1976

Facey, Paul W. **The Legion of Decency:** A Sociological Analysis of the Emergence and Development of a Social Pressure Group. First publication, 1974

Feineman, Neil. **Persistence of Vision:** The Films of Robert Altman. First publication, 1978

Feldman, Charles Matthew. **The National Board of Censorship (Review) of Motion Pictures, 1909-1922.** First publication, 1977

Feldman, Seth R. **Evolution of Style in the Early Work of Dziga Vertov.** First publication, 1977

Flanders, Mark Wilson. **Film Theory of James Agee.** First publication, 1977

Fredericksen, Donald Laurence. **The Aesthetic of Isolation in Film Theory:** Hugo Munsterberg. First publication, 1977

Gosser, H. Mark. **Selected Attempts at Stereoscopic Moving Pictures and Their Relationship to the Development of Motion Picture Technology, 1852-1903.** First publication, 1977

Harpole, Charles Henry. **Gradients of Depth in the Cinema Image.** First publication, 1978

James, C. Rodney. **Film as a National Art:** NFB of Canada and the Film Board Idea. First publication, 1977

Karimi, A.M. **Toward a Definition of the American Film Noir (1941-1949).** First publication, 1976

Karpf, Stephen L. **The Gangster Film:** Emergence, Variation and Decay of a Genre, 1930-1940. First publication, 1973

Lounsbury, Myron O. **The Origins of American Film Criticism, 1909-1939.** First publication, 1973

Lynch, F. Dennis. **Clozentropy:** A Technique for Studying Audience Response to Films. First publication, 1978

Lyons, Robert J[oseph]. **Michelangelo Antonioni's Neo-Realism:** A World View. First publication, 1976

Lyons, Timothy James. **The Silent Partner:** The History of the American Film Manufacturing Company, 1910-1921. First publication, 1974

McLaughlin, Robert. **Broadway and Hollywood:** A History of Economic Interaction. First publication, 1974

Maland, Charles J. **American Visions:** The Films of Chaplin, Ford, Capra, and Welles, 1936-1941. First publication, 1977

Mason, John L. **The Identity Crisis Theme in American Feature Films, 1960-1969.** First publication, 1977

North, Joseph H. **The Early Development of the Motion Picture, 1887-1909.** First publication, 1973

Paine, Jeffery Morton. **The Simplification of American Life:** Hollywood Films of the 1930's. First publication, 1977

Pryluck, Calvin. **Sources of Meaning in Motion Pictures and Television.** First publication, 1976

Rimberg, John. **The Motion Picture in the Soviet Union, 1918-1952.** First publication, 1973

Sanderson, Richard Arlo. **A Historical Study of the Development of American Motion Picture Content and Techniques Prior to 1904.** First publication, 1977

Sands, Pierre N. **A Historical Study of the Academy of the Motion Picture Arts and Sciences (1927-1947).** First publication, 1973

Selby, Stuart Alan. **The Study of Film as an Art Form in American Secondary Schools.** First publication, 1978

Shain, Russell Earl. **An Analysis of Motion Pictures about War Released by the American Film Industry, 1939-1970.** First publication, 1976

Snyder, John J. **James Agee:** A Study of His Film Criticism. First publication, 1977

Stuart, Frederic. **The Effects of Television on the Motion Picture and Radio Industries.** First publication, 1976

Van Wert, William F. **The Theory and Practice of the** *Ciné-Roman.* First publication, 1978

Wead, George. **Buster Keaton and the Dynamics of Visual Wit.** First publication, 1976

Welsch, Janice R. **Film Archetypes:** Sisters, Mistresses, Mothers and Daughters. First publication, 1978

Wolfe, Glenn J. **Vachel Lindsay:** The Poet as Film Theorist. First publication, 1973

Zuker, Joel Stewart. **Ralph Steiner:** Filmmaker and Still Photographer. First publication, 1978